The MICHELIN Guide

San Francisco
Bay Area & Wine Country

RESTAURANTS
2015

Michelin Travel Partner

Société par actions simplifiées au capital de 11 288 880 EUR
27 Cours de l'Ile Seguin - 92100 Boulogne Billancourt (France)
R.C.S. Nanterre 433 677 721

© **Michelin, Propriétaires-Éditeurs**

Dépôt légal septembre 2014

Printed in Canada - septembre 2014
Printed on paper from sustainably managed forests

Compogravure : Nord Compo à Villeneuve d'Ascq (France)
Impression et Finition : Transcontinental (Canada)

Dear Reader

We are thrilled to present the ninth edition of our MICHELIN guide to San Francisco, Bay Area & Wine Country.

Our dynamic team has spent this year updating our selection to reflect the rich diversity of the city's restaurants. As part of our meticulous, highly confidential evaluation process, our inspectors have anonymously and methodically eaten through all of the city's neighborhoods including the bay area and wine country to compile the finest in each category. While the inspectors are expertly trained food industry professionals, we remain consumer-driven and provide comprehensive choices to accommodate your comfort, tastes, and budget. Our inspectors dine, drink, and lodge as "regular" customers in order to experience the same level of service and cuisine that you would as a guest.

We have expanded our criteria to reflect the more current and unique elements of the city's dining scene. Don't miss the tasty "Small Plates" category, highlighting places with a distinct style of service, setting, and menu; as well as the "Under $25" listing, which includes an impressive choice at great value.

You may also follow our Inspectors on Twitter @MichelinGuideSF as they chow their way around town. They usually tweet daily about their unique and entertaining food experiences.

Our company's founders, Édouard and André Michelin, published the first MICHELIN guide in 1900, to provide motorists with practical information about where they could service or repair their cars, find quality accommodations, and a good meal. Later in 1926, the star-rating system for outstanding restaurants was introduced, and over the decades we have developed many improvements to our guides. The local team here in San Francisco eagerly carries on these traditions.

We truly hope that the MICHELIN guide will remain your preferred reference to San Francisco's restaurants.

Contents

The MICHELIN Guide

"This volume was created at the turn of the century and will last at least as long".

This foreword to the very first edition of the MICHELIN Guide, written in 1900, has become famous over the years and the Guide has lived up to the prediction. It is read across the world and the key to its popularity is the consistency in its commitment to its readers, which is based on the following promises.

→ Anonymous Inspections

Our inspectors make anonymous visits to hotels and restaurants to gauge the quality offered to the ordinary customer. They pay their own bill and make no indication of their presence. These visits are supplemented by comprehensive monitoring of information—our readers' comments are one valuable source, and are always taken into consideration.

→ Independence

Our choice of establishments is a completely independent one, made for the benefit of our readers alone. Decisions are discussed by the inspectors and the editor, with the most important decided at the global level. Inclusion in the guide is always free of charge.

→ The Selection

The Guide offers a selection of the best hotels and restaurants in each category of comfort and price. Inclusion in the guides is a commendable award in itself, and defines the establishment among the "best of the best."

How the MICHELIN Guide Works

→ Annual Updates

All practical information, the classifications, and awards, are revised and updated every year to ensure the most reliable information possible.

→ Consistency & Classifications

The criteria for the classifications are the same in all countries covered by the Michelin Guides. Our system is used worldwide and is easy to apply when choosing a restaurant or hotel.

→ The Classifications

We classify our establishments using ✗✗✗✗-✗ and 🏨🏨🏨-🏨 to indicate the level of comfort. The ✿✿✿-✿ specifically designates an award for cuisine, unique from the classification. For hotels and restaurants, a symbol in red suggests a particularly charming spot with unique décor or ambiance.

→ Our Aim

As part of Michelin's ongoing commitment to improving travel and mobility, we do everything possible to make vacations and eating out a pleasure.

How to Use This Guide

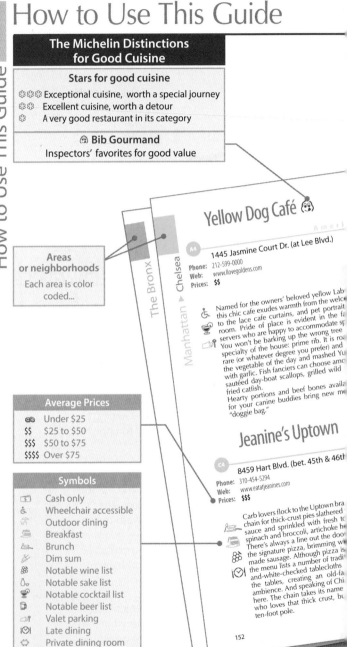

The Michelin Distinctions for Good Cuisine

Stars for good cuisine

❀❀❀ Exceptional cuisine, worth a special journey
❀❀ Excellent cuisine, worth a detour
❀ A very good restaurant in its category

⊛ Bib Gourmand
Inspectors' favorites for good value

Areas or neighborhoods
Each area is color coded...

Average Prices

🍴	Under $25
$$	$25 to $50
$$$	$50 to $75
$$$$	Over $75

Symbols

⑤	Cash only
⬆	Wheelchair accessible
⌂	Outdoor dining
🍽	Breakfast
🍽	Brunch
⅍	Dim sum
🍷	Notable wine list
⌂	Notable sake list
♆	Notable cocktail list
🍺	Notable beer list
⚑	Valet parking
|◎|	Late dining
⟺	Private dining room

Yellow Dog Café ⊛

Ameri...

The Bronx ▸ Chelsea

Manhattan ▸

A4 1445 Jasmine Court Dr. (at Lee Blvd.)

Phone: 212-599-0000
Web: www.llovegoldens.com
Prices: $$

Named for the owners' beloved yellow Lab... this chic cafe exudes warmth from the welco... to the lace cafe curtains, and pet portrait... room. Pride of place is evident in the fa... servers who are happy to accommodate sp... You won't be barking up the wrong tree... specialty of the house: prime rib. It is roa... rare (or whatever degree you prefer) and... the vegetable of the day and mashed Yu... with garlic. Fish fanciers can choose amo... sautéed day-boat scallops, grilled wild... fried catfish.

Hearty portions and beef bones availa... for your canine buddies bring new me... "doggie bag."

Jeanine's Uptown

C4 8459 Hart Blvd. (bet. 45th & 46th...

Phone: 310-454-5294
Web: www.eatatjeanines.com
Prices: $$$

Carb lovers flock to the Uptown bra... chain for thick-crust pies slathered... sauce and sprinkled with fresh to... spinach and broccoli, artichoke he... There's always a line out the doo... the signature pizza, brimming w... made sausage. Although pizza is... the menu lists a number of tradi... and-white-checked tablecloths... the tables, creating an old-fa... ambience. And speaking of Chi... here. The chain takes its name... who loves that thick crust, bu... ten-foot pole.

152

8

Restaurant Classifications by Comfort

More pleasant if in red

X	Comfortable
XX	Quite comfortable
XxX	Very comfortable
XxxX	Top class comfortable
XxxxX	Luxury in the traditional style
🍽	Small plates

Map Coordinates

Sonya's Palace ✿ ✿

Italian   XXXX

A4   100 Reuther Pl. (at 30th Street)

Dinner daily

Manhattan ▶ Chelsea

Phone: 415-867-5309
Subway: 14th St – 8 Av
Web: www.sonyasfabulouspalace.com
Prices: $$$

Home cooked Italian never tasted so good than at this unpretentious little place. The simple décor claims no big-name designers, and while the Murano glass light fixtures are chic and the velveteen-covered chairs are comfortable, this isn't a restaurant where millions of dollars were spent on the interior.

Instead, food is the focus here. The restaurant's name may not be Italian, but it nonetheless serves some of the best pasta in the city, made fresh in-house. Dishes follow the seasons, thus ravioli may be stuffed with fresh ricotta and herbs in summer, and pumpkin in fall. Most everything is liberally dusted with Parmigiano Reggiano, a favorite ingredient of the chef.

For dessert, you'll have to deliberate between the likes of creamy tiramisu, ricotta cheesecake, and homemade gelato. One thing's for sure: you'll never miss your nonna's cooking when you eat at Sonya's.

153

Lunch daily

San Francisco ▶ Nob Hill

retriever,
waitstaff
e dining
friendly
guests.
der the
edium
ed by
inged
ch as
pan-

ome
erm

eria
nara
anic

about
ouse-
here,
. Red-
adorn
aurant
choice
ughter,
with a

meat with a

107

9

Where to Eat

San Francisco

The Castro, once a cluster of farmland, is today a pulsating community punctuated by chic boutiques, hopping bars, and handsomely restored Victorians. In fact, it's a perpetual party here, with everybody waiting to sample the area's range of shabby to chic bars and dance clubs that spin tunes from multi-platinum pop icons. To feed its buzzing population of gym bunnies, leather daddies, and out-of-towners on tour to this mecca, the Castro teems with cool cafeterias. Start your day right at **Kitchen Story**, where the mascarpone-stuffed, deep-fried French toast has a following as large as the district's diversity. Then, stop in at **Thorough Bread & Pastry** if only to watch their

bakers craft *the* best almond croissant in town. Linger at **Cafe Flore**, whose quaint patio is more evocative of its Parisian namesake than the simple continental fare. Primo for a quick lunch, Chef Chris Cosentino's more casual successor, **Porcellino** is *salumi* central with murals of smoked meats donning its walls and a small front market selling the full line from **Boccalone**, Cosentino's salumeria, as well as pasta, olive oil, and other Italian staples. While gourmands may prefer **La Méditerranée**, one of the many fine-dining establishments for worthwhile cuisine, word on the street is that the best flavors here are served on the run. Look no further than the kitschy kiosk **Hot Cookie**, which is perfect for that hit of sweet.

COLE VALLEY

Neighboring Cole Valley may be small in size, but flaunts huge personality. Cradling a mix of yuppies and families, this snoot-free quarter also embraces global flavors as seen in purveyors like **Say Cheese**, filled with quality international varieties. On Monday nights, dog-lovers treat the whole family to dinner at **Zazie**. Equally fun is a visit to **Val de Cole**, a wine shop offering value table wines to go with a delish dinner. The back garden patio at quaint **Cafe Reverie** is a stroller-friendly

Castro
Cole Valley
Haight-Ashbury
Noe Valley

GOLDEN GATE PARK

THE PANHANDLE

CIVIC CENTER

Magnolia Pub

HAIGHT-ASHBURY

COLE VALLEY

BUENA VISTA PARK

Duboce Park-Duboce & Noe

Duboce-Church

UPPER MARKET

Padrecito

Cole-Carl

RICHMOND & SUNSET

ASHBURY HEIGHTS

CORONA HEIGHTS PARK

RANDALL MUSEUM

Church St.

L'Ardoise

Pesce

Starbelly

MISSION DOLORES

EUREKA VALLEY

CASTRO THEATRE

Frances

Mama Ji's

Anchor Oyster Bar

CASTRO DISTRICT

Church-18 St

MISSION DOLORES

MISSION

TWIN PEAKS

NOE VALLEY

Saru
Church-24 St

Contigo

DIAMOND HEIGHTS

GLEN CANYON PARK

Church-30 St

MT. DAVIDSON

MIRALOMA PARK

San Jose-Randall

La Corneta

Glen Park

asado; or **Cha Cha Cha**, a groovy tapas bar flowing with fresh-fruit sangria. Nurse that hangover with greasy hash browns and hotcakes at **Pork Store Cafe**, or head to **Haight Street Market** for a ready-made gourmet spread. On game night, kick back with a pint and plate of wings at old-school **Kezar Pub**.

spot for a snack, whereas the 1930's throwback **Ice Cream Bar** with a soda fountain and lunch counter is mobbed by hipsters. Counterculturalists have long sought haven in the hippiefied Haight-Ashbury, where despite the onslaught of retail chains, smoke shops and record stores dominate the landscape. **Second Act** is an alluring marketplace for artisan food vendors including **High Cotton Kitchen**, packed for its ravishing spread of Southern staples. The Valley's aversion to fine dining and adoration for laid-back spots is further evident in lines that snake out the door of homey Puerto Rican favorite, **Parada 22** for authentic *pernil*

NOE VALLEY

Noe Valley is known for its specialty shops, and Italian emporium **Pasta Gina** sells everything you might need for a night in with *nonna*. **Noe Valley Bakery** is divine for a bit of bread, after which a pour of fresh coffee from the **Castro Coffee Company** is in order. Meats are all the rage at **Drewes Meats**, while **Marcello's** is a post-cocktail mecca for fast, fresh, and fab pizza. Keeping pace with this sense of "spirit," **Swirl on Castro** is a sleek space big on boutique wines, but also brimming with stemware and accessories. Seal all the booze and bites with a soothing brew at **Samovar Tea Lounge**, specializing in artisan loose-leaf teas.

Anchor Oyster Bar 🐷

Seafood ✗

B2

579 Castro St. (bet. 18th & 19th Sts.)

Phone: 415-431-3990
Web: www.anchoroysterbar.com
Prices: $$

Lunch Mon – Sat
Dinner nightly

Landlubbers seeking a taste of the sea can be found pulling up a stool at this Castro institution, where waves of waiting diners spill out the doors. This tiny, minimally adorned space filled with old-fashion charm is better for twosomes than groups.

While the menu may be petite, it's full of fresh fare like a light and flavorful Dungeness crab "burger" on a sesame bun; Caesar salad combining sweet prawns and tangy anchovy dressing; or a cup of creamy Boston clam chowder loaded with fresh clams and potatoes. As the name portends, raw oysters are a specialty, so fresh and briny that the accompanying mignonette may not be necessary. And while the cioppino is only an occasional special, it's worth ordering if available, as it's one of SF's signatures.

Contigo 🐷

Spanish ✗✗

B3

1320 Castro St. (bet. 24th & Jersey Sts.)

Phone: 415-285-0250
Web: www.contigosf.com
Prices: $$

Dinner Tue – Sun

Contigo is Spanish for "with you," and you'll certainly want to bring some of your favorite people along to linger at this Iberian charmer's warm dining room and pretty back patio. Sustainability is a watchword here: the design incorporates re-used and recycled materials, and each dish reflects the season's best ingredients.

Tempting small plates include smoky caramelized coca (flatbread) with garlicky house-made *txistorra* pork sausage, Manchego, and sliced summer squash. Simple yet delicious offerings go on to feature slices of crusty levain topped with smashed fresh peas, roasted porcini, trumpet mushrooms, and more Manchego shavings. Their outstanding pork-lamb-jamón meatballs in a tangy tomato-sherry sauce are among the best *albondigas* you'll find.

Frances

Californian ✗✗

C2

3870 17th St. (at Pond St.)

Phone: 415-621-3870   Dinner nightly
Web: www.frances-sf.com
Prices: $$$

Frances is set in a quiet, residential neighborhood that complements its effortlessly cool and casual San Franciscan vibe. Parking is non-existent, so plan to arrive on foot—all the better to sample the variety of local wine. Groups larger than four don't fit into this shoebox and even solo diners may need to wait in line during rush hour. A few bar seats serve walk-ins.

The closely-spaced tables quickly fill with beautiful ceramic dishes of Chef/owner Melissa Perello's food, which may include airy bacon beignets with maple crème fraîche and crisp baby kale with fennel, pecorino, and dates. Don't miss the delicious roasted duck breast, coated in a nutty cumin-pumpkin seed crust and served over grilled blood oranges and caramelized sweet potatoes.

La Corneta

Mexican ✗

B4

2834 Diamond St. (bet. Bosworth & Chenery Sts.)

Phone: 415-469-8757   Lunch & dinner daily
Web: www.lacorneta.com
Prices: මම

Make sure you've got cash, plenty of patience to wait in line, and a huge appetite before arriving at this massively popular spot. Inside, vivid murals and walls painted in bright hues of orange and yellow create a cheery yet very clean atmosphere. Tasty favorites like burritos (beware of anything with the word "super"—they mean it); made-to-order salmon tacos; nachos smothered in black beans, cheese, and guac; or shrimp and steak-stuffed quesadillas are all freshly made, utterly satisfying, and seriously filling. Place your order at the counter and stroll down the line to pick your protein (chicken, steak, prawns, or tofu), beans (black, pinto, or refried), and *pico de gallo* (hot or mild). If you still have room, go for a warm, sugary churro...bliss.

L'Ardoise

French ✗✗

C1

151 Noe St. (at Henry St.)

Phone: 415-437-2600   Dinner Tue – Sat
Web: www.ardoisesf.com
Prices: **$$**

Local couples do date night in high Parisian style at this long-running Duboce Triangle bistro, where a largely French staff serves up classics like coq au vin and steak frites. The seafood *cassolette* brings together plump prawns, huge (and fresh) mussels, and flaky fish together over a bed of mashed potatoes, then swaths them in a velvety lobster bisque reduction. A floating island of caramelized meringue is especially indulgent, especially when served in a pool of crème anglaise with strawberries and caramel sauce.

Set on a charming, tree-lined block, L'Ardoise's secret weapon is its softly lit back area, whose rich burgundy walls draw in diners. Given their compact space and subdued ambience, save this one for a tête-à-tête, not a big group.

Magnolia Pub

Gastropub ✗

A1

1398 Haight St. (at Masonic Ave.)

Phone: 415-864-7468   Lunch & dinner daily
Web: www.magnoliapub.com
Prices: **$$**

Situated amid the psychedelic storefronts and "medicinal" marijuana emporiums of the Upper Haight, Magnolia is an oasis of high-quality beer on an otherwise touristy strip. As out-of-towners pack the black banquettes for a hearty lunch and locals shoot the breeze at the well-worn back bar, pints of the house-brewed beers, from IPAs to English-style ales, can be seen everywhere.

That said, Magnolia is a prime food destination, specializing in tempting treats like crunchy, garlicky Scotch quail eggs and a surprisingly refreshing fried chicken sandwich with fennel-cabbage slaw, fennel honey, pickled jalapeños, and aïoli. Be sure to save room for the moist, none-too-sweet sticky toffee pudding, topped with delicious Humphry Slocombe beer ice cream.

Mama Ji's

Chinese ✗

B2

4416 18th St. (bet. Douglass & Eureka Sts.)

Phone: 415-626-4416   Lunch & dinner daily
Web: www.mamajissf.com
Prices: 💰

Dim sum options outside of Chinatown and the Avenues are rare, which explains why this cute little Cantonese spot has become a Castro favorite in its first year. While the crowd may not draw Chinese expats craving a taste of home, the bilingual menu is nonetheless full of authentic treats, from the tender and flavorful *xiao long bao* to meltingly soft tofu topped with steaming shrimp in a soy-ginger broth.

Service is basic but very friendly, and the mini, simple space is full of natural light from the quiet tree-lined street outside. Large groups should head elsewhere; but smaller ones will delight in sharing chewy, spicy cold noodles loaded with vegetables and chili paste, or roasted eggplant stuffed with gingery shrimp—especially at these prices.

Padrecito

Mexican ✗✗

A1

901 Cole St. (at Carl St.)

Phone: 415-742-5505   Dinner nightly
Web: www.padrecitosf.com
Prices: $$

Like its baby sib Mamacita, this easygoing cantina serves modern Cal-Mex food crafted with excellent, locally sourced ingredients. Padrecito bears a bohemian, south-of-the-border spirit with a buzzy cocktail bar that pours a remarkable list of tequilas. Its dining room is rife with reclaimed wood; but climb a few colorful steps to arrive in the lovely mezzanine decked in chandeliers glinting over the main room.

Adept, smiling servers whirl around diners cradling such specials as *sopa Azteca*, a purée of ancho chilies and tomato bobbing with meltingly tender *queso* Oaxaca and avocado; or grilled Arctic char tacos sauced with crimson-red achiote and crowned with mango-jicama slaw. Warm, sugary churros with mascarpone-coffee *crema* offer mucho fulfillment.

Pesce

Italian ✗✗

C1

2223 Market St. (bet. 15th & 16th Sts.)

Phone: 415-928-8025   Dinner nightly
Web: www.pescebarsf.com
Prices: **$$**

Like any good SF renter, when Pesce saw an opportunity for more space, it made the move and uprooted from Polk Street to the Castro. Its commodious new home is minimalist yet warm, with wood tables, bistro chairs, and a pressed-tin ceiling. But some things stay the same, namely, the Venetian-inspired, seafood-heavy cuisine and wonderfully warm service for which it's known.

As the Market Street crowds pass by, groups of friends sip wine and share small plates like seafood *fritto misto*; or caramelized potato gnocchi with shreds of milk-braised pork, sage, and crispy pancetta. The silky hamachi crudo is a must-order, accented with citrus-infused olive oil and a tangle of micro greens. Creamy, none-too-sweet panna cotta is a comforting conclusion.

Saru

Japanese ✗

C3

3856 24th St. (bet. Sanchez & Vicksburg Sts.)

Phone: 415-400-4510   Lunch & dinner Tue – Sun
Web: www.akaisarusf.com
Prices: **$$**

A handful of seats along the L-shaped counter and a smattering of high and low tables are all the comforts one needs at this petite Noe Valley sushi bar. The talented team works behind a display case of fresh and appetizing fish, topped with little jars of powders and seasoned salts.

The menu focuses on excellent quality and judiciously embellished maki, nigiri, and sashimi. The signature tasting spoons reveal a duo of sushi bar preparations, such as *ankimo* (monkfish liver) lightly torched and set atop cool but spicy daikon, coupled with raw sea scallop dressed with finely diced wasabi root and a touch of yuzu zest. Nigiri from the day's offerings has brought pristine white salmon, Japanese yellowtail, and incredibly rich, fatty slices of tuna.

San Francisco ▲ Castro

Starbelly ☺

Californian 🍴🍴

C1

3583 16th St. (at Market St.)

Phone: 415-252-7500
Web: www.starbellysf.com
Prices: $$

Lunch & dinner daily

Oh, Starbelly, you devilish creature. Must you tempt us with your salted caramel *pot de crème*, your rosemary cornmeal cookies (limiting us to one at brunch), your orange blossom doughnuts, and your roasted butternut squash pizza with black garlic and chèvre?

It's no wonder this local darling is forever packed—the dynamite menu, welcoming staff, and cheery, kick-back vibe make for a winning combo—and we can't get enough. It's a tough table to score, so expect a line and know it's worth the wait. Freshly fried and golden-crisp spuds; broccoli *de ceccio* scramble; or a grilled steak sandwich are among the delicious options. If all else fails, go for their popular house-made pizza highlighting chorizo, a soft sunny-side-up, and fragrant cilantro.

Red=Particularly Pleasant.
Look for the red 🍴 symbols!

23

Civic Center

Anchoring this old, new, and now fashionable district is the gilded beaux arts-style dome of City Hall, whose architectural splendor gleams along the main artery of the Civic Center. Following in these footsteps, refined details grace the neighborhood's prized cultural institutions like the War Memorial & Performing Arts Center, as well as the Asian Art Museum. On Wednesdays and Sundays, SF's oldest market, **Heart of the City**,

Asian ingredients like young ginger and Buddha's hand. Ground zero for California's marriage equality movement and countless political protests, City Hall's plaza is also home to galas like LovEvolution; the SF Symphony's biennial Black & White Ball; and the Lao New Year Festival held every year, in April.

Neighboring Tenderloin successfully alleviates this region's now-defunct repute

erupts in full form on the vast promenade outside City Hall. This independent and farmer-operated arcade is a hit among locals thanks to an extensive offering of high-quality, locally sourced, and attractively priced produce—not to mention rare

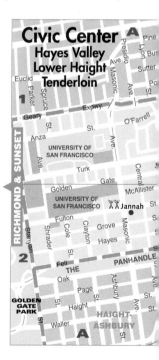

as a "food desert." Akin to Manhattan's Meatpacking District and home to a vast Asian—particularly Vietnamese—population, this once tough but now trendy "underbelly" boasts an incredible array of authentic ethnic eateries. Gone are those gangs of organized crime, and in place Larkin Street (also known as "**Little Saigon**") is crowded with mom-and-pop shops like **Saigon Sandwich**—leading the way with spicy *bánh mì* made from fresh, crusty baguettes for only $3.25 a pop. Nearby, **Turtle Tower** has amassed quite a patronage (celebrity chefs included) for fragrant *pho ga*; while romantic little **Bodega Bistro** is best known for bold aromas, French flavors, and more *pho*. Score points among family and friends by treating them to an authentic and

elaborate Vietnamese spread at the **Four Seasons Restaurant**. After indulging in a shining plate of their garlicky noodles, savor an equally excellent selection of classic cocktails reinterpreted at **Bourbon & Branch**—a sultry hideaway and former speakeasy. For a more sober and substantial meal, local suits head to **Elmira Rosticceria** for a range

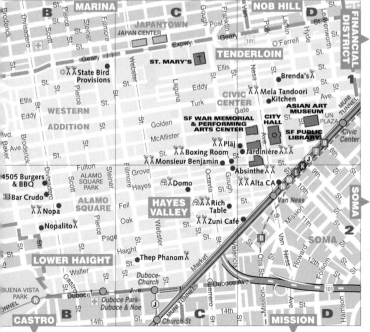

delicacies like cheeses and cured meats (*paleta ibérico de bellota* rules the roost here). Sate such salty treats with a sip from **True Sake**, a super-cool, all-sake joint, whereas caffeine junkies can get their daily dose of **Blue Bottle** straight from the kiosk on Linden Street. Finish with a tour of Europe at **Miette**, an impossibly charming confiserie jammed with rare chocolates, salted licorice, taffy, and gelées; or **Christopher Elbow Artisanal Chocolate** for a smidge of bliss.

LOWER HAIGHT

Steps to the west, the Lower Haight attracts sporty troupes and hipster groups for sake-infused cocktails at **Noc Noc**, followed by fantastic live tunes at The Independent, a standing room-only music venue. Some dress to impress the über-cool scene at **Maven**, where inventive cocktails, tasty bites, and groovy tunes guarantee a great night out. Speaking of beats, the Fillmore Jazz District continues to seduce (and save) music lovers today. Settled by African-American GI's at the end of World War II, the Lower Haight hummed with jazz greats like Billie Holiday and Miles Davis. With the attempted resurgence of the jazz district, the Fillmore today goes on to resound with tunes from rock icons like Jimi Hendrix and The Dead. Of course, the annual Fillmore Jazz Festival is a must-see celebration of musical magnificence.

of Italian-inspired eats—take advantage of their flourishing take-out business during the lunch rush. Come nightfall, the Tenderloin's muddle of strip clubs and bars becomes a hot hub for a decadent nightlife. Completely dark and eerie, yet thoroughly enlightening, **Opaque** is a literal dining-in-the-dark establishment where guests rely on their every sense, save sight, to appreciate an entire meal.

HAYES VALLEY

West of the Civic Center, Hayes Valley is undeniably polished, with a coterie of designer boutiques set amid a medley of sleek retreats. Some residents find themselves smitten by **Chantal Guillon Macarons**, which spotlights exquisitely flavored macarons served in a French-style setting. Others may choose to country hop to Spain by way of **Nosa Ria**, a prized market selling imported

Absinthe

Mediterranean ✗✗

C2

398 Hayes St. (at Gough St.)

Phone: 415-551-1590
Web: www.absinthe.com
Prices: $$$

Lunch & dinner daily

The original colonist of Hayes Valley's now-bustling restaurant row, this "green fairy" still has plenty of sparkle, thanks to its timeless brasserie atmosphere and classic French- and Mediterranean-inspired menu. Even a lowly chicken breast gets the magic treatment here, with crunchy skin, perfectly wilted lacinato kale, and swirls of luscious bourbon-yam purée. The same goes for a little gem lettuce salad with fine herbs dressed in red wine-shallot vinaigrette.

Perched between formal and casual, the restaurant draws relaxed alfresco lunchers with dogs by day and stylish symphony or opera patrons by night. In either incarnation, it's a lovely place for a cocktail—a few may earn you a wink from those fairies, flitting across the dining room mural.

Alta CA

Californian ✗✗

D2

1420 Market St. (bet. Fell St. & Van Ness Ave.)

Phone: 415-590-2585
Web: www.altaca.co
Prices: $$

Lunch Mon – Fri
Dinner nightly

This newish mid-Market destination radiates California cool from every pore, with its hip reclaimed-wood décor (including dramatic floor-to-ceiling shelving) and young foodie crowd from the nearby tech offices. A large, angled bar provides the heart of the room, while tables face big, light-filled windows overlooking bustling Market Street.

Owner Daniel Patterson (of Coi) offers more casual, but still complex cuisine here at Alta, with a menu of plates in every size for sharing. Pair a creative cocktail with the crispy chickpea and oxtail fritters over creamy herb aïoli, or the warm root vegetable salad with ribbons of fried parsnip and carrot. Another must-order: the crispy, caramelized pork trotter terrine crowned with a slow-cooked egg.

Bar Crudo

B2

Seafood

655 Divisadero St. (bet. Grove & Hayes Sts.)

Phone: 415-409-0679
Web: www.barcrudo.com
Prices: $$

Dinner Tue – Sun

Seafood, and plenty of it, is the specialty at this Divisadero hot spot. As the name suggests, their crudo is supreme: whether it's Arctic char with horseradish crème fraîche, wasabi tobiko, and dill; or perhaps raw scallop with sweet corn purée, tarragon oil, and popped sorghum, the combinations are fresh and delicious. Platters of shellfish are available, and there are a few hot dishes like head-on Louisiana prawns in a lobster broth, served beside a baby fennel-pea shoot salad. This small and largely popular restaurant is often standing-room-only, with only a handful of tables; most guests pack in at or around the bar. Grab a glass of wine or a beer, peek into the open kitchen, and be sure to check out the futuristic mermaid art on the walls.

Boxing Room

C1

Southern

399 Grove St. (at Gough St.)

Phone: 415-430-6590
Web: www.boxingroom.com
Prices: $$

Lunch & dinner daily

A trip to the real-life Big Easy may be short on veggies (unless fried okra counts), but northern California balances the Cajun and Creole indulgences on offer at this lively restaurant, leading to dishes like a spicy-sweet fig and arugula salad with spiced pecans and pan-seared goat cheese. Casual and sleek, it draws business types for lunch and happy hour, when they cluster around the oyster bar with beers and boiled peanuts. All the classics can be found here including gumbo, fried alligator, and a perfect jambalaya studded with spicy andouille and tender roasted duck. The simple and high-ceilinged dining room encourages lingering—as does the airy angel-food "strawberry shortcake" with lemon verbena ice cream and tangy whipped yogurt.

Brenda's

Southern ✗

D1

652 Polk St. (at Eddy St.)

Phone: 415-345-8100
Web: www.frenchsoulfood.com
Prices: $$

Lunch daily
Dinner Wed – Sun

Big portions and even bigger flavors are the draw at this taste of New Orleans, helmed by Louisiana-bred Chef/owner Brenda Buenviaje. Chicken étouffée offers a smoky, dark roux packed with vegetables, while a flawless *muffuletta* is packed with savory meat, provolone, and spicy olive salad (it's great with an ice-cold Abita beer). Sweet and salty golden beignets, filled with cheesy crawfish or molten Ghirardelli chocolate, could be a meal on their own.

The Tenderloin address is rough around the edges, but Brenda's interior is quite lovely, with a light-filled dining room, bright murals, and high ceilings. Count on a wait here now that the secret is out, particularly at lunch and brunch—and don't plan on lingering, as the staff are expert table-turners.

Domo 😊

Japanese ✗

C2

511 Laguna St. (bet. Fell & Linden Sts.)

Phone: 415-861-8887
Web: www.domosf.com
Prices: $$

Lunch Mon – Fri
Dinner nightly

The cat's out of the bag: this tiny, unembellished spot is foodie paradise. And it's no surprise as über fresh sushi at affordable prices plus long waits to boot make for a killer combo. It's a get in-get out affair here at Domo—there's no trying to linger over sake—where a small interior with wood counters and a sprinkling of sidewalk tables keep things simple.

A tidy list of specialty rolls are spelled out on a mirror—try the Apollo Roll, avocado, cucumber, and shiso topped with caramelized scallops, crab, and tobiko; or the Alpha, filled with smoky *unagi*, mango, and avocado, crowned with spicy tuna and pickled jalapeño. Delectable nigiri are another spot-on option like silky and oily aji or firm Spanish mackerel enhanced with fresh wasabi.

4505 Burgers & BBQ

Barbecue ✗

B2

705 Divisadero St. (bet. Fulton & Grove Sts.)

Phone: 415-231-6993   Lunch & dinner daily
Web: www.4505meats.com
Prices: 🌰

With lines out the door and the scent of wood smoke heavy in the air, one thing is clear: this Civic Center barbecue spot is smokin' hot. And with no service or ambience to speak of (diners order at the counter, claim a spot at one of the picnic tables arranged in the parking lot, and then dig in), the focus is firmly on the food.

Chef and butcher Ryan Farr offers succulent fare by the plate or pound. Select a trio and revel in a meaty heap of pork ribs, super moist pulled chicken, and the Bay Area's best brisket accompanied by a Parker House roll, pickles, and sliced onion. Sides like the *frankaroni* (a mac and cheese fritter studded with hot dog) are average, but follow the crowd and pair your platter with 4505's "best damn grass-fed cheeseburger."

Jannah

Middle Eastern ✗✗

A2

1775 Fulton St. (bet. Central & Masonic Aves.)

Phone: 415-567-4400   Lunch & dinner Tue – Sun
Web: www.yayacuisine.com
Prices: $$

The name of Yahya Salih's lovely Middle Eastern restaurant translates to "heaven," a concept echoed by its blue walls and ceiling, adorned with puffy white cloud paintings and glowing chandeliers. From the large front bar to the back patio, it's an airy and inviting choice for groups or families.

Paradise extends to the plate, where seasonal California ingredients are highlighted in Kurdish and Iraqi specialties like grilled, mint-marinated lamb kabobs with outstanding accompaniments including creamy hummus, ultra-fresh tabbouleh, and crisp *lavash*. But diners veer towards more unique dishes like the *perdaplow*, a richly flavorful, *basteeya*-like phyllo pastry enclosing tender shredded chicken, fragrant cardamom, and sweet golden raisins.

Jardinière

D1

300 Grove St. (at Franklin St.)

Phone: 415-861-5555
Web: www.jardiniere.com
Prices: $$$

Dinner nightly

For a memorable night on the town, don your best dress, find a hand to hold, and head to this longtime favorite, tinged with a sense of bygone romance. Stop off at the circular bar and join the well-heeled couples sipping cocktails pre- or post-opera. Snag a seat upstairs where tables dot a candle-lit balcony overlooking the lower levels, and stunning arched windows show off views of the bustling street.

Delectable dishes like wild fennel pappardelle with oxtail ragout, cherry tomatoes, and Niçoise olives; or ravioli bursting with autumnal squash, roasted bell peppers, provolone, and crisp sage keep locals happy. The Monday night three-course prix-fixe (with wine pairings) for $55 is a steal, while the chef's nightly tasting menu makes for a fine feast.

Mela Tandoori Kitchen

D1

536 Golden Gate Ave. (bet. Polk St. & Van Ness Ave.)

Phone: 415-447-4041
Web: N/A
Prices: $$

Lunch Mon – Fri
Dinner Mon – Sat

If *"mela"* means "fair" in Hindi, then Tandoori Kitchen is aptly named. As fun and lively as a carnival, this welcoming spot sports brightly striped walls and colorful splashes of paint set aglow by stylish pendant lights. Its menu displays a vast litany of eats, and obliging servers are happy to lend a hand with useful recommendations.

The overwhelming lunch buffet is a hit among office workers for hot, crispy samosas with sweet tamarind chutney, or fiery *tandoori* wings baked until smoky and juicy. The area takes a bit of a dive at sunset, but that doesn't curb this kitchen's appeal. Families keep coming to devour huge portions of *aloo gobi* in an onion-and-tomato masala along with intensely spicy lamb *vindaloo*—and inevitably leave toting leftovers.

Monsieur Benjamin

French ✗✗

C1

451 Gough St. (at Ivy St.)

Phone: 415-403-2233 Dinner nightly
Web: www.monsieurbenjamin.com
Prices: $$$

This highly anticipated newcomer delivers superb bistro fare in an inspired setting. The casual vibe means that it is welcoming to families with children; the chic space, anchored by a large central bar with flattering pendant lighting, makes it just as popular for date-night.

Towards the back, note the exhibition kitchen's meticulous team at work, preparing their beautifully executed French classics. Begin with tasty, golden-brown croquettes with a decadent potato-leek-Gruyère filling. Then move on to an absolutely standout ragout of sweet lobster meat, reduced stock, mirepoix, and fine herbs twirled with spaghetti. Equally impressive desserts include the gateau Marjolaine layering hazelnut and almond meringue, praline mousse, and chocolate ganache.

Nopa

Californian ✗✗

B2

560 Divisadero St. (at Hayes St.)

Phone: 415-864-8643 Lunch Sat – Sun
Web: www.nopasf.com Dinner nightly
Prices: $$

Before you're able to enjoy a single forkful at this Bay Area sensation, you'll have to secure a table—and that takes some serious effort. Reservations are snapped up at lightning speed, and hopeful walk-ins must lineup prior to the start of service to add their name to the list.

The good news? Your efforts will be well rewarded. Inside, an open kitchen, soaring ceilings, and hordes of ravenous sophisticates produce a cacophonous setting in which to relish Nopa's wonderful, organic, wood-fired cuisine. Dig in to a bruschetta of grilled *levain* spread with smashed avocado, pickled jalapeños, lemon-dressed arugula, and shaved *mezzo secco*, or go for the roasted King salmon fillet over creamed corn, smoky maitakes, crisp green beans, and sweet tomato confit.

Nopalito

Mexican   ✗

B2

306 Broderick St. (bet. Fell & Oak Sts.)

Phone: 415-437-0303   Lunch & dinner daily
Web: www.nopalitosf.com
Prices: 🪙🪙

Whether they're digging into a griddled corn *panucho* stuffed with earthy black beans and zesty citrus-marinated chicken or tender *mole* enchiladas garnished with tangy *queso fresco*, local couples and families adore this sustainable Mexican spot. Sister to Cal-cuisine icon Nopa, Nopalito is so beloved that an equally good and popular Inner Sunset location is thriving.

The small, cheerful space with reclaimed wood and bright green accents doesn't take reservations; call ahead to get on the list, or try takeout. Once seated, friendly servers will guide the way with house-made *horchata* for the kids and an extensive tequila selection for grown-ups. Both groups will certainly agree on a sweet finish: Mexican chocolate and seasonal fruit *paletas* are a favorite.

Pläj

Scandinavian   ✗✗

D1

333 Fulton St. (bet. Franklin & Gough Sts.)

Phone: 415-863-8400   Dinner nightly
Web: www.plajrestaurant.com
Prices: $$

This attractive spot located inside the Inn at the Opera is the love child of Swedish-born Chef/owner Roberth Sundell. Strutting a small bar and two dining areas, inflections like white linen-topped tables and orange accents give the space a stylish yet low-key atmosphere.

The menu is Scandinavian featuring classic ingredients and flavor combinations mingled with Californian influence. Meals may start with toasted rye bread and proceed to pillow-soft potato dumplings arranged atop onion confit, sweet lingonberry sauce, brown butter, and smoky lardons. Try a herring tasting paired with marinades like saffron-tomato and an Asian-inspired ginger and smoked soy, ideally complemented by a Scandinavian wine, beer, or soda—lingonberry-elderflower anyone?

Rich Table

Contemporary ✗✗

C2

199 Gough St. (at Oak St.)

Phone: 415-355-9085   Dinner nightly
Web: www.richtablesf.com
Prices: $$

Its rustic-chic décor, highlighting reclaimed and raw wood, gives Rich Table a farmhouse feel, and the crowds that pack it are equally shabby-sleek. Reserve early or expect a long wait, as there's serious competition for seats that quickly fill with young professionals in designer casualwear.

The contemporary American food from Chef/owners Evan and Sarah Rich is highly engaging with menu mainstays like crispy sardine chips and porcini-salted doughnuts set alongside a warm raclette dip. Snap peas are arranged beside grapefruit segments, pecans, and nasturtium blossoms; while seasonal mains include a tangy strawberry gazpacho topped with crunchy chicken skin and burrata. Also irresistable is a smoky pork chop posed atop wheat berries and pork-*garum* jus.

Thep Phanom

Thai ✗

C2

400 Waller St. (at Fillmore St.)

Phone: 415-431-2526   Dinner nightly
Web: www.thepphanom.com
Prices: $$

A good Thai spot is as essential to an SF neighborhood as air to breath, and Lower Haighters have long pledged their allegiance to Thep Phanom's interpretation of the sweet and spicy cuisine. Whether they crave sinfully crisp, golden-brown chicken wings with sweet-chili dipping sauce or a range of healthy vegetarian options, they've yet to be disappointed.

Tucked just off bustling Haight and Fillmore, the location is no friend to drivers (prepare to circle), but once inside, it's dimly lit and low-key, ideal for a quiet date night or even solo dining. Spice levels are adjustable—and hot means hot—for all the dishes ranging from creamy red pumpkin curry, to "Thaitanic" tofu, eggplant, and string beans in a lemongrass-ginger- and Thai basil-sauce.

State Bird Provisions ✿

B1

Contemporary ✗✗

1529 Fillmore St. (bet. Geary Blvd. & O'Farrell St.)

Phone: 415-795-1272   Dinner nightly
Web: www.statebirdsf.com
Prices: $$

&

One of the city's toughest tickets, State Bird's nightly lines begin forming late afternoon. The restaurant expanded in an attempt to accommodate the crowds, but scoring a reservation is still a coup. The space is casual, raw, and feels like one big party with industrial pegboard walls and concrete floors. Most of the menu isn't so much ordered as paraded from table to table on dim sum-style carts and trays.

Though it lacks the comforts of traditional fine dining, State Bird is both an innovator and lots of fun. It's hard not to order everything that the friendly, efficient staff rolls by. Duck liver mousse boasts a subtler pleasure as it softens and almost melts into warm almond financiers. Wide ribbons of yuba "pasta" primavera may tangle with soft poached egg, snap peas, tiny green leaves, and smoked egg yolk, but that kimchi tucked at the bottom of the bowl skyrockets it to greatness. Push the limit with one extra round of buttery deep-fried garlic fry bread with a creamy slice of burrata—pure and total gluttony at its finest.

Do try to save room for dessert, namely the ice cream sandwich in rotating flavors like soft rosemary shortbread with chicory-coffee ice cream and fudge sauce.

Zuni Café

Mediterranean ✕✕

D2

1658 Market St. (bet. Franklin & Gough Sts.)

Phone:	415-552-2522
Web:	www.zunicafe.com
Prices:	$$

Lunch & dinner Tue – Sun

Over thirty years young and still thriving, locals and tourists alike remain drawn to this renowned favorite, famous for its laid-back Cali vibe and great, locally sourced eats. The iconic space is styled with exposed brick, contemporary paintings, and a wood-burning fireplace at the center of the action. Located near the Civic Center, Financial District, and SoMa, Zuni Café makes for a perfect lunch destination. Indeed, many local business folk can be found noshing on wood-fired pizzas (try the pecorino, pancetta, and arugula); or the grass-fed hamburger on grilled rosemary focaccia, smothered with garlic aïoli. Swing by at dinner for the likes of pork tenderloin and fennel sausage with sautéed rapini, cannellini beans, and breadcrumb salsa.

Bib Gourmand 🐷
indicates our inspectors'
favorites for good value.

Financial District

Booming with high-rises and corporate headquarters, San Francisco's Financial District is world-renowned. While the city itself may be known for its easygoing attitude, the financial sector is bustling, given its concentration of Fortune 500 companies, multi-national banks, and law firms. Settled along

the west of the waterfront, on weekdays expect to see streetcars, pedestrians, and wildly tattooed bicycle messengers clogging the routes of the triangle bounded by Kearny, Jackson, and Market streets. Come noon, lines snake out the doors of better grab-and-go sandwich shops and salad bars. And yet, irrespective of time

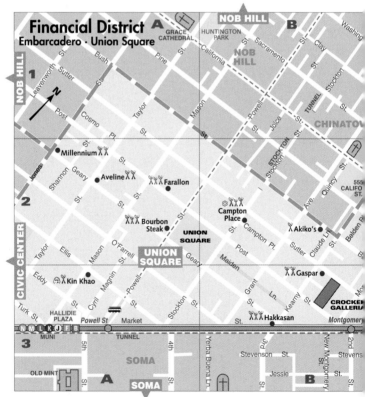

Financial District
Embarcadero · Union Square

NOB HILL

NOB HILL

CIVIC CENTER

CHINATOWN

Millennium

Aveline

Farallon

Campton Place

Akiko's

Bourbon Steak

UNION SQUARE

UNION SQUARE

Kin Khao

Gaspar

CROCKER GALLERIA

Hakkasan

Montgomery

MUNI

TUNNEL

SOMA

OLD MINT

SOMA

Stevenson St.

Jessie St.

555 CALIFO ST.

HALLIDIE PLAZA

Powell St

Market

GRACE CATHEDRAL

HUNTINGTON PARK

of day, steady streams of expense-account clients patronize the FiDi's host of fine-dining establishments. Along Market Street, casual cafés and chain restaurants keep the focus on families, tourists, and shoppers alike.

EMBARCARDERO

Despite all that this area has to offer, its greatest culinary treasures lies within the famed **Ferry Building**. This 1898 steel-reinforced sandstone structure is easily recognized by its 244-foot clock tower that rises up from Market Street and way above the waterfront promenade—also called **The Embarcadero**.

It is among the few survivors of the 1906 earthquake and fire that destroyed most of this neighborhood. Thanks to a 2004 renovation, the soaring interior arcade makes a stunning showcase for regional products, artisanal foods, rare Chinese teas, and everything in between. Popularly referred to as the **Ferry Building Marketplace**, every diligent foodie is destined here for the likes of Lauren Kiino's **Il Cane Rosso,** a quick-serve rotisserie-cum-casual hangout serving weekday brunch (the olive oil-fried egg sandwich is a particular thrill); or lunch standbys like salads, soups, and sammies. Their three-

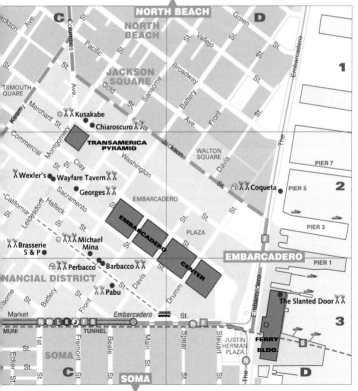

course, family-style dinners are attractively pegged at $30. This emporium also pays homage to the surrounding food community by highlighting small producers. Two of the most popular among them are **Cowgirl Creamery**'s farmstead cheeses, and Berkeley's **Acme Bread Company**—whose organic breads are a sight (and smell) to behold! Following this philosophy, find numerous organic and exotic mushrooms, medicinal herbs, and themed products at **Far West Fungi**. Here, patient enthusiasts can even

While such world-class food shopping may whet the appetite of many, more immediate cravings can be satisfied at the Building's more casual dining delights like **DELICA**, popular for beautifully prepared Japanese fusion food, from signature sushi rolls to savory croquettes. Join the corporate lunch rush seated at picnic tables in **Mijita** (run by Traci Des Jardins of **Jardinère** fame) to sample such treats as *queso fundido* or Baja-style fish tacos. Or, perch atop a barstool at **Hog Island Oyster Company** to get

purchase logs on which to grow their own harvest. Legendary **Frog Hollow Farm** is also stationed nearby, offering pristine seasonal fruit alongside homemade chutneys, marmalade and fresh-baked pastries. Known for their Parisian-style chocolates and caramels, **Recchiuti Confections** has elevated their craft to an art form that can only be described as heavenly. And, completing this gourmet trend are gleaming bottles of **McEvoy Ranch Olive Oil** from their Petaluma ranch that also includes an impressive array of olive oil-based products.

first dibs on their plump bivalves, plucked fresh from Tomales Bay. While this is a great spot to sit, slurp, and take in the view, the most decadent takeout option is still **Boccalone Salumeria**, for their comprehensive charcuterie. Whether purchasing these salty eats by the platter, pound, or layered in a single-serving "cone," prepare for an unapologetically carnivorous treat. On Tuesday, Thursday, and Saturday mornings, high-minded chefs share laughs with the locals at **Ferry Plaza Farmer's Market**, dealing in everything from organic produce

and baked goods to fresh pastas and tons more. On market days, open-air stands and tents line the picturesque sidewalk in front of the Ferry Building and rear plaza overlooking the bay.

Tourists and unwearied locals are sure to enjoy some visual stimulation at The Bay Lights—an undulating light installation by artist Leo Villareal—illuminating the west span of the Bay Bridge until March 2015. **The Embarcadero** (or "embarking place" in Spanish) promenade boasts the best view of this beautiful piece. Meanwhile, groups of suits know to head to the **Embarcadero Center** (spanning five blocks in the heart of the commercial district with reduced parking rates on weekends) to get their midday shopping fix in the sprawling three-story indoor mall, or to grab a quick lunch at one of the thirty-some eateries ranging from mini-chains to noodle shops. A speck of sweet from **See's Candies** or caffeine from **Peet's** makes for an ideal finale.

UNION SQUARE

Upscale department stores like Barneys, Neiman Marcus, and Saks preside over Union Square, where foodies gather for a gourmet experience and fashionistas flock to designer shops. Just as noodle lovers form a queue outside **KATANA-YA** for steaming bowls of slurp-worthy ramen, shopaholics and local bargain hunters pop into **Tout Sweet Patisserie** (housed inside Macy's) for a pick-me-up in the form of pastries, candies, and macarons. Take home a few extra goodies, if only to appreciate their beautiful packaging.

Akiko's

Japanese ✗

B2

431 Bush St. (bet. Grant & Kearny Sts.)

Phone: 415-397-3218   Lunch Mon – Fri
Web: www.akikosrestaurant.com   Dinner Mon – Sat
Prices: $$$

Akiko's is hard to find. In addition to sharing a name with a lesser nearby sushi bar, it's hidden just off an alleyway and has no sign. The cool clientele is probably happy to avoid any more competition for the mere handful of tables and seats at the small sushi bar.

Arrive at dinner, sit at the counter, toss aside that à la carte menu, and opt for an omakase feast created by the very talented chefs. Expect them to take liberties and leave tradition behind; yet the quality remains high with pristine nigiri featuring fluke, scallop, or geoduck clam minimally garnished and perched atop rice with a touch of nutty red rice vinegar. Bookend the meal with rich tuna poke with sesame, or a lightly torched slice of A5 Wagyu beef with black truffle shavings.

Aveline

Contemporary ✗✗

A2

490 Geary St. (at Taylor St.)

Phone: 415-345-2303   Dinner nightly
Web: www.avelinesf.com
Prices: $$$

Former *Top Chef* contestant Casey Thompson has lived up to her televised reputation at this Warwick Hotel beauté, which boasts some of the prettiest plates of food in town. And if the dishes could have been ripped out of a food magazine, the sophisticated space, decorated in a palette of grays, creams, and taupes, is every bit as worthy of a home-décor spread.

The menu groupings may sound quirky, but they often sing, as in the red abalone with pepperoni coulis, seafood foam, and roasted mushrooms, or those "deconstructed" baked potato bites with dehydrated and powdered bacon, cheese, sour cream, and onion. A delicious tomato pie with whipped bananas, parsley ice cream, and bourbon is another weird-in-theory, works-in-practice winner.

Barbacco

Italian XX

C3

220 California St. (bet. Battery & Front Sts.)

Phone: 415-955-1919
Web: www.barbaccosf.com
Prices: ⊖⊖

Lunch Mon – Fri
Dinner Mon – Sat

A sleek urban haunt with the feel of a local trattoria, Barbacco buzzes with suit-donning execs at lunch and post-work revelers at dinner. Grab a spot in the modern dining space—replete with low ceilings, track lighting, dark woods, and steel touches—and peruse the digital wine list while noshing on an antipasto.

Tasty pastas include *maccheroni alla chitarra* tossed in an herbaceous ragù, studded with hearty chunks of braised pork, and dusted with *Parmigiano Reggiano*. Sicilian-style pork and beef *polpette* are absolutely delicious, combining garlic, raisins, fresh herbs, and toasted pine nuts, submerged in tangy tomato sugo with a side of braised chard. End with a refreshing scoop of lemon *sorbetto*.

Also try Barbacco's neighboring sister, Perbacco.

Bourbon Steak

Steakhouse XXX

A2

335 Powell St. (bet. Geary & Post Sts.)

Phone: 415-397-3003
Web: www.bourbonsteaksf.com
Prices: $$$$

Dinner nightly

There may be no better way to start a fun yet swanky steakhouse meal than with a trio of crisp duck-fat fries with seasoning and sauce pairings—think vanilla-parsley fries with sour-cherry ketchup. The primo space is perched up a short flight of stairs on one side of the Westin St. Francis's lobby, where a heavily marbled entrance leads to a stylish bar and spacious dining room filled with columned pillars, soaring ceilings, and a business crowd using their expense accounts. Tables are laden with contemporary steakhouse fare like ultra-tender barbecue short ribs with kimchee and sides like potato purée in copious amounts of butter and cream. Pricey steaks and Wagyu by the ounce are rounded out with Michael Mina signatures, such as lobster pot pie.

Brasserie S & P

Contemporary ✗✗

222 Sansome St. (bet. California & Pine Sts.)

Phone: 415-276-9888   Lunch & dinner daily
Web: www.mandarinoriental.com/
sanfrancisco
Prices: $$

In honor of her 25th anniversary, the Mandarin Oriental recently received a facelift that included a lobby renovation, where this new dining venue now draws hotel guests and San Franciscans alike. Inlaid flooring, plush carpets, and blonde wood tables furnished with butterscotch-colored leather armchairs provide a luxurious backdrop for casual dining. Sample one of the specialty cocktails from the gin-focused list to settle in completely.

Creamy clam chowder and lamb sliders with mint aïoli are among the enjoyable starters. Then, try the Vietnamese pork burger dressed with basil and mint-flecked mayonnaise on a brioche bun, next to excellent sea salt- and paprika-sprinkled French fries; or roasted duck breast with aged balsamic and farro.

Chiaroscuro

Italian ✗✗

550 Washington St. (bet. Montgomery & Sansome Sts.)

Phone: 415-362-6012   Lunch Mon – Fri
Web: www.chiaroscurosf.com   Dinner Mon – Sat
Prices: $$

Chiaroscuro flies a bit under the radar in the Financial District, but those in the know frequent this place for its fantastic homemade pastas. The chef is from Rome and his menu reflects the rich culinary history of Lazio. Lunch sees a bigger business clientele, but dinner is a mix of young and old. The charming "cement barn" vibe of the décor with its cushioned concrete banquettes reflects the food as grounded, solid, and contemporary, yet well-rooted in its history.

A tasting of signature pastas should be mandatory and may include wonderful vermicelli mingled with pecorino-coated prawns, mussels, sun-dried tomato, and arugula; or a unique and sublime monkfish dressed with potato foam and perfectly paired with a black disk of squid terrine.

Campton Place ♝

Contemporary 🍴🍴🍴

B2

340 Stockton St. (bet. Post & Sutter Sts.)

Phone: 415-955-5555   Lunch & dinner daily
Web: www.camptonplacesf.com
Prices: $$$$

Dress up and lower your voice, Campton Place is refined, serene, and quietly formal from first glance. Lodged in the namesake Taj Hotel, the dining room blends intimate booths and tables against a wall of windows with a beige and cream color scheme, as if to heighten the effect of dramatic florals and a blown glass orchid chandelier hanging from the coffered ceiling.

That sense of refinery greeting each guest at the door is true to the contemporary menu, which hints of Indian spices yet prizes superb skill and taste over drama or innovation. The art of combining delicate flavor and texture is clear from the first spoonful of velvety sunchoke velouté poured tableside over toasted hazelnuts, micro herbs, and woodsy matsutake mushrooms. Expertly balanced dishes include day boat scallops that are plump, succulent, and seared just until the very moment of readiness, served with Madras-spiced potatoes, Brussels sprout leaves, and turmeric-scented whey powder and cream.

Meat dishes feature spice-rubbed grilled lamb tenderloin over a streak of boldly seasoned eggplant purée redolent of *garam masala*, cumin, and cardamom, accompanied by caramelized pineapple, mint-flecked millet and pea pods.

Coqueta 😊

D2

Pier 5 (at The Embarcadero)

Phone: 415-704-8866
Web: www.coquetasf.com
Prices: $$

Lunch Tue – Sun
Dinner nightly

Local diners have a full-blown infatuation with Michael Chiarello's city-side spot, though its name is Spanish for "flirt." The handsome dining room is a rustic-chic and masculine display of cowhides, distressed wood, and stone, with huge windows overlooking the Embarcadero. All this makes the crowded Pier 5 restaurant a highly coveted reservation.

The Spanish fare has some California lightness (order extra). Begin with oblong crunchy fried and *chicharrón*-encrusted chicken croquetas filled with English pea mousse. Toasted sandwiches of smoked salmon with *queso fresco* and truffle honey are tasty little bites. Desserts are a slam dunk with a touch of sweet—don't miss the lush Manchego cheesecake dipped in caramel-white chocolate with caramel corn.

Farallon

A2

450 Post St. (bet. Mason & Powell Sts.)

Phone: 415-956-6969
Web: www.farallonrestaurant.com
Prices: $$$

Lunch Tue – Sat
Dinner nightly

Union Square's lauded seafood respite is an aquatic-themed fantasy at every turn. Dive in and enjoy an extravagant platter of *fruits de mer* while admiring its thematic, custom-made chandeliers and bar stools in The Jellyfish Lounge. Also known as the Jelly Bar, it's a San Francisco institution unto itself. Then head to the Pool Room (it once served as the pool room of the Elks Club) to dine on the kitchen's coastal cooking amid sparkling mosaics and a vaulted ceiling.

A raw first course unearths yellowtail sashimi adorned with garlicky aïoli, finely chopped piquillo peppers, and dollops of basil chantilly. Following that is an entrée of crisp-skinned grilled salmon, accompanied by torn croutons, heirloom tomatoes, red onions, and balsamic vinegar.

Gaspar

B3   French   ✗✗

185 Sutter St. (bet. Kearny & Montgomery Sts.)

Phone: 415-576-8800   Lunch Mon – Fri
Web: www.gasparbrasserie.com   Dinner Mon – Sat
Prices: $$

In a sea of faux-rustic restaurant décor, this recruit stands out for its sexy, intimate vibe, complete with dark-tufted banquettes, soft lighting, and an intimate downstairs bar. It's the kind of place where you'll see FiDi brokers rehash deals over pre-dinner cocktails, before being joined by their well-dressed dates for a swanky dinner party upstairs.

The menu of French brasserie favorites is prepared with skill, from grand plateaux of *fruits de mer* to perfectly cooked flatiron steak with well-seasoned pommes frites and a red wine bordelaise. Don't miss the outstanding *Paris-Brest*, golden-hued pastry filled with creamy rose-mascarpone filling and juicy raspberries. Or if you'd rather skip sweets, opt for their well-curated cheese plate.

Georges

C2   Seafood   ✗✗

415 Sansome St. (bet. Commercial & Sacramento Sts.)

Phone: 415-956-6900   Lunch Mon – Fri
Web: www.georgessf.com   Dinner Mon – Sat
Prices: $$

When it was said that Luca Brasi "swims with the fishes" it was bad news. However, this Italian kitchen thrives on such fortune. Set in a former gold rush-era bank, Georges' rush is from financial types for lunch and happy hour. Handsome aesthetics await in the form of a wasabi green bar, sleek paneling, and tables of reclaimed wood.

A John Dory sculpture underlines the menu's focus on sustainable seafood. From the ice cold raw bar, try premium Kusshi oysters served on the half shell with a rosé mignonette; or super fresh ono ceviche neatly topped with hearts of palm and crispy shallot rings. Savor bold fenugreek-dusted albacore placed atop a crunchy chickpea pancake flecked with carrot-*harissa*. Leave the gun and take the citrus-and-semolina *zeppole*.

Hakkasan

B3

1 Kearny St. (at Market St.)

Phone: 415-829-8148   Lunch & dinner daily
Web: www.hakkasan.com
Prices: $$$$

A mixed crowd of businesspeople, cocktailing hipsters, and Chinese tourists descends on the SF outpost of this upscale international chain, housed in the historic One Kearny building. Carved wood screens, dramatic lighting, and a striking V-shaped bar fashion a distinct style and sultry glamor. The ambience is not formal but still worthy of your date-night best, especially in the evening.

The professional, gracious staff proffers beautifully plated Cantonese favorites, like a steamer basket full of tasty prawn-chive and black pepper duck dumplings. The signature *pipa* duck boasts tender meat and lacquered skin, while tea-smoked short ribs are smoky and rich. A three-course lunchtime prix-fixe is a good option for the time- or budget-conscious.

Kin Khao

A3

55 Cyril Magnin (Entrance at Ellis & Mason Sts.)

Phone: 415-362-7456   Lunch & dinner daily
Web: www.kinkhao.com
Prices: $$

There is no peanut sauce, sweet coconut curry or Americanized fare at this authentic Thai retreat, which serves the family recipes of Bangkok-reared food blogger and chef *extraordinaire*, Pim Techamuanvivit. Here, sample spicy, herbaceous, and uniquely refined curry mushroom mousse with crisp rice cakes and thick coconut milk. Complex, aromatic dishes include braised rabbit and eggplant in rich green curry; as well as spicy and beautifully browned Thai pork sausage with sticky rice and pepper relish.

The Parc 55 Wyndham location is a bit odd (and the restaurant's entrance is actually at Ellis and Mason), but the low-key decor, convivial vibe, and intricately spiced food make it worth the effort. Bring a group, order family-style, and get ready for a ride.

Kusakabe

Japanese 𝒴𝒴

C1

584 Washington St. (bet. Montgomery & Sansome Sts.)

Phone:	415-757-0155
Web:	www.kusakabe-sf.com
Prices:	**$$$$**

Dinner Tue – Sun

This is a place for serious, dedicated sushi lovers. Serene and tranquil with warm wood, clean lines, and a strong sense of minimalism, Kusakabe brings distinctive creativity to sushi-focused, kaiseki-style dining. The stunning sushi counter is cut from a single piece of live-edge elm. High-back oyster colored leather chairs, exposed brick, and a ceiling of wood slats complete the Japan-chic look.

The nightly omakase menu showcases Chef Mitsunori Kusakabe's style, employing myriad cooking techniques to ensure that every bite is deliciously balanced and memorable. After awakening the palate with a cup of warm kelp tea, begin with a sushi prelude featuring soy-cured and lightly torched tuna, cold-smoked bonito with a pinch of garlic salt, and buttery halibut topped with bits of liver mousse. A soup course may bring tender meatballs of duck meat and liver bobbing in nutty miso broth mingling with herbaceous mitsuba leaves. A superb rendition of barbecued sushi yields velvety Wagyu beef that has been torched just enough to melt a bit of fat, resulting in a salty bacon-like richness.

The finale of wild Alaskan Copper River salmon with a simple brushing of soy will leave you amazed.

Michael Mina ✿

Contemporary ✕✕✕

C2

252 California St. (bet. Battery & Front Sts.)

Phone: 415-397-9222
Web: www.michaelmina.net
Prices: $$$$

Lunch Mon – Fri
Dinner nightly

Michael Mina now curates an empire of restaurants that spans the country, but his eponymous home base remains his crown jewel. Housed in a stately grey stone building, it's a magnet for nearby business folk, who broker deals over dinner or relax with a glass of Mina's private-label cabernet after a stressful workday. The elegant, high-ceilinged dining room features huge foliage arrangements and oversized framed mirrors that lend added splendor to the space.

The French- and Asian-influenced food emphasizes luxury ingredients as seen in meaty Maine lobster pocked in a sunny carrot risotto with creamy Parmesan mousse. *Vadouvan*-spiced cauliflower purée enlivens a plate of short-rib tortelloni with roasted maitake mushrooms, while perfectly cooked Liberty duck breast is accompanied by a rich artichoke paste and Meyer lemon marmalade. For those who'd prefer to leave their meal to the chef's discretion, four- and nine-course tasting menus are primo.

The expense-account crowd always saves room for dessert, and for good reason: a cassis crémeux with ribbons of chocolate cake and cocoa nib-port ice cream, or passion fruit cream with coconut ice cream, lime, and rum are worth those extra calories.

Millennium

Vegan ✗✗

A2

580 Geary St. (at Jones St.)

Phone: 415-345-3900   Dinner nightly
Web: www.millenniumrestaurant.com
Prices: $$

Vegan dining isn't just a fad; it's a way of life at this sleek site, grandly operating since 1994. Influenced by countless cultures, Chef Eric Tucker's brand of animal-free cooking will please even fervid carnivores with its bonanza of sustainable products ripe with flavor and refined by creativity. A trendy bar adds to the overall festivity.

Millennium offers numerous set menus including a raw tasting which must be ordered 48 hours in advance. The seasonal harvest menu was recently fixated on spring's arrival via a chilled purée of green tomato-and-cucumber dotted with fried corn and pickled green strawberries; miso-glazed *onigiri* in a sake- white tea- and cherry-broth; or *huitlacoche*-stuffed tamales atop black beans and leafy *broccoli di Ciccio*.

Pabu

Japanese ✗✗

C3

101 California St. (bet. Davis & Front Sts.)

Phone: 415-668-7228   Lunch Mon – Fri
Web: www.pabuizakaya.com   Dinner nightly
Prices: $$$

Michael Mina and Ken Tominaga have gone big with their Japanese offspring and baby boy is quite a looker. Encompassing a stunning, high-ceilinged bar, gleaming sushi bar, several dining rooms, and a casual ramen joint (The Ramen Bar, next door), Pabu is enormous in space but serene in atmosphere. The warm service is highly personal.

If you can fork over the requisite gobs of cash, the massive menu will accommodate seemingly any Japanese craving—from whole grilled squid and *izakaya*-style skewers of smoky chicken tails or thick trumpet mushrooms, to a sweet, salty, and savory burdock salad. Sushi fans can opt for the omakase or stick to à la carte treats like a tender *kanpyo* squash roll. The top-notch sake and Japanese whiskey lineup is worth exploring.

Perbacco 🎭

Italian ✕✕

C3

230 California St. (bet. Battery & Front Sts.)

Phone: 415-955-0663   Lunch Mon – Fri
Web: www.perbaccosf.com   Dinner Mon – Sat
Prices: $$

Slick investment bankers enjoy power meals at this Northern Italian haunt where dishes are executed with care—from starters like exquisite house-made *salumi* to hand-stuffed *raviora*. The polished décor belies a hearty menu of hand-crafted pastas (*rabaton* is a light, very fluffy herb-and-spinach gnocchi dressed with tasty leek *fonduta*); or American models like roast chicken and braised lamb shank for lunch. Dinner features slightly more refined interpretations.

Perbacco is larger than it looks, with plenty of booths and seats at the marble bar up front, whereas buzzy tables dominate the back. Well-clad servers encourage saving room at the end—follow suit as the cheese display, remarkable range of *grappe*, and inventive desserts are all highlights.

The Slanted Door

Vietnamese ✕✕

D3

1 Ferry Building (at The Embarcadero)

Phone: 415-861-8032   Lunch & dinner daily
Web: www.slanteddoor.com
Prices: $$

The crown jewel of owner Charles Phan's restaurant empire, this tourist favorite is known for long waits—even for those with reservations. Luckily, its location at the northern end of the Ferry Building allows for some pre-meal shopping and snacking at various nearby vendors (including The Slanted Door's own take-out offshoot, Out the Door), or a top-notch cocktail at their bar.

A sizable menu offers modernized takes on Vietnamese classics, like honey-hoisin glazed pork spareribs, vermicelli noodles with grilled lemongrass-marinated pork shoulder, and spicy soy-sesame tuna tartare accompanied by shrimp chips for scooping. Ultra-modern design, stunning views of the Bay Bridge and capacious seating make it a perfect, if noisy, setting for group dining.

Wayfare Tavern

Gastropub ✗✗

C2

558 Sacramento St. (bet. Montgomery & Sansome Sts.)

Phone: 415-772-9060   Lunch & dinner daily
Web: www.wayfaretavern.com
Prices: $$

Though it feels like it's been around for decades, celebrity chef Tyler Florence's FiDi favorite is actually a toddler—at least in tavern years. Nonetheless, it's become a standby for business types doing deals or enjoying post-work cocktails. Complete with dark wood and leather furnishings, a private billiards room, and bustling bar, Wayfare Tavern has the air of a gastropub-turned-private club.

Hearty Americana with seasonal accents defines the menu, like a take on biscuits and gravy that integrates plump dayboat scallops and spicy chili oil. Buttermilk-brined fried chicken, grilled hanger steak, and baked macaroni and cheese are pure comfort, as is a decadent TCHO chocolate cream pie with salty caramel ganache and devil's food cake crumble.

Wexler's

American ✗

C2

568 Sacramento St. (bet. Leidesdorff & Montgomery Sts.)

Phone: 415-983-0102   Lunch Mon – Fri
Web: www.wexlerssf.com   Dinner Tue – Sat
Prices: $$

Wexler's has a discreet façade, but those who've discovered this friendly, casual spot simply love it. Local business folk come here to rest their weary legs under a dark, undulating art installation, nicely contrasted with vibrant red chandeliers. Their barbecue-inspired bill of fare is not for the purists, but tender, smoked chicken wings bathed in signature hot sauce and paired with Greek yogurt and tangy Pt. Reyes blue cheese, deserves to be a meal on its own. Barbecue brisket *bánh mi* may be a westernized version of the classic filled with pickled cabbage and Fresno chiles, but when coupled with a macaroni salad studded with bacon, the experience is magical. Complete this meaty feast with a slice of cheddar cheese-crusted apple-huckleberry pie.

Marina

Following the havoc wreaked by the 1906 earthquake, San Francisco began reconstructing this sandy marshland by selling it to private developers. They, in turn, transformed the Marina into one of the most charming residential bubbles in town. Picture young families, tech wealth, and an affluent vibe straight out of a 21st century edition of The Yuppy Handbook,

and you're in the Marina! Pacific Heights is considered the area's upper echelon—known for older family money and members who couldn't care less about being edgy. Here, bronzed residents adore jogging with their dogs at Crissy Field, or sipping aromatic chocolate from the **Warming Hut**. Parents can be seen pushing Bugaboos in haute couture boutiques or vying for parking in German-engineered SUVs.

CASUAL EATS

Members of this community are always on the go, and quick-bite cafés are their calling card. Pacific Heights denizens gather at **Jane** for pastries and paninis to nibble along with sips from a range of excellent teas, coffees, and smoothies. **Cafe GoLo** brings to life a classic American coffeehouse replete with expected breakfast specials, salads, and sandwiches; and **Liverpool Lil's** is a welcoming gastropub boasting an impressive bevy of bites and brews. True burger buffs in the Marina seem

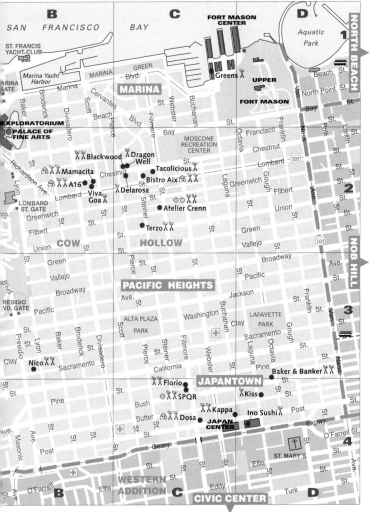

to have an insatiable appetite for locally founded **Roam Artisan Burgers**. Equally popular and sought-after are the contemporary American-infused offerings at SoCal favorite, **Umami Burger**. In truth, quality cuisine has little to do with a Marina restaurant's success: the locals are unapologetically content to follow the buzz to the latest hot spot, where the clientele's beauty seems to be in direct proportion to its level of acclaim and popularity.

However, in the Presidio (home to Lucasfilm headquarters) squads of tech geeks opt for convenience at nearby **Presidio Social Club**, cooking up tasty, regionally focused fare in a classic northern Californian setting. "**Off the Grid-Fort Mason**" is California's most coveted street food fair that gathers every Friday night and features a fantastic collection of vendors and food trucks—from **Curry Up Now** and **Magnolia Brewery** to **Rocko's Chocolate Tacos** and everything in between. Then again, food is mere sustenance to some, and simply a sponge for the champagne and chardonnay flowing at the district's numerous watering holes. The bar scene

here is not only fun but also varied, with a playground for everyone. Oenophiles plan far in advance for the annual **ZAP Zinfandel Festival** in January; while preppy college kids swap European semester stories at sleek wine spots like **Ottimista Restaurant & Bar** or **Nectar**. Couples can find more romance by the fireplace at posh **MatrixFillmore**.

JAPANTOWN

Evident in the plethora of restaurants, shopping malls, banks, and others businesses, the Asian community in the Marina is burgeoning. Thanks to the prominent Japanese population and abundant cultural events, **Japantown** is an exceptional and unique destination. The Northern California Cherry Blossom Festival and **Nihonmachi Street Fair** bring to life every aspect of Asian-American heritage and living. Date night is always memorable at the **Sundance Kabuki Cinema**, which happens to be equipped with two full bars. For a post-work snack, prepared meals, or even authentic imported ingredients, **Super Mira** is a market that offers a host of traditional eats. But for lunch on the run, grab excellent sushi, sashimi, or bento boxes at nearby **Nijiya Market**. Visitors and laid-back locals sojourn to **Shiki** (in the Kintetsu Mall) if only to admire their assortment of beautiful Japanese ceramics, cast iron teapots, sake sets, and glazed bowls. Just a couple blocks from Japantown is perhaps the best spice shop in the country. Featuring walls lined with stacks of jars, **Spice Ace** boasts of extensively curated spices, extracts, and salts, that can all be sampled before purchase.

A16

B2

Italian ✕✕

2355 Chestnut St. (bet. Divisadero & Scott Sts.)

Phone: 415-771-2216
Web: www.a16sf.com
Prices: $$

Lunch Wed – Fri
Dinner nightly

Here's how to do it: a glass of *vino*, a hearty bowl of pasta, and a seat at a table facing the energetic exhibition kitchen. Named after a highway that runs from Naples to Canosa, A16 spins out the kind of exquisitely simple stuff that keeps the place packed night and day.

The menu creates a lovely homegrown feel as it features local, seasonal ingredients. Begin with Neapolitan-style *salsiccia* pizza, wood-fired and topped with tomato sauce, mozzarella, fennel seed sausage, rapini, and chilies; or *scialatielli*, pasta ribbons tossed in chili oil and studded with bits of rich pork. Conclude with a Medjool date cake, a buttery sensation served with amaretto sauce and crème fraîche.

A16 Rockridge also buzzes in its tony neighborhood of Oakland.

Baker & Banker

D3

Californian ✕✕

1701 Octavia St. (at Bush St.)

Phone: 415-351-2500
Web: www.bakerandbanker.com
Prices: $$$

Dinner nightly

Named for married owners Lori Baker (appropriately, the pastry chef) and Jeff Banker (the executive chef), this Pacific Heights restaurant boasts numerous regulars, whom the chefs personally greet on strolls through the dining room. The square space, with leather banquettes, wood furnishings, and vintage accents, has a charming European feel. The best local ingredients star on the menu in unfussy preparations that highlight their excellence. House-made ramp fettuccine is swirled with truffle butter and topped with fresh favas and roasted chanterelles; while corn soup is garnished with shishito peppers and an addictive lobster fritter. Baker's breads and desserts, like a fried peach pie with cinnamon ice cream, are a fine accompaniment to Banker's food.

Atelier Crenn ✿ ✿

C2

Contemporary 🍴🍴

3127 Fillmore St. (bet. Filbert & Pixley Sts.)

Phone: 415-440-0460   Dinner Tue – Sat
Web: www.ateliercrenn.com
Prices: **$$$$**

Neutral gray and very discreet, Atelier Crenn is almost camouflaged in plain sight. Inside, gracious servers keep the dining room low key and very serene. The décor follows suit with a ceiling comprised of a backlit reed canopy, twig-like fixtures, and unadorned wood tables. This is a place for celebrants as well as serious foodies—reservations are a must.

Chef Dominique Crenn's cooking is at once whimsical and deeply accomplished, based on elemental expressions of the earth or sea. Expect dishes with names like "a walk in the forest" to arrive as a woodsy and absolutely delicious arrangement of roasted wild mushrooms strolling amid pine syrup meringues and foraged greens.

Try the umami-rich porridge of assorted sprouted grains and seeds mixed with fresh herbs and a quenelle of *yuzu kosho*, finished tableside with earthy konbu dashi. The seafaring "flavors of Brittany" unite as fresh mussels, tomato concassé, kelp gelée, and tender clams beneath a dome of razor clam broth foam. Explore the tastes of the "land" in a seared venison loin medallion served with roasted chestnuts, crumbled bits of honeycomb, and parsnip purée beneath a tent of crisp-fried cabbage and parsnip leaves.

Bistro Aix

Mediterranean ✗✗

C2

3340 Steiner St. (bet. Chestnut & Lombard Sts.)

Phone: 415-202-0100   Dinner nightly
Web: www.bistroaix.com
Prices: $$

In the competitive Marina market, lovely Bistro Aix remains a charming and relatively affordable neighborhood option for thoughtfully made Southern French fare with a California touch. The dining room offers two distinct culinary experiences, beginning with seats in front at the convivial marble bar and small bistro tables. Beyond this, find the sunny bubble of the intimate back atrium, verdant with olive trees and flooded with natural light. A well-heeled crowd enlivens the space.

Dishes are simple and well executed, like roasted eggplant with grilled sesame seeds, gypsy peppers, and a topping of creamy burrata; or the perfectly grilled ahi tuna with fried baby spinach and a spicy Port reduction. Nicely chosen French wines complement each dish.

Blackwood

Fusion ✗✗

C2

2150 Chestnut St. (bet. Pierce & Steiner Sts.)

Phone: 415-931-9663   Lunch & dinner daily
Web: www.blackwoodsf.com
Prices: $$

For a hip, fusion-y take on Thai fare, Marina locals beeline to this stylish spot, which offers classic dishes like shredded mango salad with cilantro, scallions, and smoky tiger prawns, as well as more mod items such as grilled Wagyu flank steak massaged with a five-spice sauce, set atop ginger rice and garlicky long beans. Empanada-like samosas come stuffed with potato, caramelized onions, and carrots, accompanied by a light and refreshing cucumber-avocado salad.

The sleek interior features tufted banquettes and enormous mirrors, but the prime perch is at their lovely front patio, with two fireside communal tables that face the hustle and bustle of Chestnut Street. Allow extra time for parking and for a wait at weekend brunch—the most popular service.

Delarosa

C2

2175 Chestnut St. (bet. Pierce & Steiner Sts.)

Phone: 415-673-7100   Lunch & dinner daily
Web: www.delarosasf.com
Prices: $$

It's hard to miss the sleek grey and orange façade or the sexy signage, summoning pizza and beer lovers from afar. Inside, the color scheme continues: steel stools sit under long wooden tables dotted with orange votive holders; a twelve-seat wood-topped bar is backed by neat, cubicle shelving and a rectangular steel slab studded with beer taps. Above, fiery, flame-like light fixtures dangle from high ceilings.

Packed with well-heeled locals and families, Delarosa spins out terrific wood-fired and generously sized pizzas, with fourteen types of beer to complement. Not in the mood for pie? Choose an antipasto like chicken sausage with red grapes and mustard; Dungeness crab arancini; or soulful pastas like *garganelli* with porcinis, pancetta, and sage.

Dosa

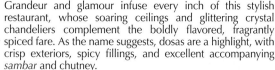

C4

1700 Fillmore St. (at Post St.)

Phone: 415-441-3672   Lunch Wed – Sun
Web: www.dosasf.com   Dinner nightly
Prices: $$

Grandeur and glamour infuse every inch of this stylish restaurant, whose soaring ceilings and glittering crystal chandeliers complement the boldly flavored, fragrantly spiced fare. As the name suggests, dosas are a highlight, with crisp exteriors, spicy fillings, and excellent accompanying *sambar* and chutney.

Welcoming servers will help translate street favorites like *bhel puri* (a delicious sweet-spicy blend of puffed rice, crispy noodles, green mango, and chutney); or shake up a tangy Bengali gimlet with gin, curried nectar, and lime. Desserts are every bit as exotic as the rest of the menu and include *rasmalai*—delicate patties of fresh cheese in sweet cream flavored with cardamom and rosewater.

Find a second, smaller location on Valencia Street.

Dragon Well

C h i n e s e 🍴

2142 Chestnut St. (bet. Pierce & Steiner Sts.)

Phone: 415-474-6888   Lunch & dinner daily
Web: www.dragonwell.com
Prices: 💰

This Marina mainstay nestled among the posh boutiques of Chestnut Street has been at it for over a decade. Westernized classics crafted with fantastically fresh ingredients are the secret to their ongoing success. Inside, high ceilings with sunny skylights and butter-yellow walls evoke an airy feel, while framed photos depict the everyday life of the vast Chinese culture.

Pop in for a shopping break and nosh on tasty tea-smoked duck, served with hand-made steamed buns, thick hoisin sauce, and julienned leeks; or Chinese chicken salad, freshened with cilantro and lemon-soy vinaigrette. The *Kung Pao* chicken, stir-fried with roasted peanuts and chili sauce, is fiery but never overpowering. Sweeten things up with a chocolate (or traditional) fortune cookie.

Florio

Italian 🍴🍴

1915 Fillmore St. (bet. Bush & Pine Sts.)

Phone: 415-775-4300   Dinner nightly
Web: www.floriosf.com
Prices: $$

Florio is a sparkling Italian jewel set amid the chic boutiques on Fillmore Street. The atmosphere is inviting, service is friendly, and the crowd is mostly local. The softly lit dining room is elegant but easygoing, and there is a front bar where you can snag a seat on jam-packed nights.

Flavorful, hearty comfort food is well-prepared and not the slightest bit fussy. Nightly additions to the menu might reveal well-seasoned meatballs beautifully golden brown and tossed in a deliciously spicy herb-infused tomato sauce; or fat ribbons of pappardelle spiraling around caramelized pancetta, fresh rosemary, and earthy cranberry beans. A wedge of zucchini bread topped with a tangy-sweet Meyer lemon glaze will have you calling this place home in no time.

San Francisco ▶ Marina

Greens

C1

Building A, Fort Mason Center

Phone: 415-771-6222
Web: www.greensrestaurant.com
Prices: $$

Lunch Tue – Sun
Dinner nightly

Annie Somerville's pioneering vegetarian restaurant has been around since 1979, but neither the menu nor the surroundings show Greens' age. Instead, fresh, energetic cuisine abounds, with a light touch and a slight Italian bent. Brunch draws a big crowd, so be prepare to wait for those perfectly fried eggs over griddled potato cakes. Vegetarians and carnivores will rejoice after sampling the honest, colorful, down-to-earth seasonal entrées at dinner, followed by delightful desserts like an huckleberry upside down cake with a subtle kick from Meyer lemon.

Housed in historic Fort Mason, the warehouse-style space is rustic yet refined, with sweeping views of the Golden Gate Bridge and sailboats on the Bay.

For a quick lunch, there's also a to-go counter.

Hong Kong Lounge II

A4

3300 Geary Blvd. (at Parker Ave.)

Phone: 415-668-8802
Web: N/A
Prices: $$

Lunch & dinner daily

While lesser Chinese restaurants struggle to balance quality dim sum with equally tasty dinner entrées, Hong Kong Lounge II does it all. As a result, it's become one of the Richmond's biggest draws, with big crowds on weekends and Chinese families packing the round banquet tables at lunch and dinner. The pretty interior's rose walls, wood screens, and white tablecloths are another attractive step up from the competition.

Bring a group to fully sample the array of winning dishes, including handmade soup dumplings, tender honey-glazed barbecue pork, salt-and-pepper tofu fritters, and an excellent mushroom rice-noodle roll. Skip the steamed pork buns and opt for the fluffy baked ones—their crisp, slightly sweet, and very unique topping is a real highlight.

Ino Sushi

Japanese ✗

D4

22 Peace Plz., Ste. 510 (bet. Buchanan & Laguna Sts.)

Phone: 415-922-3121   Dinner Tue – Sat
Web: N/A
Prices: $$

A traditional entrance with cream-colored shades framed in wood sets just the right tone for this petite, reservations-required *sushi-ya*. Inside, find a blonde wood sushi bar and handful of tables run by a serious chef and his wife, the very polite server. Meals may seem to progress slowly but their dedication and knowledge is clear in every slice of supremely fresh fish. Nigiri begin with textbook-perfect mounds of well-seasoned, slightly warmed rice. These are then topped with pristine aji, *tai* (red seabream), or kanpachi (amberjack) and a light swipe of wasabi. The *ankimo* (monkfish liver) may be the best in California.

Do feel free to pick up each morsel with your fingers, but if you dunk the rice-side in soy, expect a gentle correction from the chef.

Kappa

Japanese ✗✗

C4

1700 Post St. (at Buchanan St.)

Phone: 415-673-6004   Dinner Mon – Sat
Web: www.kapparestaurant.com
Prices: $$$$

Located in Japantown on the second level of a small shopping complex, Kappa has a discreet sign that is easy to miss. However, once inside, the kimono-clad hostess offers a warm greeting. Reservations are an absolute must here as there is a loyal patronage (read: regulars) of Japanese business people and local gourmands.

The small space has an arching counter that faces the chef's workspace. His wife is the sole server and explains each course of the nightly Koryori menu that has included super fresh sashimi, nigiri, and a hot dish combo of a crispy corn fritter, breaded and fried pork, *tsukune*, roasted duck, *tamago*, firefly squid, and crunchy green beans dressed in miso paste. A bowl of red bean gelée completes this delicious ensemble.

Kiss

D4

1700 Laguna St. (at Sutter St.)

Phone: 415-474-2866   Dinner Wed – Sat
Web: N/A
Prices: **$$$**

In a sea of trendy and flashy Japanese restaurants, this mom-and-pop standby sometimes gets drowned out—but one taste of its top-quality fish will have you hooked. Traditional nigiri, ranging from giant clam and halibut to bluefin tuna, arrives minimally dressed and served atop excellent rice. Appealing non-sushi options include a delicate *chawan mushi* custard filled with flaky white fish and buttery gingko berries, with an umami-rich dashi broth.

Adjacent to Japantown's Peace Plaza, tiny Kiss is easy to miss (look for the sign on the door), and reservations are recommended. Expect a quiet, sparse, and decorous atmosphere, with polite service from the husband-and-wife owners. The contemplative vibe encourages savoring each delicious morsel.

Mamacita

B2

2317 Chestnut St. (bet. Divisadero & Scott Sts.)

Phone: 415-346-8494   Dinner nightly
Web: www.mamacitasf.com
Prices: **$$**

Marina hipsters flock to Mamacita for its flavor-packed Cal-Mex fare that is not 100% authentic, but is 200% delicious. The vibe is casual and the wood furnishings, large tequila-lined bar, oversized mirrors, and starburst pendant lights hint of Mexico.

Mexican-inspired dishes utilize fresh, local ingredients but still somehow taste like delicious south-of-the-border grub. Mamacita's menu may feature *chiles rellenos* filled with fava beans and goat cheese; achiote-spiced prawn tacos with grilled pineapple and watercress; and an enchilada casserole of pork meatballs, spicy tomato salsa, refried black beans, and melted *queso*. For a bit of sweet, try the cheesecake "flan" with a tequila-strawberry purée—likely spiked from its vast list of tequilas.

Nico

Contemporary   ✗✗

B3

3228 Sacramento St. (bet. Lyon St. & Presidio Ave.)

Phone: 415-359-1000   Dinner Tue – Sat
Web: www.nicosf.com
Prices: $$

Its gorgeously plated French-contemporary food seems like chichi fine dining, but newish Nico takes great pains to maintain its approachable neighborhood bistro vibe. Well-dressed Pac Heights locals skip the scene at flashier area spots and come here for a more relaxed good time, joining friends and family over a glass of wine from the compact, well-curated list.

Dishes rotate seasonally, but a meal here might start with delicate, mild trout rillettes on a crunchy crouton, then segue into a butter-braised beet salad with shaved hazelnuts and whey. Mains include a crispy rock-cod fillet over clams, broccoli, and turnips. Meanwhile, dessert offers the option of an oh-so-French cheese course, or a sweet finish like the white chocolate-rhubarb composition.

Sociale

Italian   ✗✗

A4

3665 Sacramento St. (bet. Locust & Spruce Sts.)

Phone: 415-921-3200   Lunch Tue – Sat
Web: www.sfsociale.com   Dinner Mon – Sat
Prices: $$

Sociale is perfect for an intimate rendezvous. A subtle awning marks the spot and a brick path transports you to this sunny, bucolic sanctuary. Inside, find a comfy room decked with framed photos on buttery yellow walls. The cozy bar is lovely for a sip of refreshing prosecco. Seats in the heated courtyard patio are coveted, so be sure to reserve them.

Chef Tia Harrison looks to Northern Italy for inspiration in starters, like duck meatballs in a sugo with hints of dried cherry, that are perfect to share. But if you dine like an Italian, pastas like homemade pappardelle tossed with braised duck and laced with porcinis may serve as a primer before pan-seared petrale sole stuffed with shrimp and served atop fingerling potatoes in chive-beurre blanc.

SPQR ❀

Italian 🍴🍴

C4

1911 Fillmore St. (bet. Bush & Pine Sts.)

Phone: 415-771-7779
Web: www.spqrsf.com
Prices: $$$

Lunch Sat – Sun
Dinner nightly

Pleasant, casual, and homey with excellent Italian cooking, there is little wonder why this highly popular destination is always bustling. Book in advance and assume that the dining counter reserved for walk-ins is already overflowing for the night. The space itself is narrow with tightly packed wood tables and furnishings; it would seem cramped were it not for the soaring ceiling, skylights, and open kitchen to keep the mood bright. This is a place where passion and enthusiasm for Italian specialties are palpable—if not contagious.

From *piccolo* (snacks) to *dolce*, the extensive menu evolves with the seasons, yet remains consistently good. Antipasti deliver pure pleasure, balancing crunchy fried chicken in a sweet honey glaze arranged with shaved and pickled radish, serrano chili powder, a quenelle of ice lettuce remoulade, and drizzles of honey and chili cream. Twirls of homemade pasta are always memorable, as in mustard capellini with an extraordinary guinea hen ragù, chopped Savoy cabbage, and melting mimolette.

However, desserts are true showstoppers, so save room for luscious blond chocolate panna cotta with sweet coconut cream *espuma*, almond brittle, and salted caramel cubes.

Spruce ✿

Californian 𝄞𝄞𝄞

A4

3640 Sacramento St. (bet. Locust & Spruce Sts.)

Phone:	415-931-5100	Lunch Mon – Fri
Web:	www.sprucesf.com	Dinner nightly
Prices:	**$$$**	

Set in one of San Francisco's toniest neighborhoods, Spruce draws a regular crowd of wealthy retirees and corporate types by day, segueing into couples on date nights in the evening. Its dining room is masculine yet modern, with velvet banquettes, studded leather chairs, and splashes of charcoal and chocolate. A small front café serves morning coffee and pastries, while the marble bar lures happy-hour crowds for a cocktail or glass of wine from their impressive list.

Highly seasonal and delightfully Californian, Spruce's food spotlights ingredients like asparagus in a creamy bisque, accented by toad-in-the-hole toast with a soft-cooked Jidori egg yolk. Sweet, succulent scallops are served with snap peas, pickled green strawberries, turnips, and onion soubise, all uniting into a delicate harmony. For the less daring palates, salads and an excellent burger are also perennial options.

The attentive staff is always at the ready with another piece of house-made cranberry bread or wine recommendation. Teetotalers can enjoy a delicious spritzer, with raspberry, mint, lime, and ginger, alongside the white-chocolate mousse with olive-oil cake and berry compote for a light and refreshing finish.

Tacolicious

C2

Mexican ✗

2031 Chestnut St. (bet. Fillmore and Steiner Sts.)

Phone: 415-346-1966   Lunch & dinner daily
Web: www.tacolicious.com
Prices: ⊕⊕

Born out of a farmer's market stand, this local mini-chain now has four locations and legions of fans willing to wait in line for its famed tuna tostada. It's still filled with barely seared tuna, crisp leeks, and topped with chipotle mayo, but somehow it tastes better each year. Overstuffed tacos require a head dip to relish the delicious *guajillo*-braised short ribs and crisp rock cod with cabbage slaw. Just remember to douse them with plenty of the smoky, tangy house-made salsas. A solid kids' menu draws families, and some parents can be seen taking advantage of the extensive tequila selection as their youngsters dine.

At the Chestnut Street original, the pressed-copper ceiling and religious votive candles provide a colorful atmosphere.

Terzo

C2

Mediterranean ✗✗

3011 Steiner St. (bet. Filbert & Union Sts.)

Phone: 415-441-3200   Dinner nightly
Web: www.terzosf.com
Prices: $$

The third time's a charm as the saying goes and Terzo, the third restaurant from the group that owns Rose Pistola and Rose's Café, gets it right. Filament bulbs cast a cool light over the dark contemporary interior where chocolate leather covers the banquettes and a central communal table bustles with noshing regulars. Wall-mounted racks display a good selection of global wines, with many available by the glass— de rigueur for washing down these Mediterranean-inspired small plates.

Start with grilled Monterey Bay calamari with lentils, fennel, and a dusting of pimentón; or try the luscious hummus and beet salad. Hearty appetites should look for larger entrées like roasted mahi mahi with garbanzo beans and almonds.

Terzo is romantic, so do bring a date.

Viva Goa

B2

Indian ✗

2420 Lombard St. (bet. Divisadero & Scott Sts.)

Phone: 415-440-2600   Lunch & dinner daily
Web: www.vivagoaindiancuisine.com
Prices: 💰💰

The Portuguese-influenced cuisine of Goa typically gets less play in the States than that of its northern neighbors. But Goan food takes center stage in this sparse, low-key dining room decked with burgundy booths and preparing delicious dishes like spicy bronzed curry with prawns and coconut milk or *channa xacutti*, a creamy concoction of chickpeas, fresh coconut, onion, carrot, and poppy seeds.

The less adventurous can opt for more familiar Indian fare like crisp, golden-brown samosas filled with potato and peas, and chewy, smoky naan strewn with garlic and fresh cilantro. Takeout and delivery are the core of the restaurant's dinner business, so those in search of a lively scene might prefer the crowd-drawing (and budget-friendly) lunch buffet.

Couverts (✗... ✗✗✗✗✗) indicate the level of comfort found at a restaurant. The more ✗'s, the more upscale a restaurant will be.

It's like the sun never goes down in the Mission, a bohemian paradise dotted with palm trees and doted on by scores of artists, activists, and a thriving Hispanic community. Here, urban life is illustrated through graffiti murals decorating the walls of funky galleries, thrift shops, and indie bookstores. Sidewalk stands burst with fresh plantains, nopales, and the juiciest limes this side of the border. Mission markets are known to be among the best in town and include **La Palma Mexicatessen** teeming with homemade *papusas*, chips, and fresh cheeses. **Lucca Ravioli** is loved for its legion of imported Italian goods; and the petite grocer, **Bi-Rite**, is big on prepared foods and fresh flowers. Across the street, **Bi-Rite Creamery** is a cult favorite for ice cream. Moving on from markets to hip coffee haunts, **Ritual Coffee Roasters** is the leader of the pack. Join their fan base in single file outside the door, order a special roast from the Barista, and find yourself thoroughly in awe of this pleasing, very potent berry. Coffee connoisseurs also pay their respects at the original **Philz Coffee** for fresh brews that cannot be beat.

CLASSIC MEETS CUTTING-EDGE

The Mission is home to many contemporary hangouts, although those bargain *mercados* and dollar stores might suggest otherwise. **Dynamo Donuts** over on 24th Street is a dreamy retreat for these fried and sugary parcels of dough, complete with delectable flavors such as lemon-buttermilk and chocolate-star anise. **Walzwerk** charms with East German kitsch and is the go-to spot for traditional delights; while carb fiends know to stop by **Magic Curry Kart** for $5 plates of steaming rice dishes. Here in the Mission, pizza reigns supreme and thin-crust lovers are happy to wait in line at **Pizzeria Delfina** for wickedly good slices with crisped edges. A destination in its own right, **Tartine Bakery's** exceptional breads, pastries, and pressed sandwiches are arguably unmissable. However, to best experience this region's range of culinary talents, forgo the table and chairs and pull up at a curb on Linda Street, where a vigilant street food scene is brimming with a wealth of international eats.

DAYTIME DELIGHTS

The city's hottest 'hood also offers a cool range of sweets. A banana split is downright retro-licious when served at the Formica counter of 90-year-old **St. Francis Fountain**, whose sundaes are made with Mitchell's Ice Cream, famous since 1953. Modish flavors like grasshopper pie and Kahlua mocha cream are in regular rotation at the newer **Humphrey Slocombe**; while **Mission Pie** is another local gem that tempts with a spectrum of pies—both sweet and savory. For more bold plates, **Plow** in Potrero Hill is a top breakfast and brunch hit. The space is small but insanely popular, so expect to wait a while before your first bite of lemon-ricotta pancake—there's even a menu for the little "plowers" who arrive by stroller. At lunch head to Peru by way of abuela-approved **Cholo**

Soy for authentic, homemade, and always-affordable fare. **La Taqueria**'s carne asada burrito is arguably the most decadent around, but when it comes to tacos, it's a tossup on whether **El Gallo Giro** or **El Tonayense** takes the title for best truck in town.

NIGHT BITES

The **Abbot's Cellar** on Valencia brags a beer list beyond par, with a massive selection available by the bottle and on tap. But if cocktails are what you crave, then dash over to **Trick Dog** for tantalizing concoctions and creative small plates. Sate a late-night appetite at **Pig & Pie**, offering an array of tasty eats including daily desserts, before dancing off these indulgences on Salsa Sunday at **El Rio**, the dive bar with a bustling back patio. Growling stomachs seem game to brave the harsh lighting at the many taquerias around (some open until 4:00 A.M.) including **Cancún** for a veggie burrito or **El Farolito** for mind-blowing meats.

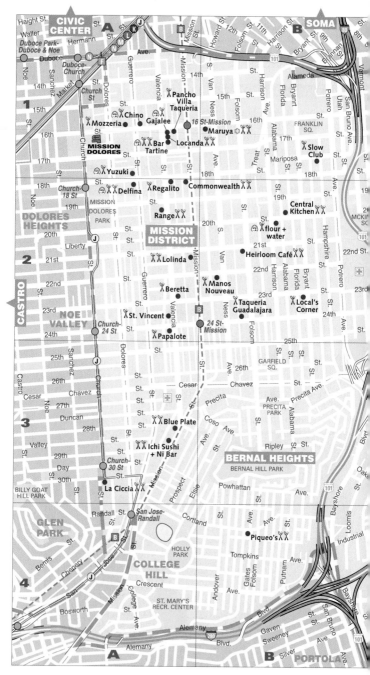

CIVIC CENTER

SOMA

Haight St.
Waller
Duboce Park-
Duboce & Noe
Hermann
Ave.
Duboce
Noe
Duboce-Church
14th
Sanchez
Market
Church St
15th
Mozzeria
Chino
Gajalee
Pancho Villa Taqueria
15th St.
Van Ness Ave.
Folsom St.
Alameda
Florida
Bryant
Utah
Potrero
San Bruno Ave.
16th
16 St-Mission
Maruya
FRANKLIN SQ.
MISSION DOLORES
Bar Tartine
Locanda
17th
Alabama
Mariposa St.
Treat St.
Slow Club
17th
Yuzuki
18th
St.
Church-18 St
Delfina
Regalito
Commonwealth
19th
Central Kitchen
DOLORES HEIGHTS
MISSION DOLORES PARK
Range
MISSION DISTRICT
20th
flour + water
Liberty
21st
Lolinda
Van
21st
Heirloom Café
22nd St.
2
CASTRO
22nd
Guerrero
Beretta
Manos Nouveau
23rd
Harrison
Florida
Bryant
Potrero
23rd
23rd
NOE VALLEY
Church-24 St
St. Vincent
Valencia
Taqueria Guadalajara
Local's Corner
24th
24 St-Mission
Papalote
Folsom
25th
25th
26th
Cesar Chavez
26th
GARFIELD SQ.
27th
Precita
Ave.
Precita Ave.
Duncan
PRECITA PARK
Blue Plate
Coso Ave.
Ripley St.
3
28th
Ichi Sushi + Ni Bar
BERNAL HEIGHTS
BERNAL HILL PARK
Valley
29th
Day
Church-30 St
La Ciccia
30th
Powhattan
Ave.
BILLY GOAT HILL PARK
Randall St.
San Jose-Randall
Cortland
Elsie
GLEN PARK
Bemis
Chenery
HOLLY PARK
COLLEGE HILL
Piqueo's
Tompkins
Gates
Folsom
Putnam
4
Crescent
Andover Ave.
ST. MARY'S RECR. CENTER
Bosworth
Alemany
Alemany
Blvd.
Silver
PORTOLA

72

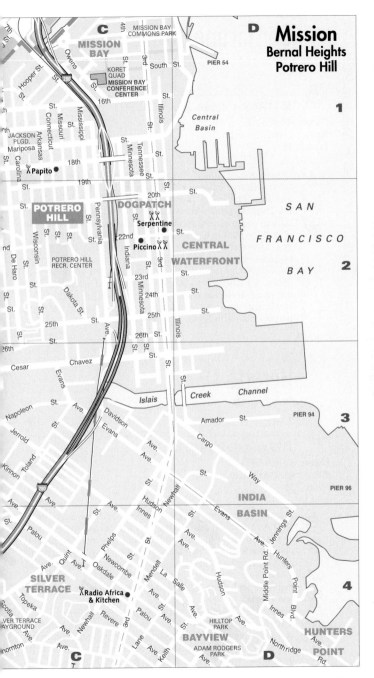

Mission
Bernal Heights
Potrero Hill

C   4th   MISSION BAY COMMONS PARK   D

MISSION BAY

7th St.

Owens St.

Hooper St.

280

3rd St.

KORET QUAD
MISSION BAY CONFERENCE CENTER

South St.

PIER 54

16th St.

Illinois St.

Central Basin

Connecticut
Missouri
Mississippi

JACKSON PLGD.
Arkansas
Mariposa
Carolina

Minnesota
Tennessee

St.

18th

Papito

19th

St.

20th St.

POTRERO HILL

Pennsylvania

DOGPATCH

Serpentine

22nd St.

3rd St.

Piccino

De Haro

Wisconsin

POTRERO HILL RECR. CENTER

Indiana

CENTRAL WATERFRONT

S A N

F R A N C I S C O

B A Y

Dakota St.

23rd

Minnesota

24th St.

25th St.

25th

26th St.

Illinois St.

26th

St.

Cesar

Chavez

St.

Islais

Creek   *Channel*

Evans

Napoleon

St.

Davidson

Evans

Ave.

Amador St.

PIER 94

Jerrold

Cargo

St.

Way

PIER 96

Kinnon
Toland

Ave.

St.

Hudson

Innes

Newhall

Evans Ave.

INDIA BASIN

Palou

Ave.

St.

Ave.

Ave.

Phelps

St.

Ave.

Middle Point Rd.

Hunters

Jennings St.

Quint
Ave.

Newcombe

Oakdale

Mendell
La Salle

Hudson

Point

Innes

Blvd.

SILVER TERRACE

Topeka

Radio Africa & Kitchen

Newhall
Revere

Palou

St.

Ave.

Scotia

VER TERRACE AYGROUND

Ave.

Ave.

Lane
Ave.
Keith

Palou

HILLTOP PARK

Ave.

HUNTERS

nornton

Ave.

BAYVIEW

ADAM RODGERS PARK

Ave.

North ridge

Ave. Rd.

POINT

C   D

Bar Tartine 😊

Eastern European ✗✗

561 Valencia St. (bet. 16th & 17th Sts.)

Phone: 415-487-1600
Web: www.bartartine.com
Prices: $$

Lunch Wed – Sun
Dinner nightly

Despite the fact that it's the restaurant sibling of the Mission's famed Tartine Bakery, Bar Tartine is far less packed with tourists. That leaves plenty of room for locals, who love the Eastern Europe-meets-California food, warm farmstead setting, and engaging service. Still, unless you plan on dining solo at the marble bar, weekend reservations are a must.

The captivating dishes rotate seasonally, but the smoked potatoes drizzled with pungent black garlic aïoli are to die for, as are the mushroom caps stuffed with ground meat, sauerkraut, and served in a vinegary broth. Delicious artisan breads are served as European-style sandwiches at lunch, but you'll want to save room for desserts like the airy steamed parsnip cake with honey and bee pollen.

Beretta

Italian ✗

1199 Valencia St. (at 23rd St.)

Phone: 415-695-1199
Web: www.berettasf.com
Prices: $$

Lunch Sat – Sun
Dinner nightly

A lively vibe, strong cocktail program, and late hours (until 1:00 A.M. nightly) ensure that the crowds have yet to abate at this five-year-old Mission hotspot. The menu is packed with flavorful Italian fare and delicious antipasti like rich and chunky eggplant *caponatina* with oozing burrata drizzled in excellent olive oil. Crisp, thin crust pizzas are another highlight, with tangy sauce and cured meats like spicy salami and *coppa*.

A handful of booths offer a more private experience, while a large communal table serves the walk-in crowd. Whether you're spending an evening amid the glow of Edison bulbs and the clink of cocktail shakers or munching on a brunch-time pizza carbonara at a sunny outdoor table, you'll exit both sated and energized.

Blue Plate

A3 American ❌❌

3218 Mission St. (bet. 29th & Valencia Sts.)

Phone: 415-282-6777   Dinner nightly
Web: www.blueplatesf.com
Prices: $$

Wedged between the Mission and Bernal Heights, this casual and quirky charmer is constructed from reclaimed and repurposed materials all dripping with local art. This draws a relaxed and funky crowd for comfort-food favorites. Dig into a vibrant heirloom-tomato salad with wedges of ripe peaches, sourdough, and creamy pecorino vinaigrette. Move onto slow-cooked pork belly with smoked-oyster Thousand Island sauce and velvety soft-cooked egg.

The American menu shifts with the seasons, but a few dishes are constants, like the blue-plate meatloaf or fried chicken with cornbread. Couples and groups of friends pack the garden patio on warm nights to share slices of tangy key lime pie. Warm up from the winter chill at tables near the vibrant open kitchen.

Central Kitchen

B2 Californian ❌❌

3000 20th St. (at Florida St.)

Phone: 415-826-7004   Lunch Sun
Web: www.centralkitchensf.com   Dinner nightly
Prices: $$$

A chic and sleek crowd of hip Mission foodies gathers at this trendy restaurant, nestled in a complex beside sister shop/deli Salumeria, cocktail bar Trick Dog, and coffee shop Sightglass. Wend your way to the central courtyard, with a trickling fountain and large glass doors leading into the main space, where a large open kitchen faces the simple wood tables.

Select inventive dishes à la carte, or opt for a five- or six-course tasting menu. Along the way, you might taste silky seared tuna topped with earthy matsutake mushrooms and a silky avocado purée, or hen roulade with confit radishes and *puntarelle*. Their delicious desserts—maybe white chocolate with kiwi and nasturtiums or strawberries and fennel with black-garlic ice cream—are compelling.

Chino

Asian ✗

3198 16th St. (at Guerrero St.)

Phone: 415-552-5771
Web: www.chinosf.com
Prices: 👓

Lunch & dinner daily

Pan-Asian dining comes to this hip district thanks to the team behind Tacolicious. Loud music fills this fun corner, along with colorful pops of avocado-green tile, turquoise booths, and pastel paper lanterns.

After ordering, a caddy of house-made chili garlic and spicy mustard sauces is brought to the table, so be prepared to dip, slather, and spice your own way to bliss once the scrumptious plates arrive. Yuba is presented as a salad of slender strips tossed with pickled shiitakes and cilantro-ginger spiked salsa verde. Skewers of lamb are served hot off the grill, appetizingly charred and seasoned with a hit of chili and cumin. Tasty *bao de chicharrón* arrive stuffed with crispy pork belly, avocado, pickled onion, cilantro, and spicy aïoli.

Commonwealth

Californian ✗✗

2224 Mission St. (bet. 18th & 19th Sts.)

Phone: 415-355-1500
Web: www.commonwealthsf.com
Prices: $$

Dinner nightly

Commonwealth is a restaurant that takes chances, starting with its edgy Mission locale. Yet the interior is minimal and serene, with a bar offering views of the open kitchen and tables spotlit by filaments. There is a sense of purpose here, both among the progressive owners who donate part of every tasting menu to charity, and the buzz of young epicureans.

This kitchen thrills in reformulating ingredients to deliver flavor and textural surprise, as in herring fillets with chicken skin breadcrumbs and beet-miso purée; egg custard with uni, seaweed brioche cubes, and wild greens; and lamb's tongue terrine with gem lettuce, Meyer lemon, artichoke hearts, and pistachio cream. At dessert, chocolate and peanut butter semifreddo tops cloud-like frozen popcorn.

Delfina 😋

Italian ✗✗

A2

3621 18th St. (bet. Dolores & Guerrero Sts.)

Phone: 415-552-4055   Dinner nightly
Web: www.delfinasf.com
Prices: $$

Delfina is one of those spots that is perennially popular with the Mission locals. The pizzeria next door does a booming business, but this spacious dining room is almost always packed, and highlights a neat arrangement of bare wood tabletops, a narrow counter (perfect for solo diners), and a semi-open kitchen. Mirrors on the side walls and a line of windows in the front give this space a larger and airy feel. There is no need to dress up for this casual, welcoming spot. Expect menu items such as hearty, chewy pappardelle tossed with flavorful pork sugo; tender-roasted and crisp-skinned quail served over creamy polenta; and chicken liver *spiedini* with *guanciale* and aged *balsamico*. Close with a lovely chocolate *budino* with salted caramel ice cream.

flour + water 😋

Italian ✗

B2

2401 Harrison St. (at 20th St.)

Phone: 415-826-7000   Dinner nightly
Web: www.flourandwater.com
Prices: $$

The moniker of this Mission mob scene says it all. With a solid lineup of homemade pastas and Neapolitan-style wood-fired pizzas, Chef Thomas McNaughton has put the building blocks of Italian cooking on a serious pedestal. Expect to wait in line if you don't have a reservation, especially since their debut of an expanded menu.

Once seated, make like the guests on a pasta pilgrimage here and dig into exquisite corn-stuffed *cappelletti* arranged with plump kernels, chocolate-mint leaves, and a drizzle of butter-honey (and if you order the pasta tasting menu, that's only the beginning). A short list of entrées leads to an incredible dessert selection, which has featured a zucchini cake with carrot purée, buffalo's milk gelato, and a fried squash blossom.

77

Gajalee 😋

Indian 🍴

A1

525 Valencia St. (bet. 16th & 17th Sts.)

Phone: 415-552-9000   Lunch & dinner daily
Web: www.gajalee.net
Prices: $$

♿ Named for the Indian term for an informal gathering, Gajalee may not appear lavish, but it's heavy on traditional flavor and ingredients. The remarkably authentic Southern Indian fare focuses on seafood, creamy curries, and delicate spices. They'll even ask just how hot you like your shrimp chili *tava* and rich, moist fish *kolhapuri*. Portions are generous; the pitch-perfect rice or *chapatti* is a meal unto itself. Finish with the light, meltingly sweet *gulab jamun*.

Though the neon signs out front aren't prepossessing, the dining room is surprisingly cheerful, with yellow walls and colorful murals. Snag a window seat for great people-watching on one of Valencia Street's most bustling corners. Those who'd rather dine at home can order takeout or delivery.

Heirloom Café

Californian 🍴🍴

B2

2500 Folsom St. (at 21st St.)

Phone: 415-821-2500   Dinner Mon – Sat
Web: www.heirloom-sf.com
Prices: $$$

♿ Though a nice selection of European vintages is a boon to this charming bistro housed in a quiet corner of the Mission, the delicate and seasonal food keeps it bustling. Fresh and elegant Mediterranean-leaning dishes are pure expressions of California's bounty. Sample the likes of seared scallops on a bed of fresh fava beans and frisée with minced bacon and shallot-butter; or pan-roasted cod with cauliflower purée, English peas, and ramps. Simple desserts display a gentle touch, as in polenta cake with macerated strawberries and tarragon cream.

The dining room features communal tables, a marble counter with a close-up view of the open kitchen, whitewashed walls plastered with European wine labels, warm candlelight, and even warmer service.

Ichi Sushi + Ni Bar

Japanese 🍴🍴

A3

3282 Mission St. (bet. 29th & Valencia Sts.)

Phone: 415-525-4750   Dinner Mon – Sat
Web: www.ichisushi.com
Prices: $$$

Gone are the days when dining here was marred by the memory of how hard it was to score a table—this new space down the street is much bigger. Relaxed and casual, with a big, fun mural on one wall, it's an über-busy smash among tech types and hipsters. Hit the central sushi bar for nigiri, or opt for izakaya dishes and sake (but no sushi) at adjacent Ni Bar.

The cognoscenti opt for the omakase, which might kick off with oysters garnished with yuzu juice and bits of caviar, followed by piping hot grilled skewers of tender and juicy miso-glazed pork. The nigiri pack punches of flavor from *yuzu kosho* or ponzu sauces and unique garnishes. The fish (think of sea bream, Hokkaido scallops, ocean trout, and uni) are always fresh and delicious.

La Ciccia

Italian 🍴🍴

A3

291 30th St. (at Church St.)

Phone: 415-550-8114   Dinner Tue – Sat
Web: www.laciccia.com
Prices: $$

Sardinian cuisine takes the spotlight at this family-run charmer, which draws a loyal crowd of Noe Valley regulars—particularly parents on a well-earned date night. The intimate, dark green dining room is always full, and is nestled right up against the kitchen, from which the chef regularly pops out to greet guests in a blend of Italianenglish.

Start with the house-made bread and the home-cured *salumi* of the day (think citron-studded mortadella). The pasta *longa* with cured tuna heart slivers twirls fresh, delicious linguini with sea urchin and tomato, and an entrée of stewed goat is gamey but tender, served alongside braised cabbage, black olives, and fried capers. For a pleasant conclusion, cap it all off with the fluffy and airy ricotta-saffron cake.

Local's Corner

Californian ✗

B2

2500 Bryant St. (at 23rd St.)

Phone: 415-800-7945
Web: www.localscornersf.com
Prices: $$

Lunch Tue – Sun
Dinner Tue – Sat

Local's Corner is exactly that—a neighborhood café set upon a corner and geared toward local foodies. This vintage-esque respite contains only a handful of tables and counter seats. Service is laid-back, but it's so much fun to watch the animated (read: skilled) team in the open kitchen.

The menu of light, well-crafted Californian fare spins to the season, so check out the framed mirror listing daily oysters and cheeses. Then embark on dishes that might feature a refreshing chicken salad mingled with yogurt, toasted almonds, raisins, and fresh cilantro; or beef tartare crowned with a quail egg and pickled cauliflower. That smoked salmon salad sandwich with a side of peppery arugula is just begging to be paired with a homemade Meyer lemon-ade.

Locanda

Italian ✗✗

A1

557 Valencia St. (bet. 16th & 17th Sts.)

Phone: 415-863-6800
Web: www.locandasf.com
Prices: $$

Dinner nightly

This chic Roman-style *osteria* packs in the hipsters with a lively scene, killer cocktails, and inspired pastas, like radiatore tossed in tomato-lamb ragù with pecorino and hints of fresh mint. None of this is surprising, considering Locanda is from the team behind Mission favorite, Delfina. Classic chicken under a brick is characteristically on-point: smoky, tender, and served with a squeeze of lemon over nutty farro, Umbrian lentil, and red quinoa salad.

Reservations here are a tough ticket, but the attire and vibe are casual and welcoming (if noisy). Can't get a table? Seats at the bar, where the full menu is served, are a solid backup. Locanda's ultra-central address makes parking a challenge, so plan on using the valet or allotting extra time.

Lolinda

Argentinian 🍴🍴

A2

2518 Mission St. (bet. 21st & 22nd Sts.)

Phone: 415-550-6970   Dinner nightly
Web: www.lolindasf.com
Prices: $$

Equal parts contemporary steakhouse and small plates spot, Argentine-inspired Lolinda is fun and sexy, loaded with twenty- and thirty-somethings gabbing over cocktails and sips of malbec. The soaring dining room with its wagon-wheel chandeliers and tufted-leather banquettes leads to a bustling second-floor mezzanine; whereas El Techo, a heated and more casual roof deck, offers sweeping views of the skyline. Sharing is encouraged and groups can be found divvying up plates of silky ono ceviche, flaky chicken empanadas, or sweet, caramelized pork belly.

Bull sculptures and murals remind diners that the chargrilled steak or crosscut beef short ribs with chimichurri are must-orders—tender and smoky, they'll transport you to Buenos Aires instantly.

Manos Nouveau

Latin American 🍴

B2

3115 22nd St. (bet. Capp St. & Van Ness Ave.)

Phone: 415-638-6109   Dinner Tue – Sun
Web: www.manosnouveau.com
Prices: $$

A welcome addition to the Mission (AKA land of a hundred taquerias), this Latin American delight serves divine plates prepared with much skill and minimal fuss. A definitive step-up from surrounding taco stands and *pupusa* spots, the small dining room allures with snug linen-topped tables as well a counter armed with additional seats for rush hour.

Colorful paintings from local artists hang on the walls, while handmade ceramic dishes carry such delicious courses as *camarones* Riviera featuring plump prawns served in a creamy *chili aji* with cubes of starchy yucca. Brought to you by a smiling staff, oven-roasted salmon paired with smoky *arroz chimole* trailed by velvet-y molten chocolate cake are heartwarming specials that warrant a revisit…or three.

Maruya ✿

B1

J a p a n e s e   ✗✗

2931 16th St. (bet. Mission St. & Van Ness Ave.)

Phone: 415-503-0702   Dinner Tue – Sat
Web: www.maruyasf.com
Prices: $$$$

This is where the local sushi-aficionado-hipsters head for a very sophisticated meal steeped in Edomae tradition. Look for the unmarked entrance beyond a Japanese screen; window views of the urban streetscape are rather artistically blocked with slats of raw wood. The small, serene dining room is furnished with black walnut tables and clear glass pendant lights; red lacquer trays and enamel chopsticks mark each place setting. Of course, the room's greatest attributes are Chefs Masaki Sasaki and Hidebumi Sueyoshi working diligently behind the honey-toned knotty cypress counter.

There is an à la carte menu, but most prefer the omakase options to fully explore this very special cuisine. A trio of delicious appetizers may feature warm and delicate house-made tofu topped with custardy uni; finely chopped and intensely rich toro with bits of caviar and a plantain chip for scooping; and a bowl of white miso-sesame dipping sauce with blanched heirloom vegetables. Raw octopus with coarse lava salt, torched mackerel, and Tasmanian ocean trout with shiso—all served over perfectly prepared rice—are among the exquisite nigiri here.

Subtly sweet desserts achieve the same level of excellence.

Mozzeria

Pizza ✗

A1

3228 16th St. (bet. Dolores & Guerrero Sts.)

Phone: 415-489-0963
Web: www.mozzeria.com
Prices: 💰💰

Lunch Fri – Sun
Dinner Tue – Sun

Oh, the pies at Mozzeria! Whether it's the traditional Margherita, oozing with mozzarella and fresh basil; the California-style slathered with decadent blue cheese, caramelized onions, and thyme; or the Asian-style crowned with roast duck, hoisin sauce, and spring onions, there's a pleaser for every palate.

Specializing in those Neapolitan-style, thin-crust pizzas (fired at a thousand degrees), this brilliant newbie's deaf owners attract a largely non-hearing patronage. But don't fret if you're not proficient in sign language as the wonderful and accommodating staff will steer your way. Though pizza is their main affair, other tasty options abound like flaky, delicate salmon topped by salsa verde, served with tangy fried capers and rosemary potatoes.

Pancho Villa Taqueria

Mexican ✗

A1

3071 16th St. (bet. Mission & Valencia Sts.)

Phone: 415-864-8840
Web: www.sfpanchovilla.com
Prices: 💰💰

Lunch & dinner daily

Around the corner from the 16th and Mission BART stop, this long-running taqueria earns high marks from locals. Upon entering, take a moment to step back and examine the menu board; the vested attendants working the flat-tops and grills will be quizzing you on the beans, condiments, and choice of ten meats you desire. That line moves quickly, so be ready. After loading up your burrito, perhaps filled with thinly sliced steak and butterflied prawns, select an *agua fresca* from the glass barrels, and hit the salsa bar. It features award-winning varieties in every range of heat and sweet to complement their thin, ultra-crispy tortilla chips. Ambience is nil and tables can be hard to snag, but the reward is a fresh and flavorful taste of the Mission.

Papalote

Mexican ✗

A2

3409 24th St. (bet. Poplar & Valencia Sts.)

Phone: 415-970-8815   Lunch & dinner daily
Web: www.papalote-sf.com
Prices: 🝰

For a lighter, more Californian take on classic taqueria fare, head to this tiny joint slightly off the Mission's beaten track. There, you'll find tortillas packed with flaky and perfectly cooked fish, plump shrimp, and flavorful carne asada, available in either burrito or taco form. (Be sure to go "super" for a hearty dose of freshly made guacamole.) Order at the counter, then snag a table and try not to fill up on chips.

Whatever you order, top it with a heaping helping of the outstanding roasted-tomato salsa, good enough to merit licking the ramekin—take-home jars are sold on-site and online. Throw in an *agua fresca* or a cold beer from the fridge, and prepare to leave stuffed and smiling from a chat with the friendly owner.

Papito

Mexican ✗

C1

317 Connecticut St. (at 18th St.)

Phone: 415-695-0147   Lunch & dinner daily
Web: www.papitosf.com
Prices: 🝰

Owned by the team behind nearby Chez Papa and Chez Maman, this taqueria has a French touch that complements its sunny, bistro-like environs on the slope of Potrero Hill. The colorful walls and tightly packed tables lead to a semi-open kitchen full of energy and movement, while servers may be snappy without sacrificing timely presentations.

Start with the zippy *ensalada* Papito, packed with avocado, crispy tortilla strips, and cilantro dressing. Then, dig into the giant mushroom quesadilla with Oaxaca cheese or crisp rock cod tacos with chipotle mayo and cabbage slaw. Well-crafted Mexican entrées, a flavorful salsa selection, and a fully-stocked bar further cement Papito's status as a neighborhood favorite spot for a quiet lunch or bustling dinner.

Piccino

Pizza ✗✗

C2

1001 Minnesota St. (at 22nd St.)

Phone: 415-824-4224   Lunch & dinner Tue – Sun
Web: www.piccinocafe.com
Prices: $$

A progenitor of the increasingly hot Dogpatch restaurant scene, Piccino embodies the neighborhood's many flavors, drawing families with kids in tow, young tech types, gregarious retirees, and more. Its memorable yellow exterior houses a relaxed, artsy-urban interior with lots of wood and natural light, a perfect venue for unwinding with friends.

Everyone comes here for deliciously blistered pizzas like the *funghi*, with roasted mushroom duxelle, sautéed wild mushrooms, *stracchino* cheese, and slivers of garlic. Though pizza is a focus, Piccino excels in appetizers like tender, skillfully prepared *polpette* (meatballs) in tomato sauce, and must-order desserts such as a delectable hazelnut-cocoa nib cake. Their adjacent coffee bar is an area favorite.

Piqueo's

Peruvian ✗✗

B4

830 Cortland Ave. (at Gates St.)

Phone: 415-282-8812   Dinner nightly
Web: www.piqueos.com
Prices: $$

Gather your friends for a trip to Peru (with a layover in Bernal Heights) at Piqueo's, where the menu of flavor-packed small plates is built for sharing. From crispy yucca balls stuffed with cheese to tender pork adobo over mashed sweet potatoes, hearty palate-pleasers abound. Sauces are a house specialty; the tender beef empanada boasts a trio of garlicky *huacatay*, creamy *huancaina*, and spicy *rocoto*. And where else can you sample a quinoa-blueberry flan?

While not as glamorous as upscale sister La Costanera, Piqueo's has its charms, thanks to a quaint atmosphere with wood floors and an open kitchen. It's a standby for Bernal families, who stroll over in the evenings to catch up with the friendly servers and dig into their favorite dishes.

Radio Africa & Kitchen

C4

4800 3rd St. (bet. Oakdale & Palou Aves.)

Phone: 415-420-2486   Dinner Tue – Sat
Web: www.radioafricakitchen.com
Prices: $$

Bayview may be one of the most crime-ridden areas in the city, however, the arrival of hot spots like Radio Africa & Kitchen strutting a unique bill of fare and bright setting, have been hugely sought-after.

This well-received haunt features Ethiopian-born Chef Eskender Aseged's original style of Afro-Mediterranean food mingled with Cali flair—the ingredients come from a local community garden. A healthy dish of green lentils is topped with roasted red beets, goat cheese, arugula, and shredded red cabbage; and baked white fish is deliciously seasoned with a fragrant spice blend and crowned with tomato confit. Heartier appetites will return time and again for the leg of lamb massaged with a unique *berbere* blend and coupled with roasted vegetables.

Range

A2

842 Valencia St. (bet. 19th & 20th Sts.)

Phone: 415-282-8283   Dinner nightly
Web: www.rangesf.com
Prices: $$

It may have been one of the first higher-end restaurants to colonize this stretch of the Mission, but Range's crowds haven't abated, despite the influx of new local dining options. Its popularity is thanks to the focused menu of seasonal cuisine that manages to be uncomplicated yet reliably delicious. Expect dishes like grilled asparagus drizzled with *harissa* and cumin-laced yogurt; pan-roasted medallions of rabbit loin with natural jus and minty gremolata; and milk-chocolate mousse cake.

This industrial-chic space combines worn wood floors, contemporary fixtures, and leather seating; knowledgeable servers are cordial and hip. The wine list may be packed with interesting choices, but innovative cocktails draw their own crowds to the light-studded bar.

Regalito

Mexican ✗

A2

3481 18th St. (at Valencia St.)

Phone: 415-503-0650
Web: N/A
Prices: $$

Lunch Sat – Sun
Dinner nightly

Regalito is Spanish for "little gift," and those who dine here will surely understand the choice of name. Instead of relying on the bold, spicy approach of local taquerias, Regalito takes a milder, ingredient-focused path, infusing dishes like chicken enchiladas with new life via handmade corn tortillas, fresh roast chicken, and a delicate green chili sauce. Familiar Mexican favorites get an upgrade here, from the super-sweet, fresh corn on the cob *elote* with tangy chili-lime mayo and *cotija* cheese, to the silky vanilla custard in a pool of caramel sauce.

The cheery, colorful space and friendly servers are welcoming, but the real charmers are the smiling cooks, who happily interact with diners in prime seats overlooking the open kitchen.

Serpentine

Californian ✗✗

C2

2495 3rd St. (at 22nd St.)

Phone: 415-252-2000
Web: www.serpentinesf.com
Prices: $$

Lunch daily
Dinner Mon – Sat

Located in the Dogpatch, Serpentine is typically SF: an urban-industrial space with worn wood floors, loft-like ceilings, and exposed ductwork. The setting coupled with Californian fare that features fresh, local, and seasonal ingredients, equals a very popular spot among locals for a business lunch, dinner, or weekend brunch.

Sociable servers may bring you an arugula salad tossed with crunchy sugar snap peas, shaved carrots, Easter Egg radishes, sliced almonds, and *ricotta salata* in a tangy red wine vinaigrette. The relaxed atmosphere is ideal for enjoying fresh food prepared with skill—that might even include a fluffy pork *rillettes* sandwich heaped with deliciously griddled crispy pork and topped with a tangy shaved fennel- and pepper-relish.

87

Slow Club

Californian ✗

B1

2501 Mariposa St. (at Hampshire St.)

Phone: 415-241-9390
Web: www.slowclub.com
Prices: **$$**

Lunch daily
Dinner Mon – Sat

Situated among the warehouses, commercial spaces, and converted lofts of the eastern Mission, Slow Club is a neighborhood standby for seasonal California cuisine in a casual, industrial setting. Businesspeople and start-up types fill the tables at lunch, while dinner and brunch draw hipster locals, occasionally with kids. Alfresco perches on the sidewalk are a favorite for nice days.

The menu is as relaxed as the vibe, boasting well-made classics like a grilled flatbread with house-made pork sausage, broccoli rabe, and *montaso* cheese. Perfectly al dente fettuccine is twirled with asparagus, spinach, king trumpet mushrooms, and crowned with a slow-cooked egg. Save room for a wedge of dark chocolate mousse cake, served with salted caramel ice cream.

St. Vincent

Contemporary ✗

A2

1270 Valencia St. (bet. 23rd & 24th Sts.)

Phone: 415-285-1200
Web: www.stvincentsf.com
Prices: **$$**

Lunch Sat
Dinner Mon – Sat

Wine lovers will fall hard for this hip, industrial spot in the Mission, which boasts 100 bottles under 100 bucks. Adding to the fun, they also offer any non-sparkling vintage as a half-bottle. Then, to the delight of thirsty brunchers, owner David Lynch (a renowned Italian wine expert previously of Quince and Cotogna) often conducts Saturday tastings with unique and affordable bottles for sale.

Bold flavors and Italian-European influences dominate the menu like chargrilled asparagus over a potato cake with an egg yolk and *crescenza* cream, or smooth pumpkin ravioli with amaretti crumbs in a gentle broth. Save room for dessert: both the feather-light lavender bread pudding and the *pasteis de nata* (Portuguese egg custard tarts) are too tempting to miss.

Taqueria Guadalajara

Mexican ✗

B2

3146 24th St. (at Shotwell St.)

Phone: 415-642-4892   Lunch & dinner daily
Web: N/A
Prices: 💰

At this Mission mainstay for Cal-Mex treats, regulars place their order at the counter, watch the action unfold in the open kitchen located just beyond, and then settle into a vibrant mural-walled dining room that charmingly evokes the countryside and its way of life. Clay roof tiles, and handmade wood and leather seats stick to the rustic, very quaint theme that locals seem to have grown so fond of.

Any item ordered 'super' is usually heaped with cheese, sour cream, and fresh avocado. Case in point: a pollo *asado* burrito packed with Mexican rice, pinto beans, and smoky, tender grilled chicken. These may be meals in themselves, but other classics like *al pastor* and *chile verde* tacos, enchiladas, and fajitas continue to thrive as tried and true favorites.

Yuzuki 😊

Japanese ✗

A1

598 Guerrero St. (at 18th St.)

Phone: 415-556-9898   Dinner Wed – Mon
Web: www.yuzukisf.com
Prices: $$

Izakaya Yuzuki's tantalizing array of grilled and fried bites is made with palpable authenticity. Note the number of dishes that are prepared with *koji* (fermented rice mixed with water and salt) to impart umami. Taste this in *yaki surume ika*, marinated Hokkaido squid—the body grilled until tender with crisped, chewy tentacles—served with excellent yuzu mayonnaise for dipping. Morsels of dark meat chicken are also marinated in *koji* and then fried until golden for enticing *kara-age*. House-made tofu or *nukazuke*, vegetables pickled in fermented rice bran, are among the delightful *otsumami* to savor with sake or frosty sweet potato beer.

The modest interior showcases simple white walls hand-painted with outlines of vegetables and an amicable staff.

Nob Hill

Thanks in large part to its connection to the Gold Rush industry magnates, Nob Hill is San Francisco's most privileged neighborhood. Its plush mansions, strategic location complete with breathtaking views of the Bay, and accessible cable car lines that chug up to the top ensure that it remains home to the upper crust. Speaking of which, note the familiar tinkle from wind chimes and postcard-perfect

brass rails checking tourists who dare to lean out and take in the sights. Despite the large scale devastation following the 1906 earthquake, this iconic part of town bordering the gorgeous Golden Gate Bridge and Alamo Square's "Painted Ladies" was able to retain its wealthy reputation thanks to an upswell of swanky hotels, door-manned buildings, and opulent dining rooms. Unsurprisingly, "Snob Hill" today continues to echo of mighty egos and wealthy families who can be seen making the rounds at **Big 4**, cradled within The Huntington Hotel. Named after the 1800s railroad titans, this stately hermitage is known for antique memorabilia and nostalgic chicken potpie. A stop at **Swan Oyster Depot** for some of the finest seafood in town is a sure way to impress your out-of-town, tourist-trapped friends, but be prepared to wait up to several hours on busy days for one of their coveted few seats. Cocktails and small plates ensure epic levels of enjoyment at the extravagant **Top of the Mark** restaurant, boasting a sleek, lounge-like vibe and panoramic vistas of the sun setting over the cityscape. Moving from day to night, a handful of food-centric saloons fortuitously sate the tastes of young professionals with pennies to spare. At the top is **Cheese Plus**, showcasing over 300 international cultures, artisan charcuterie, and of course, chocolate for added decadence. Across the street, **The Jug Shop** is an old-time, reliable, and very personable destination among locals who can be seen lapping up micro-brew beers and global wines. For a total departure, kick back with a mai tai (purportedly invented at Oakland's Trader Vic's in 1944) at **Tonga Room & Hurricane Bar**—a tiki spot in the *très* chic Fairmont, decked out with an indoor swimming pool that also functions as a floating stage.

RUSSIAN HILL

Slightly downhill and north toward Polk Street, the vibe mellows on the approach to Russian Hill, named after a Russian cemetery that was unearthed up top. Chockablock with cute boutiques, dive bars, and casual eateries, this neighborhood's staircase-like streets are scattered with predominantly un-Russian groups and singles that seem more than willing to mingle. Good, affordable fare abounds here, at such popular haunts as **Caffé Sapore** serving breakfast specials, sandwiches, soups, and salads; as well as **Street** for fine, seasonal American cuisine. Tacky taqueria-turned-nighttime disco, **Nick's Crispy Tacos**, is a perennial favorite. The

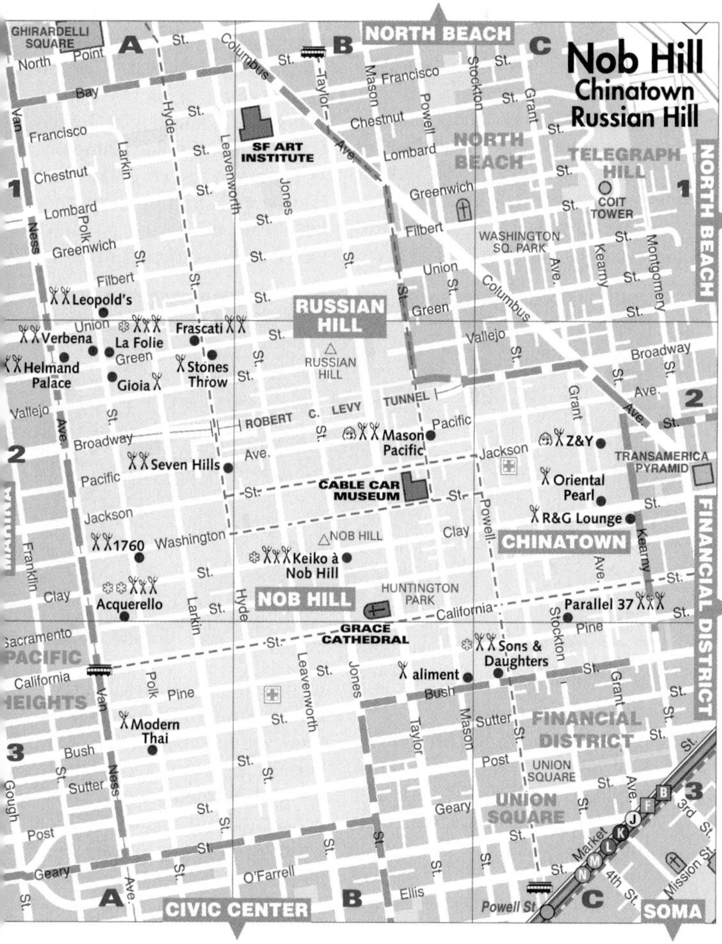

Nob Hill
Chinatown
Russian Hill
NORTH BEACH
GHIRARDELLI SQUARE
SF ART INSTITUTE
RUSSIAN HILL
TELEGRAPH HILL
COIT TOWER
WASHINGTON SQ. PARK
Leopold's
Verbena
La Folie
Frascati
Helmand Palace
Gioia
Stones Throw
Seven Hills
Mason Pacific
Z&Y
TRANSAMERICA PYRAMID
CABLE CAR MUSEUM
Oriental Pearl
R&G Lounge
CHINATOWN
1760
Keiko à Nob Hill
NOB HILL
Acquerello
HUNTINGTON PARK
Parallel 37
GRACE CATHEDRAL
Sons & Daughters
aliment
PACIFIC HEIGHTS
Modern Thai
FINANCIAL DISTRICT
UNION SQUARE
CIVIC CENTER
SOMA
Powell St
ROBERT C. LEVY TUNNEL

downright sinful and delicious chocolate earthquake from **Swensen's Ice Cream**'s flagship parlor (in business since 1948) is undoubtedly the town's most treasured dessert. From flashy finds to tastefully decorated destinations, **Bacchus Wine Bar** is an elegant and ever-alluring Italian-style spot lauded for both its beautiful interiors and exceptional wine, beer, and sake selections.

CHINATOWN

Scattered with large parks— Huntington Park is perhaps the city's most coveted stretch of greenery—Nob Hill's scene begins to change as you venture east to the country's oldest **Chinatown**. Here, authentic markets, dim sum palaces, sum houses where jam-packed dining is the name of the game. Even gastronomes flock here to scour the shelves at family-owned and operated **Wok Shop**, bursting with unique cookware, linens, tools, and all things Asian. Others may prefer to avoid the elbow-to-elbow experience and take home a slice of Chinatown by way of juicy dumplings, buns, and sweets from **Good Mong Kok Bakery**. Soldier on from this excellent and inexpensive take-out spot only to spin out a sugar-rush over creamy, oven-fresh custard tarts at **Golden Gate Bakery**; or prophetic little samples in the making at **Golden Gate Fortune Cookie Company**. The amazing and very affordable **House of Nanking** is another rare (read: necessary) pleasure. Don't bother ordering from the

souvenir emporiums, banks, and other businesses employing scores of the immigrant community spill down the eastern slope of the Hill in a wash of color and vibrant Chinese characters. Amid these steep streets find some of the city's most addictive and crave-worthy barbecue pork buns at old, almost antique dim menu—the owner will usually grab them from your hands and take over the ordering. But really, nobody is complaining. Finally, the **Mid-Autumn Moon Festival** brings friends and families together over mooncakes—a traditional pastry stuffed with egg yolk and lotus seed paste—and to reflect upon summer's bounty.

Acquerello ✿✿

Italian 🍴🍴🍴

A2

1722 Sacramento St. (bet. Polk St. & Van Ness Ave.)

Phone: 415-567-5432   Dinner Tue – Sat
Web: www.acquerello.com
Prices: $$$$

Elegant but never overdone, Chef/co-owner Suzette Gresham delivers classic dining with more than a flash of modern savvy. From the host who greets you to the attentive servers and expert sommeliers, every member of this service team is remarkably personable and able to read each table. Spectacular collector wines available by the glass are equally impressive.

The superb Italian cuisine does have contemporary touches, but never sacrifices flavor and style for the sake of innovation. Memorable pastas may not be pasta at all—don't miss the cuttlefish cut into the shape of *tagliatelli* tossed with a powerful yet perfectly balanced blend of lobster, capers, chili flakes, and a pile of fresh *agretti*. Veal loin is beautifully roasted and sliced, accompanied by a subtle roasted garlic and potato foam, topped with mushroom confit and micro-greens dressed in truffled bone marrow sauce. It sounds heavy, but it's not.

Modern desserts are noteworthy, so don't be mislead by a humble title. Here, "chocolate mousse" is actually frozen sweet cream gelato studded with crushed hazelnuts and dots of vanilla foam, all coated in bittersweet chocolate mousse for a fun play on the best *tartuffo* you've ever had.

aliment

American 🍴

B3

786 Bush St. (bet. Mason & Powell Sts.)

Phone: 415-829-2737   Dinner nightly
Web: www.alimentsf.com
Prices: $$

Named for the Latin term for nourishment, this chic and comforting newcomer feeds the soul as well as the body. Cheery, upbeat service, a small but compelling wine list, and an eye-catching stainless steel and wood design make it a pleasant retreat from the heart of Union Square, located just blocks away.

The brief menu is saturated with flavor-packed, hearty options like a thick and succulent grilled pork chop over roasted fingerling potatoes and apple chutney, or seared diver scallops in green curry cream with crispy quinoa. Weekend brunch boasts hangover helpers like a Gruyère-stuffed knockwurst with sauerkraut on a brioche bun. For dessert, the custardy cheesecake, served on a cookie-crumb base with chopped yuzu jelly and peel, is obligatory.

Frascati

Mediterranean 🍴🍴

A2

1901 Hyde St. (at Green St.)

Phone: 415-928-1406   Dinner nightly
Web: www.frascatisf.com
Prices: $$

Forget circling for parking and hop on a cable car instead to reach this quaint Mediterranean standby, where you'll see more of the iconic vehicles pass by their large front windows. Inside, closely-spaced tables are ideal for an intimate meal, and local residents definitely know it, because reservations are always hard to come by.

Frascati's fare may not be the city's most innovative, but it is very satisfying, thanks to well-made classics like tender potato gnocchi with asparagus and peas in thyme-white truffle butter, or grilled duck breast in pomegranate sauce over hearts of palm and herb spaetzle. Split the luscious *pain perdu*, caramelized sponge cake soaked in citrusy crème anglaise, and let the friendly servers and soft lighting work their magic.

Gioia

A2

Pizza ✗

2240 Polk St. (bet. Green & Vallejo Sts.)

Phone: 415-359-0971   Lunch & dinner Tue – Sun
Web: www.gioiapizzeria.com
Prices: **$$**

With its large space and casual vibe, Gioia has become a Russian Hill standby, drawing families with kids, groups of friends, and even solo diners (there's lots of counter seating). The rustic décor features white subway-tile walls, an open kitchen, and wood and metal furniture. Be warned: the noise level can be a bit high for any intimate conversation.

The highlight here is pizza, with creatively topped pies like summer squash with pesto, burrata, and Calabrian chili, or sausage, broccoli, leeks, pecorino, and olives. They're pricey, but worth it. A selection of salads and antipasti make for great starters. Otherwise, opt for *rigatoncini* in a meaty pork ragù with fresh, creamy ricotta and more Calabrian chili.

A second location dwells in Berkeley.

Helmand Palace

A2

Afghan ✗✗

2424 Van Ness Ave. (bet. Green & Union Sts.)

Phone: 415-345-0072   Dinner nightly
Web: www.helmandpalacesf.com
Prices: **$$**

A drab exterior and an awkward Van Ness address haven't always worked in Helmand Palace's favor, but the food-savvy know it's one of the Bay Area's best for Afghan cuisine. The well-appointed interior is worlds away from the busy thoroughfare's steady stream of traffic, with linen-draped tables, big blue-cushioned armchairs, and warm, inviting service.

Every meal here kicks off with a basket of fluffy flatbread, served with three irresistible dipping sauces. The *kaddo*, caramelized baby pumpkin and ground beef in a garlic-yogurt sauce, is a perennial favorite, as is the *chapendaz*, marinated beef tenderloin over a tomato-pepper purée, rice, and lentils. Vegetarians will find numerous dishes to enjoy, all of them just as flavorful as the carnivorous feast.

Keiko à Nob Hill

Fusion XXX

B2

1250 Jones St. (at Clay St.)

Phone:	415-829-7141	Dinner Tue – Sun
Web:	www.keikoanobhill.com	
Prices:	**$$$$**	

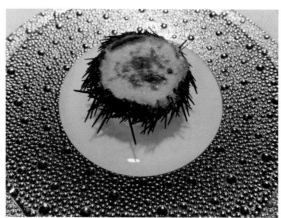

Luxurious, sophisticated, and intimate, Keiko blends unique culinary style with traditional appeal. Cushioned banquettes wrap the square dining room, outfitted with mirrored panels, decorative sconces, and heavy brown trim.

Just be prompt: seatings are limited and all are served at the same time. Arriving late means holding up the entire dining room (and making enemies). This place takes its service, its mission, and itself very seriously.

In the kitchen, Chef Keiko Takahashi performs her own superb balancing act combining very traditional Japanese ingredients with classic French technique. This signature style is immediately clear in the first bite of *kinmedai* sashimi served on a bed of aerated vinegary, peppery Hollandaise sauce with quenelles of briny sturgeon caviar. Fresh, clean flavors highlight silky wild salmon, lightly smoked with cherry wood, presented with fresh cherries, tangy yogurt, trout roe, and dill flowers. Tremendous skill and care are clear in buttery Wagyu beef that has been slowly cooked and cooled four times to retain fat, then complemented with yuzu-soy foam, freshly grated wasabi, and a few threads of insanely spicy Japanese chili to temper the meat's richness.

La Folie ✿

French ✕✕✕

2316 Polk St. (bet. Green & Union Sts.)

Phone: 415-776-5577
Web: www.lafolie.com
Prices: $$$$

Dinner Mon – Sat

Classic French technique and a hint of Japanese influence informs the refined food at Roland Passot's Russian Hill stalwart, which draws an older crowd of wealthy regulars and a younger set celebrating birthdays, anniversaries, and other milestones. Begin with a cocktail in the next-door lounge, before making your way into the warm, persimmon-and-bronze dining room, where an elegant, white-clothed table awaits.

Food is consistently delicious and well-balanced, as an oozy tempura-fried duck egg over a fluffy sweetbread pancake with wild mushroom salad ably showcases. The three-four- and five-course set menus allow for plenty of choice, whether you're seeking a rich take on duck à l'orange with quince purée, or a more clean-lined seared black cod in fragrant miso dashi with shiitakes and pickled chilies. A tarte Tatin with buttery caramelized apples, kabocha crème caramel, and Maker's Mark ice cream is the best of both worlds.

Their thorough wine selection is easy to navigate thanks to the polished staff, who'll also explain each element of the complex dishes. From the first bite of house-made bread to the final chocolates and cannele, a meal at La Folie is celebratory and gratifying.

Leopold's

Austrian ✗✗

A1

2400 Polk St. (at Union St.)

Phone: 415-474-2000
Web: www.leopoldssf.com
Prices: $$

Lunch Sat – Sun
Dinner nightly

The boisterous spirit of an Austrian *gasthaus* is alive and well in Russian Hill. All thanks are due to Leopold's, which draws a young crowd to its slice-of-Vienna dining room, adorned with wood booths, deer antlers, and attended to by cheerful female servers in dirndls. If dinner alone is your goal, go early; convivial groups lend the space a communal mien, but also get larger and louder as the night wears on and the boots of beer are drained.

The carte du jour is rife with well-executed classics like golden-brown pork Weiner schnitzel with a cucumber salad, vegetable strudel, and delectable raspberry Linzer torte. If you've got a group in tow, the *choucroute garni* platter, laden with pork ribs, sausage, potatoes, and sauerkraut, is a crowd-pleaser.

Mason Pacific 😊

American ✗✗

B2

1358 Mason St. (at Pacific Ave.)

Phone: 415-374-7185
Web: www.masonpacific.com
Prices: $$

Dinner Tue – Sun

Though it debuted in 2013, this smart American bistro is already the darling of Nob Hill with swarms of Teslas and Maseratis lining up at the valet station. The stylish occupants, from tech millionaires to white-haired society matrons, stream into the light-filled dining room where they angle for a seat at the semi-private banquette facing the street or in the front room at the marble bar.

The menu is prepared with skill and top-notch ingredients and includes a note-perfect fried chicken and caramelized Alaskan halibut with grated cauliflower and *peperoncini*. The burger, served on a pretzel bun with smoked tomato, is also a terrific choice. And while the friendly, smartly attired staff keeps the handful of tables moving, reservations are still a must.

Modern Thai

A3

Thai ✗

1247 Polk St. (at Bush St.)

Phone: 415-922-8424

Lunch & dinner daily

Web: www.modernthaisf.com

Prices: ⏚⏚

Cheery flowers, greenery, and walls painted in shades of lime and raspberry make this spot look like a tropical oasis, complete with affordable lunch specials and flavorful Thai dishes. Grab a seat on the enclosed porch (weather permitting) and check out the ample vegetarian offerings or specialties like pad Thai. Start with "golden bags," six deep-fried egg wrappers stuffed with a yellow curried mix of sweet potatoes, peas, and taro, served with refreshing cucumber salad; or crisp-fried calamari, tossed with fresh vegetables and peanuts in a dynamic chili-fish sauce. Craving a kick of spice? Request a hot sauce caddy, stocked with three fiery condiments made from different chilies.

Desserts venture into the less exotic, with pan-fried blueberry roti.

Oriental Pearl

C2

Chinese ✗

760 Clay St. (bet. Grant Ave. & Kearny St.)

Phone: 415-433-1817

Lunch & dinner daily

Web: www.orientalpearlsf.com

Prices: ⏚⏚

Named to honor Hong Kong "The Pearl of the Orient," Oriental Pearl is more elegant than its Chinatown brethren: white tablecloths, intricately carved chairs, and polite servers make for a pleasant atmosphere. Street parking is at a premium, so park at Portsmouth Square Garage across the street.

This sparkling "pearl" offers an array of dim sum, à la carte, and set combo menus. Lauded as a signature for good reason, meatballs of minced chicken, mushrooms, and ham are wrapped in egg white crêpes and tied at the top with chive slivers—like tasty little beggar's purses. Wide, chewy *chow fun* are tossed with tender beef in a savory black pepper-black bean gravy; while flash-fried string beans with tofu doused in a chili-garlic sauce is a tasty veggie option.

Parallel 37

Californian 𝄞𝄞𝄞

C2

600 Stockton St. (bet. California & Pine Sts.)

Phone: 415-773-6168   Lunch & dinner daily
Web: www.parallel37sf.com
Prices: $$$

The recently renovated dining room of The Ritz-Carlton has taken a comfortable, brasserie-style turn but remains upscale with leather sofas and glowing walls. The menu is less classic French, with a contemporary farm-to-table philosophy and hints of Asian influence. Hotel guests and locals alike can be seen grabbing cocktails at the busy bar, while the adjoining dining room is slightly more sedate.

The food traverses a range of culinary styles and influences, as in roasted Alaskan halibut with yuzu and stinging nettle flatbread; or sautéed lamb with chorizo and bamboo rice. The professional staff will happily guide you through selecting one of the innovative entrées and that perfect Napa wine. A tasting menu is available by request.

R & G Lounge

Chinese 𝄞

C2

631 Kearny St. (bet. Clay & Sacramento Sts.)

Phone: 415-982-7877   Lunch & dinner daily
Web: www.rnglounge.com
Prices: ☺☺

R & G Lounge has been a longtime Chinatown fave for Cantonese food. The space is clean, while the service is a bit better than mediocre. Sure the décor is dated and the dropped ceiling of beige ribbons is rather strange, but really who's looking up when delicacies (perhaps tender, falling-off-the-bone honey spare ribs glazed in a sweet and tangy sauce) await on your plate?

Tanks of fish signal fresh seafood and fittingly, their signature dish is salt and pepper crab. At lunch, the wood-paneled den downstairs is crammed with families and businessmen. Find them chowing on fresh mixed vegetables delicately stir-fried in garlic sauce; or lamb sautéed with leeks in a mildly-spiced, aromatic gravy of ginger and garlic, teamed with steamed *bao*.

Seven Hills

Italian ✗✗

A2

1550 Hyde St. (at Pacific Ave.)

Phone: 415-775-1550   Dinner nightly
Web: www.sevenhillssf.com
Prices: $$

The dense sidewalk foliage, closely packed tables, and attentive service at this Russian Hill neighborhood favorite will transport you to Italy—that is, until you see the cable car rumbling its way up Hyde, and remember you're in San Francisco. The happy crowd of regulars wouldn't have it any other way.

They come to share bowls of house-made pasta, like a *tagliolini* mingled with asparagus and creamy buffalo ricotta (made fresh on-site). A thick grilled pork chop with gigante beans and charred Calçot onions sates heartier cravings, as do a few offal-centric dishes like rabbit tongues and roasted bone marrow. Finish with a creamy vanilla-blood orange panna cotta, or order a more superlative ricotta for dessert—this time drizzled with honey.

1760

Contemporary ✗✗

A2

1760 Polk St. (at Washington St.)

Phone: 415-359-1212   Dinner nightly
Web: www.1760sf.com
Prices: $$$

The Acquerello team further enriches Nob Hill's diningscape with the arrival of this newcomer and rousing adjunct to their upscale destination a block away. Awash in shades of grey, the dusky space closely seats a hip crowd, rife with bonhomie.

Creative plates that progress from lightest to heartiest start off with bracing tastes of hamachi crudo seasoned with diced Satsuma, *sriracha* meringues, and *bulgogi* vinaigrette. The unorthodox rendition of steak tartare is composed of zesty Thai-spiced dressing and a swipe of buttery Marcona almond purée. The carte goes on to reveal *maccheroni* tossed with a bright serrrano chili pesto and sweet Dungeness crab. The fried duck sandwich graced by slaw and pickles has become a house specialty.

Sons & Daughters 🌢

Contemporary   🍴🍴

C3

708 Bush St. (bet. Mason & Powell Sts.)

Phone: 415-391-8311   Dinner Wed – Sun
Web: www.sonsanddaughterssf.com
Prices: $$$$

From the moment you step into their inviting corner space, the young staff of Sons & Daughters will be dedicated to your comfort. Everyone is warmly professional and service is precise, well timed, and never stuffy. Add in the lovely, architecturally detailed dining room, done in black and cream with plush leather banquettes and polished vintage chandeliers, and you'll dream of returning time and again to sample the delights from the open kitchen.

The seven-course nightly fixed menu is ever-changing and seasonal, but consistently pleasing. A meal might begin with garden herbs that reflect a burst of spring in a wooden bowl teeming with nasturtium, corn flowers, red wood clover, and more, set over delicate cheese curds, favas, and peas topped with whey foam. Then transition to roasted baby beets richly accented by yogurt, mustard, and an outstanding vadouvan spice blend. Gently cooked and pan-finished Petaluma chicken gets an earthy touch from mushroom-fennel purée balanced with fennel pollen, onions, and crunchy batons of poached fennel.

The stunning Alpine strawberry tart filled with smooth polenta cream in a technically perfect crust alongside a scoop of polenta ice cream is captivating.

Stones Throw

A2

1896 Hyde St. (bet. Green & Vallejo Sts.)

Phone: 415-796-2901
Web: www.stonesthrowsf.com
Prices: $$

Lunch Sun
Dinner Tue – Sun

A good neighborhood restaurant should only be a stone's throw away, and this model has clearly hopscotched into Russian Hill's affections. Its terra-cotta floors, yellow walls, and chunky wood tables have a Mediterranean air, but the menu is more eclectically American, with a sizable beer and wine selection that makes the front bar great for a spur-of-the-moment drink and bite.

Clever takes on approachable dishes abound on the menu, from "toad in the hole" lasagna with a poached egg at dinner, to asparagus and duck confit hash at brunch. The creamy smoked salmon mousse, with bagel chips and crème fraîche, is rich and delicious. And pillowy doughnuts, topped with PB&J at dinner or pumpkin spice and pumpkin butter at brunch, are a delightful surprise.

Verbena

A2

2323 Polk St. (bet. Green & Union Sts.)

Phone: 415-441-2323
Web: www.verbenarestaurant.com
Prices: $$$

Lunch Sat – Sun
Dinner nightly

Inventive, vegetable-centric fare expands minds and explodes palates at this second spot from Berkeley's Gather team. While there are carnivorous options like pork trotter terrine with a tangy-sweet apricot mustard and crunchy strips of roasted padrón pepper, the dishes that sing are vegetarian. Think: umami-rich mushrooms with celeriac cream and lovage. Beautifully plated roasted parsnips and cardoons with kale and chermoula are also irresistible.

Located on a commercial block of Polk in Russian Hill, Verbena is stylish yet casual with wood tables, simple place settings, and a boisterous bar. Attentive servers tend to the loud crowd, bathed in colorful light from a jewel-like central wall of house-made pickles awaiting their debut on your plate.

Z & Y

Chinese   ✗

C2

655 Jackson St. (bet. Grant Ave. & Kearny St.)

Phone: 415-981-8988   Lunch & dinner daily
Web: www.zandyrestaurant.com
Prices: $$

Some like it hot, and here they are in heaven. Be forewarned: timid palates should steer clear of the super-spicy Sichuan dishes that have made Z & Y a Chinatown smash hit. Nearly every dish is crowned with chilies, from the huge mound of dried peppers that rest atop tender, garlicky bites of fried chicken to the flaming chili oil anointing tender, flaky fish fillets in a star anise-tinged broth with Sichuan peppercorns aplenty.

The well-worn dining room may seem unremarkable and the service perfunctory, but the crowds are undeterred. Plan to wait among eager fans for a taste of delicate pork and ginger wontons swimming in spicy peanut sauce and more chili oil. Allot more time to navigate the precarious parking situation and score a seat.

The sun is out – let's eat alfresco! Look for 🛖.

North Beach

Relatively compact yet filled with cool restaurants, casual cafeterias, and a hopping nightlife, North Beach has that authentic Californian vibe that makes it just as much a local scene as a tourist mecca. Steps away from the docks and nestled between bustling **Fisherman's Wharf** and the steep slopes of Russian and Telegraph Hills, this neighborhood owes its vibrant nature to the Italian immigrants who passed through these shores in the late 1800s. Many were fishermen from the Ligurian

mid-June, a celebrity pizza toss, Assisi Animal Blessings, and Arte di Gesso (chalk art) also pay homage to this region's Italian roots. Foodies however can rest assured that dining here isn't all

coast, and their seafood stew (cioppino) that they prepared and perfected on the boats evolved into a quintessential San Francisco trademark. Though Italians may no longer be in the majority here, classic *ristorantes*, pizzerias, and coffee shops attest to their idea of the good life. At the annual **North Beach Festival** held in about lasagna-loving, red-sauce joints. Brave the crowd of locals and visitors for some of the most fantastic fish and chips this side of the pond and fish tacos this side of the border, at **The Codmother Fish and Chips**. This veritable local favorite is essentially a small kiosk with a window to place your order and a handful of tables on the front patio. Clearly, it isn't about the dining experience here, and most people get their fish and chips to-go—perhaps for a stroll along the wharf?

Cutting its angle through North Beach, Columbus Avenue is home to the neighborhood's most notable restaurants, bars, and lounges. Thanks to **Molinari's**, whose homemade salami has garnered a fanatic following since 1896, whimsical, old-world Italian delicatessens are a regular fixture along these streets. Pair their impressive range of imported meats and cheeses with some *vino* for a perfect picnic in

North Beach
Fisherman's Wharf
Telegraph Hill

nearby Washington Square Park. Preparing wood-fired pizzas with classic combinations since 1935, **Tommaso's Ristorante Italiano** is another citywide institution, situated on the southern end of North Beach. The décor and ambience may be a vestige from the past, but that hasn't prevented devoted locals from cramping its quarters. Fine-dining can also come with a throwback feel and **Bix** is a grand example. This bi-level arena with a balconied dining room, classic cocktails, and jazz club ambience makes for date-night *extraordinaire*. Getting acquainted with North Beach is a never-ending but very telling experience. After all, these neighborhood venues were also home to a ragtag array of beret-wearing poets in the 1950s and remain a popular excursion for the Beat Generation. Those so-called beatniks—Allen Ginsberg and Jack Kerouac to name a few—were eventually driven out by busloads of tourists. Nonetheless, bohemian spirits still linger on here, at such landmarks as the City Lights bookstore and next door at **Vesuvio**, the quintessential boho bar.

FEASTING IN FISHERMAN'S WHARF

Fisherman's Wharf, that mile-long stretch of waterfront at the foot of Columbus Avenue, ranks as one of the city's most popular sites. There aren't many locals here and it teems with souvenir shops, street performers, and noisy rides, but you should go if only to feast on a sourdough bread bowl crammed with clam chowder, or fresh crabs cooked in huge steamers right on the street. Then, sample a bite of culinary history at **Boudin Bakery**. While this enchanting haunt has bloomed into an updated operation complete with a museum and bakery tour, it stays true to its roots by crafting fresh sourdough bread every day, using the same mother first cultivated here in 1849 from local wild yeast. Not far behind, **Ghirardelli Square** preserves another taste of old San Francisco. This venerable chocolate company, founded by Domenico "Domingo" Ghirardelli in 1852, flaunts a host of delectable wares at the equally famous **Ghirardelli Ice Cream and Chocolate Manufactory**. When visiting here, don't forget to glimpse their original chocolate manufacturing equipment, while enjoying a creamy hot fudge sundae. On your way out, be sure to take away some sweet memories in the form of those chocolate squares.

Albona

Italian ✗✗

B2

545 Francisco St. (bet. Mason & Taylor Sts.)

Phone: 415-441-1040   Dinner nightly
Web: www.albonarestaurant.com
Prices: $$

This brightly painted mid-century bungalow is nestled on a street with high-rises. Inside, find a petite, cozy, and brasserie-like dining room outfitted with velvet curtains and effusive waiters donning traditional waistcoats. Photographs on the walls depict the Istrian village from which the restaurant takes both its name and cuisine inspiration: the focus here is on the peninsula's cooking, where classic Roman and Venetian styles meet Croatian influences.

The menu reveals delicious but somewhat unfamiliar dishes like pork *involtini* stuffed with sauerkraut and enhanced by preserved-fruit sauce; or cured sardines with raisins and pine nuts. While presentations aren't overly refined, it's the ultimate in comfort fare—deeply satisfying and very flavorful.

Café Jacqueline

French ✗

C2

1454 Grant Ave. (bet. Green & Union Sts.)

Phone: 415-981-5565   Dinner Wed – Sun
Web: N/A
Prices: $$$

This petite bistro specializes in soufflés—and what incredibly light and flavorful creations they are. Her space may not dazzle with tables packed like sardines, but Café Jacqueline's faithful French treats certainly will.

Not ideal for large gatherings or groups-on-the-go (meals here may take hours), the café is patronized by those who have time on their hands—and delicious, fluffy soufflés on their mind. Start with the staple French onion soup, but with such a surfeit of savory soufflés on offer, it seems only right to follow suit with a towering chanterelle mushroom rich with Gruyère; or lobster soufflé that is at once decadent and fresh. Moving on—the warm dark chocolate is so plush and moist, you may wonder how you lived before it.

Coi ✿ ✿

C3

373 Broadway (bet. Montgomery & Sansome Sts.)

Phone: 415-393-9000   Dinner Tue – Sat
Web: www.coirestaurant.com
Prices: $$$$

As innovative as it is beautiful, Daniel Patterson's cooking eschews traditional, luxury ingredients for a focus on technique and a sense of place that shifts with the seasons.

Over the eight courses of his tasting menu, the talented chef can make broccoli seem like a delicacy beyond comparison, as evidenced in a dish of lightly cooked brassica florets over vibrant dandelion-potato purée, charred onion broth, and new olive oil that bursts with freshness and flavor. Even the classic combination of beets and goat cheese gets an update, via beet "caviar" over rye crackers and goat cheese mousse. Of course, there's real caviar, too—smoked and served over a slow-poached egg yolk with crème fraîche.

Coi's dining room recently underwent a renovation, adding more seating and a slightly more contemporary vibe to the serene, Zen-like space. A tangle of branches on the ceiling of the entryway leads to a long, narrow feasting area in the former lounge, while the main room now boasts an intricate wood-block ceiling overhead. Beautiful earthenware dishes can be as conversation-worthy as the food itself, and the genuinely warm, yet unobtrusive staff echoes the quality of each plate sent out by the kitchen.

Cotogna 🌮

Italian ✗✗

490 Pacific Ave. (at Montgomery St.)

Phone: 415-775-8508
Web: www.cotognasf.com
Prices: $$

Lunch Mon – Sat
Dinner nightly

Though rustic compared to Quince, its high-end sibling, Michael and Lindsay Tusk's casual Italian offshoot would be elegant by any other standard. Stylish, bright, and a hot ticket reservation-wise, the space centers around an exhibition kitchen, from which crisp pizzas and hearty roasted meats emerge.

Cotogna's absolutely delicious menu highlights Chef Tusk's pristine pastas, like rolled *casconcelli* stuffed with velvety pumpkin purée in sage butter, as well as seasonal starters that include a beautiful chicory salad with sweet red apple, pomegranate, and Piave cheese. And there's always that three-course prix-fixe delight: an exceptional value that features a dessert like pitch-perfect butterscotch *budino* with sea salt and *muscovado* custard.

the house

Asian ✗

1230 Grant Ave. (bet. Columbus Ave. & Vallejo St.)

Phone: 415-986-8612
Web: www.thehse.com
Prices: $$

Lunch Mon – Sat
Dinner nightly

This perennially popular Asian bistro provides a welcome alternative to the Italian-heavy streets in North Beach. The décor is minimal with blonde wood tables and there's no menu, so listen closely to the efficient staff as they recite the bounties of the day. A versatile drinks list completes the enticing spread in addition to offering a happy reprieve to those who've endured a long wait for limited tables.

Dishes like delicately prepped scallops in saffron sauce, and crispy halibut tempura propped atop roasted cauliflower may vary by the day. But a playful, fusion element remains a steady feature in all items, including house-specialties, of which warm wasabi noodles topped with flank steak or teriyaki-glazed salmon are perfect examples.

Gary Danko

Contemporary ✗✗✗

A1

800 North Point St. (at Hyde St.)

Phone: 415-749-2060
Web: www.garydanko.com
Prices: $$$$

Dinner nightly

It is clear what all the fuss is about, right from the moment one enters this polished wood veneer sanctum of Chef Danko's revered dining room. Dressed-up occupants in the mood to celebrate are bathed in flattering light and surrounded by a rainforest's worth of orchids. Service is without reproach and displays an uncommon loyalty; diners here experience a level of hospitality usually reserved for luxury hotels.

Customizable tastings allow guests to mix and match their own three- to five-course meals from a menu of classic cooking layered with global inspiration. Pan-seared quail salad features a crispy rosemary-scented potato cake, sautéed maitake mushrooms, and wild greens—an eye-catching composition united by a warm pomegranate-sweetened dressing. Intensely crisp soft-shell crabs are even easier to love when nestled in a bed of white polenta scattered with black sesame seeds, enhanced with pickled ginger and zesty lime to cut the richness.

Banana tart with rum pastry cream, caramel sauce, and coconut sorbet is a fine choice for dessert, made even sweeter when paired with an after-dinner selection from the outstanding wine list boasting more than 2,000 bottles from around the globe.

Kokkari Estiatorio 😊

Greek ✗✗

200 Jackson St. (at Front St.)

Phone: 415-981-0983
Web: www.kokkari.com
Prices: $$

Lunch Mon – Fri
Dinner nightly

Praise the Greek Gods as Kokkari is one of those places that consistently serves delicious food—no wonder this ample space is forever packed. Roaring fireplaces, wood accents, and iron light fixtures give the tavern an old-world feel that complements its fresh and flavorful carte.

In keeping with its spirit, warm servers cradle such exquisite Greek dishes as a mixed green salad mingling apple shavings, golden beets, and salty feta with oregano-infused vinaigrette; or large chunks of grilled yogurt- and herb-marinated chicken souvlaki and red bell peppers served with cool, creamy *tzatziki* and warm homemade pita strewn with herbs and sea salt. End with a filo shell filled with sweet semolina custard, topped with tangy blood orange segments.

Maykadeh

Persian ✗✗

470 Green St. (bet. Grant Ave. & Kearny St.)

Phone: 415-362-8286
Web: www.maykadehrestaurant.com
Prices: $$

Lunch & dinner daily

Tucked on the inclines leading to Telegraph Hill, this Persian tavern can be a parking challenge for some, but those who've perfected their 90-degree skills will be rewarded with a Middle Eastern oasis in pasta-heavy Little Italy. For 20 years, families have gathered at Maykadeh's linen-lined tables for warm flatbreads spread with a classic mix of onion, basil, and feta; followed by juicy chicken kebabs; lamb and beef skewers; or hearty lamb stew beside fragrant saffron-infused basmati rice.

With tunes and a crowd to match, the aura here is homey featuring dreamy lighting and red roses atop each table. Sour chicken with roasted walnuts and pomegranate may sound esoteric to some palates, but don't fret—like Maykadeh itself, it's surely worth trying.

Park Tavern

American ✗✗

C2

1652 Stockton St. (bet. Filbert & Union Sts.)

Phone: 415-989-7300
Web: www.parktavernsf.com
Prices: $$$

Lunch Fri – Sun
Dinner nightly

North Beach favorite Park Tavern has a menu that spoils diners. Should you stick with the beloved Marlowe burger, or opt for a new plate like roasted sea bass with braised fennel and celeriac purée? The choices are plenty. Go another round with the time-honored Brussels sprout chips, or sample the newer lemon chips with burrata? Whatever you decide, you're unlikely to be disappointed.

Options also abound in terms of seating—the sidewalk tables, window seats, and marble-topped bar counter are equally appealing. In terms of drinking: the house-concocted cocktails, local beers, and varied global wines will each call your name. The good news is that a second visit will allow you to try more, provided you can snatch a table away from the other regulars.

Piperade

Basque ✗✗

D2

1015 Battery St. (bet. Green & Union Sts.)

Phone: 415-391-2555
Web: www.piperade.com
Prices: $$

Lunch Mon – Fri
Dinner Mon – Sat

Basque Chef Gerald Hirigoyen blends the region's French and Spanish roots at this popular restaurant and favorite for business lunches. His roasted lamb gets a touch of Middle Eastern flavor thanks to merguez sausage and a sweet-smoky cumin-date relish, served with tender and caramelized roasted fennel bulb. A solidly Gallic apple galette is deliciously none-too-sweet, combining puff pastry, finely shaved apple slices, and decadant caramel sauce.

Located among historic warehouses in a commercial district, this charming dining room features wood floors, brick walls, and chandeliers made from empty wine bottles. Hold a confab at the eight-person round table, or enjoy a solo glass of wine on the covered front patio and while away a warm afternoon.

Quince ✿ ✿

C3

Italian XXXX

470 Pacific Ave. (bet. Montgomery & Sansome Sts.)

Phone: 415-775-8500

Web: www.quincerestaurant.com

Prices: $$$$

Dinner Mon – Sat

Situated on a tree-lined street amid upscale galleries and design firms, Quince is never bogged down by formality. Make your way inside this elegant establishment to be greeted by a well-versed, passionate, and black-suited service team—clearly one of the best in the city.

Each fixed menu option promises fine-tuned, elevated, and inspired cooking. Pasta courses are a highlight here, like enticing cocoa-flavored tagliatelle, topped with crunchy cocoa nibs, attractively spiraled over a buttery root vegetable reduction and *brunoised* turnip, beet, and radish. Meals may reach their height with the vibrant red beet-infused *cappeletti* filled with creamy smoked ricotta, dressed in a beet reduction beneath fragrant black Perigord truffle shavings. But, even a well-trimmed cutlet of Watson Farm lamb is cooked until deliciously tender and perfectly flavorsome, with a piece of loin coated in crunchy almond crumbs and rye berries, simmered in liquor and adding a splendid layer of texture and flavor.

Expert desserts may balance sheets of bitter chocolate ganache with smooth Sicilian pistachio paste, served with dark chocolate foam, pistachio-vanilla bean ice cream, and candied kumquats.

Roka Akor

Japanese XXX

C3

801 Montgomery St. (at Jackson St.)

Phone: 415-362-8887
Web: www.rokaakor.com
Prices: $$$

Lunch Mon – Fri
Dinner nightly

Contemporary Japanese small plates are the draw at this fancy chain's first California outpost, where business lunchers and fashionable duos can be found answering the call. Whether diners are craving an omakase, steak, sushi, or a snack with cocktails, there's something for everyone on the vast menu. From crunchy chicken *karaage* to *robata*-grilled black-cod skewers and meaty tiger prawns, flavors are terrific and consistent. Sleek and retro, the décor emphasizes soothing blonde woods amid this noisy space. The downstairs lounge offers a darker, sexier vibe. And while this address has housed several restaurants over the years, Roka Akor will hopefully be the last tenant for a while given their extensive, innovative, and very thrilling array of items.

The Square

Californian XX

B2

1707 Powell St. (at Union St.)

Phone: 415-525-3579
Web: www.thesquaresf.com
Prices: $$

Lunch Sat – Sun
Dinner Wed – Sun

The former home of the Washbag, where Herb Caen traded drinks and barbs, this Washington Square Park icon has been reimagined as a casual sequel to Sons & Daughters. The laid-back dining room boasts chocolate-brown leather banquettes and twinkling pendant lights. In the front, a large bar attracts hip locals for cocktails and bites like warm olives or *gougères*. Meals here are full of captivating Californian fare, much of which comes from the restaurant's own farm in Santa Cruz. Pan-fried chicken thighs, alternately crisp and juicy, get a hit of heat from Calabrian chilies, while a well-caramelized pork chop arrives draped with apricots, baby fennel, and toasted almonds. For dessert, the plum tart with vanilla ice cream and honey is deliciously rustic.

Tony's Pizza Napoletana

C2

Pizza

1570 Stockton St. (at Union St.)

Phone: 415-835-9888

Web: www.tonyspizzanapoletana.com

Prices: $$

Lunch & dinner Wed – Sun

 A veritable polymath of pizza, Tony Gemignani serves every variety imaginable at his North Beach institution, from wood-fired Neapolitan to gas-cooked New York to 1,000-degree coal-fired. Tucked into the ground floor of a quaint Victorian, the sparse décor directs focus to the 12 styles of pizza on offer. It's always crowded, so expect a wait—and don't bring a big group.

Pies and Italian-American dishes are as rich and complex as the space is simple, from the tangy, herbaceous tomato sauce lapping tender beef meatballs to the delicious interplay of soft quail eggs, smooth potato, and crisp *guanciale* atop a wood-fired pie. Can't wait? Gemignani also owns a quick-fix slice shop right next door, plus nearby Capo's, which focuses on Chicago-style pie.

Tosca Café

C3

Italian

242 Columbus Ave. (bet. Broadway & Pacific Ave.)

Phone: 415-986-9651

Web: www.toscacafesf.com

Prices: $$$

Dinner Tue – Sun

 This historic bar has been expertly revived under NYC stars, April Bloomfield and Ken Friedman, who spent millions to add a kitchen and make its old-school charm seem untouched. White-coated bartenders shake and stir behind the glorious carved wood bar, while diners feast in the cushy red leather booths. Reservations aren't accepted and tables are few, so expect a wait.

The food is Italian-American with Bloomfield's signature meaty influences, like flavorful, gamey grilled lamb ribs that nearly fall off the bone. Pastas are strong, from creamy *gemelli cacio e pepe* to rich, spicy *bucatini all'Amatriciana*, but don't neglect their vegetables: a dish of tender cauliflower and potatoes in a rich taleggio sauce with crunchy breadcrumbs is a showstopper.

Trattoria Contadina

Italian ✕

B2

1800 Mason St. (at Union St.)

Phone: 415-982-5728
Web: www.trattoriacontadina.com
Prices: $$

Lunch Sun
Dinner nightly

This old-school charmer dispenses Italian-American dishes in a quaint trattoria donning a faux-balcony overhead. Rife with a nostalgic vibe (framed photos of celebs hang throughout), it's no wonder that this homey tavern has such a loyal following. But, don't be surprised if the occasional visitor wanders in looking for an escape from the Italian tourist traps nearby.

The rustic menu is concise, but the portions are hearty. Start with *rigatoncelli* swirled with caramelized pancetta, porcini mushrooms, and sun-dried tomatoes in a tomato-cream sauce; before tucking into a juicy chicken breast covered with smoked mozzarella, prosciutto shavings, and served in a pool of Madeira wine sauce. Still need a drop of sweet? The lemon cheesecake is exemplary.

Remember, stars
(✿✿✿…✿) are awarded
for cuisine only! Elements
such as service and décor
are not a factor.

Richmond & Sunset

Named after an Australian art dealer and his home (The Richmond House), quiet yet urban Richmond is hailed for the surf that washes right up to its historic Cliff House and Sutro Baths. Springtime adds to the area's beauty with Golden Gate Park's blushing cherry blossoms and whimsical topiaries—nevermind those bordering pastel row houses in desperate need of a lick of paint. More than anywhere else in the city, this sequestered northwest enclave is ruled by a sense of Zen, and residents smoked, cured meats, sausages, pickles, sauerkraut, and more.

NEW CHINATOWN

While Richmond does cradle some western spots, it is mostly renowned for steaming bowls of piping-hot *pho*, as thick as the marine layer itself. This area has earned the nickname "New Chinatown" for good reason—deliciously moist and juicy plates of *siu mai* are meant to be devoured at **Shanghai Dumpling King** or **Good Luck Dim Sum**. Speaking

seem deeply impacted by it— from that incredibly stealthy sushi chef to über-cool Sunset surfer dudes. Given its multi-cultural immigrant community, Richmond's authentic cuisine options are both delicious and very varied. Begin with an array of European specialty items at **Seakor Polish Delicatessen and Sausage Factory**, proffering an outstanding selection of to this neighborhood's new nickname, **Wing Lee Bakery** is famed for a comprehensive selection of dim sum—both sweet and savory. And while you're at it, don't miss out on Frisco's finest roast duck, on display at **Wing Lee BBQ** next door. Those looking to replicate this Asian extravaganza at home should start with a perfect wok, stockpot, noodle bowl,

and rice cooker among other stellar housewares and kitchen supplies available at **Kamei**. If that doesn't make you feel like a kid in a candy store, Hong Kong–style delights (on offer even late at night) at **Kowloon Tong Dessert Café** will do a bang-up job. Clement Street, also an inviting exposition for the adventurous home cook and curious chef, features poky sidewalk markets where clusters of bananas sway from awnings and the spices and produce on display are as vibrant as the nearby **Japanese Tea Garden** in bloom. While the Bay Area mantra "eat local" may not be entirely pertinent here, a medley of global goodies abound and everything from tamarind and eel, to live fish and pork buns are available for less than a buck. There is a mom-and-pop joint for every corner and culture. In fact, this is *the* 'hood to source that 100-year-old egg or homemade kimchi by the pound. The décor in these divey stops is far from remarkable and at times downright seedy, but really, you're here for the food, which is always authentic and on-point. Buses of Korean tourists routinely pull up to **Han Il Kwan** for a taste of home. The space may be congested and service can be a disaster, but the kitchen's nostalgic cooking keeps the homesick coming back for more. Native-born aficionados can be found combing the wares at **First Korean Market**, poised on Geary Boulevard and packed with every prepared food and snack under the sun. Meanwhile, culture vultures gather for an intense Burmese feast at **B Star Bar**, after which a refreshing sip at **Aroma Tea Shop** is nothing if not obligatory. Their owners even encourage free tastings of exclusive custom blends of individually sourced teas from around the world.

SUNSET

A dash more updated than bordering Richmond, Sunset—once a heap of sand dunes—retains a small-town vibe that's refined but still rough around the edges. Here, locals start their day with fresh-baked pastries at **Arizmendi Bakery** and then stroll around the corner for some much-needed caffeine at the **Beanery**. Asian appetites routinely patronize **Izakaya Sozai** for juicy *yakitori*, followed by cooling and fresh sashimi. Tourists taking in the sights at the de Young Museum or Academy of Sciences love to linger over lunch at **Wooly Pig Café**. Their namesake "Wooly Pig" sandwich, crafted from toasted challah and overflowing with pork belly, mizuna greens, and pickled shallots, is guaranteed to knock your socks off. Yes, the space

Richmond & Sunset

A   **B**   **C**

South Bay

CHINA BEACH

1

LAND'S END

COASTAL TRAIL

PACIFIC

OCEAN

THE LEGION OF HONOR

LINCOLN PARK

SEA CLIFF

Lincoln Blvd

THE PRE

Washing

Lake St.

Lake

27th 25th 23rd 21st 19th St. 17th

California

Pizzetta 211

Kappou Gomi

Clem

SUTRO BATHS RUINS

Seal Rock Dr.

Clement

35th 33rd 31st 29th

Aziza

Point Lobos Ave.

Blvd.

Sutro's

CLIFF HOUSE

SUTRO HEIGHTS PARK

Geary

48th 47th 45th 43rd 41st 37th

Anza

St.

Khan Toke Thai House

Sich Hor

RICHMON

Balboa

RICHMOND

St. Ave. Ave. Ave. Ave. Ave. Ave.

Cabrillo

Balboa

2

OCEAN BEACH

La Playa

Cabrillo

Ave. Ave. Ave. Ave.

St.

47th Ave.

Fulton

Great

Chain of Lakes Dr.

Spreckels Lake

John F. Kennedy Dr.

Park Presidio

St La

GOLDEN GATE PARK

John F. Kennedy Dr.

West Dr.

Luther King Jr. Dr.

Highway

Martin Luther King Jr. Dr.

Middle Dr.

Martin Way

Lincoln

Lincoln

48th 45th 43rd 41st 37th 35th 33rd 31st 29th 27th 25th 21st 19th

Irvi

La Playa

Irving

St.

Ocean Beach

Judah

Judah-Sunset

Judah

Judah-19 Av

Kirkh

3

Kirkham

Ave. Ave. Ave. Ave. Ave. Ave.

St. St. St. 36th St. 22nd Ave.

Lawton

Lawton

St.

Moraga

Moraga

Guddu de Karahi

OCEAN BEACH

Noriega

St.

Noriega

SUNSET

Ortega

Ortega

St.

Sunset Reservoir

24th

43rd St.

37th

Pacheco

Pacheco

Quintara

21st

PACIFIC

48th

Quintara

47th 45th

41st

St.

39th

35th 33rd 31st 29th 27th 25th

Rivera

Quintar

Rivera

Ave.

Ave.

Santiago

Santiago

Taraval-22 Av

Ta

OCEAN

Ave.

Taraval-Sunset

St.

23rd 19th

4

Taraval

Ave.

Ulloa

PARKSIDE

Ave. Ave. Ave.

Ulloa

GOLDEN GATE NATIONAL RECREATION AREA

Ave.

Vicente

Sunset

St.

Vicente

Ave.

SF Zoo

Wawona

Blvd.

Wawona

PINE LAKE PARK

Sloat

Yorba

Crestlake Dr.

Sloat

Blvd.

A   **B**   **C**

is tiny with only a smattering of tables, but with gorgeous Golden Gate Park just a block away, their offerings make for perfect picnic treats. Over on Noriega Street, the line lengthens out the door and down the sidewalk at **Cheung Hing**. If that isn't a sign that something special is going on here, sample their Chinese barbecue including whole roast duck, or take slices of tender-charred pork to-go. In fact, those leaving with bags of roasted meat can be assured of envious glares from the crowds waiting around. As the sun sets in Sunset, savor some dinner at **The Moss Room**, flaunting distinctive dishes composed of local, seasonal, and nutritious ingredients. Reflecting the same philosophy, **San Tung** on Irving Street has gained a substantial local fan-base who seem unperturbed at the thought of waiting endlessly for their famously crispy dry-fried chicken wings. Outer Sunset residents who are at the mercy of time may rest assured as **Noriega Produce** resides only steps around the corner, and is as immaculate as any farmer's market for sustainable local and organic produce. Finally, no repast can be termed "regal" without a bit of sweet at **Holy Gelato!**—a quirky shop serving coffees, teas, and creamy gelatos in a wide range of flavors—maybe crème brûlée, goat cheese, and honey-lavender? Top off such sweet satisfaction at age-old, Asian kitsch fave, **Polly Ann Ice Cream**, with such inventive flavors as durian, jasmine tea, and taro, and know that nothing but sweet dreams can follow.

Aziza ✿

San Francisco ▶ Richmond & Sunset

C1

5800 Geary Blvd. (at 22nd Ave.)

Phone: 415-752-2222
Web: www.aziza-sf.com
Prices: **$$$**

Dinner Wed – Mon

The flavors of Morocco get a contemporary upgrade at Mourad Lahlou's lovely and exotic restaurant, nestled in a quiet corner of the Outer Richmond. The attractive, dimly lit dining room is divided into a variety of niches, from an alcove of booths and banquettes in front, to a Moroccan-style lounge with low seating in the rear. Bartenders stir up a host of quenching cocktails at a teal side bar, producing striking combinations like cantaloupe with pisco, pink peppercorn, and Chartreuse.

Sweet and savory elements intertwine in the skillfully prepared food, like a tangy lentil soup accented by ripe Medjool dates. The *basteeya*, a masterful signature, envelops rich duck confit, caramelized onions, olives, and raisins in a flaky phyllo pastry with hints of cinnamon and orange-flower water. Fluffy couscous arrives with caramelized cauliflower, soft currants, and spicy *harissa*; while tender lamb loin and belly gain depth from wilted chard, apple purée, and roasted beets. A nightly tasting menu offers a full tour of the fare.

From neighborhood couples to European tourists, the accommodating staff makes everyone feel comfortable, and are happy to explain an unusual dish or endorse a compelling drink.

Burma Superstar

Burmese ✗

D1

309 Clement St. (bet. 4th & 5th Aves.)

Phone: 415-387-2147   Lunch & dinner daily
Web: www.burmasuperstar.com
Prices: $$

Like any celebrity, it's easy to recognize this Inner Richmond superstar from the eager crowds swarming like paparazzi. Everyone endures this no-reservations policy to Instagram their favorite Burmese dishes. See the iPhones poised over the famed rainbow and tea-leaf salads and *samusa* soup (available as a lunchtime combo). In-the-know diners stick to traditional dishes, marked by asterisks on the menu.

Palate-tingling options include rice noodles with pickled daikon and tofu in a spicy tomato-garlic sauce, or pork and kabocha squash stewed in a gingery broth with coconut sticky rice. A creamy Thai iced tea is the perfect counterbalance to the spicy, boldly flavored fare. The food is as unusual as the dark-wood space while basic service is ho-hum.

Chapeau! ☺

French ✗✗

D1

126 Clement St. (bet. 2nd & 3rd Aves.)

Phone: 415-750-9787   Dinner Tue – Sat
Web: www.chapeausf.com
Prices: $$

For an oh-so-French experience on Asian food-centric Clement, denizens head to Philippe Gardelle's authentic bistro, where tightly spaced tables and paintings of the titular hats create a convivial atmosphere. Packed with regulars receiving *bisous* from the chef, Chapeau is warm and generous, a vibe that's aided by its strong Gallic wine list.

Dishes are traditional with a bit of Californian flair, like fingerling potato chips in a frisée and duck confit salad or salted-caramel ice cream that tops the *pain perdu*. The cassoulet, wholesome with braised lamb, rich with smoky sausage, and earthy with white beans, is perfect for a foggy night in the Avenues. Come before 6:00 P.M. for a $36.95 early bird prix-fixe, or create your own from their many set menus.

Guddu de Karahi

C3

Indian ✗

1501 Noriega St. (at 22nd Ave.)

Phone: 415-759-9088   Lunch & dinner Wed – Sun
Web: www.guddudekarahi.com
Prices: 💰💰

When Chef Guddu Haider departed the Tenderloin's Lahore Karahi a few years back, a sizable flock of devotees were bereft at the loss of his flavorful, rustic Indian and Pakastani fare. Fortunately, his cooking is back and better than ever at a tidy little no-frills home in the Sunset. Just don't expect to be in and out, the small kitchen and staff struggle to keep up during prime meal times—off-hours are the best time to go.

Your wait will be rewarded with some of the city's most flavorful homemade Indian and Pakastani cuisine. Delicious, affordable dishes include earthy, tender *dal makhany* (lentils stewed with spices, tomato, and cream) and tangy-spicy vindaloo loaded with chunks of tender lamb. Smoky naan and golden-brown samosas are equally alluring.

Kappou Gomi 😊

C1

Japanese ✗

5524 Geary Blvd. (bet. 19th & 20th Aves.)

Phone: 415-221-5353   Dinner Tue – Sun
Web: N/A
Prices: $$

Sushi-seekers should take a pass, but those seeking elegant, traditional Japanese food will find kindred spirits at this precious gem. The serene, ultra-minimalist dining room isn't fancy, with only a few shelves of ceramics as décor. But, older Japanese women in traditional garb who run the show are endlessly polite and attentive so long as you're not raising a din—or requesting a spicy tuna roll.

If you're able to go with the flow, you'll find much to adore on their menu, like umami-rich wilted mizuna salad with fresh fava beans and bonito sauce, or pale green edamame tofu with fresh cherries, cherry blossom noodles, and a sour-salty cherry paste. The exquisitely moist and flaky black cod, grilled with a slightly sweet sake marinade, is revelatory.

Khan Toke Thai House

Thai ✕

C2

5937 Geary Blvd. (bet. 23rd & 24th Aves.)

Phone: 415-668-6654
Web: N/A
Prices: 🍜

Lunch & dinner daily

Don your best dinner socks for this traditional Thai restaurant, where diners are asked to remove their shoes before perching on low cushions at the intricately carved tables. Service is as slow as a glacier, making it more suited to casual dining than business lunch. Still, Khan Toke is worth the wait.

Awaken the senses with a bowl of enticingly pungent and spicy-sour *tom yum* soup, loaded with tomato, onion, and sliced lemongrass, finished with fresh cilantro. Then dive into *gai ga prou*, a delicious stir-fry of chicken and bell peppers studded with sliced Thai chilies. Indeed, chili-lovers who order dishes "very spicy" will get what they want. There is no shortage of firepower in the bamboo shoots with chili sauce and excellent Penang curry.

Lavash

Persian ✕✕

D3

511 Irving St. (bet. 6th & 7th Aves.)

Phone: 415-664-5555
Web: www.lavashsf.com
Prices: $$

Lunch & dinner Tue – Sun

You'll feel like you've dined in a Persian home after leaving family-run Lavash, which has become a neighborhood fixture thanks to warm service and sizable portions. Painted in hues of orange, gold, and rose, the casual and flower-filled space is inviting, and throughout a meal here, you'll see locals dropping in for takeout or just to chat.

Begin your feast with *sabzi panir*, a plate of fresh herbs, feta, cucumber, tomato, walnuts, and grapes that's perfect for ad hoc toppings on the cracker-like namesake bread. Then order up a skewer or two of tender and smoky ground beef and lamb *koobideh*, served over fluffy basmati rice. Finally, don't miss the crispy, sticky-sweet *baghlava*—it's available in traditional pistachio or as a chocolate "choclava."

Mandalay

Burmese 🍴

D1

4348 California St. (bet. 5th & 6th Aves.)

Phone: 415-386-3895 Lunch & dinner daily
Web: www.mandalaysf.com
Prices: 🍪

A block from the hustle and bustle of Clement St., this long-running, intimate restaurant flaunting various Burmese influences provides a quieter alternative to its jam-packed neighbors. Though the '70s-style décor is a bit worn-out, you'll gain renewed energy from the earnest staff dressed in classic sarongs who eagerly attend to a spate of regulars. Beer and wine are available, but don't count out a ginger-mint lemonade or iced tea with condensed milk.

Steer clear of the Chinese dishes and dive straight into a pickled ginger salad with toasted lentil seeds; followed by the nation's favorite food—*mohinga*—ground catfish chowder floating noodles, fried onions, and dried chilies; or *nan gyi dok*, round rice noodles paired with spicy coconut chicken curry.

Park Chow

 American 🍴

D2

1240 9th Ave. (bet. Irving St. & Lincoln Way)

Phone: 415-665-9912 Lunch & dinner daily
Web: www.chowfoodbar.com
Prices: $$

Steps from the Golden Gate Park museums, Park Chow draws locals and tourists alike with its approachable and well-priced organic American comfort food. No matter the mood or time of day, something here will appeal. Options abound from kid-friendly mini-pizzas to lighter and healthier fare like a tangy beet and endive salad with creamy avocado and salty goat cheese. Find straightforward pleasure in the grilled free-range chicken BLT on a griddled bun with crisp fries. For dessert, don't miss the rustic ginger cake with pumpkin ice cream and caramel.

The homey space is full of appealing nooks, including a dog-friendly front patio and sunny roof deck. Remember to call ahead to get your name on the wait list (especially for weekend brunch).

Pizzetta 211

Pizza ✕

C1

211 23rd Ave. (at California St.)

Phone: 415-379-9880
Web: www.pizzetta211.com
Prices: $$

Lunch & dinner daily

This shoebox-sized pizzeria may reside in the far reaches of the Outer Richmond, but it's easily identifiable by the crowds hovering on the sidewalk to score a table. Once inside, you'll be greeted by *pizzaiolos* throwing pies in the tiny exhibition kitchen—ask for a counter seat to get a better view.

The thin, chewy, blistered *pizzettas* each serve one, making it easy to share several varieties. Weekly specials utilize ingredients like seasonal produce, house-made sausage, and fresh farm eggs, while standbys include a pie topped with wild arugula, creamy mascarpone, and San Marzano tomato sauce. Whatever you do, arrive early: once the kitchen's out of dough, they close for the day, and the omnipresent lines mean the goods never last too long.

Sichuan Home 🍤

Chinese ✕

C2

5037 Geary Blvd. (bet. 14th & 15th Aves.)

Phone: 415-221-3288
Web: N/A
Prices: $$

Lunch & dinner daily

The snug Sichuan Home lures diners far and wide to its bright, clean room with walls covered in shellacked wood panels and shiny mirrors. Décor aside, it's really all about their superb range of Sichuan food. Above the tables, find such smart accents as framed photos and descriptions of some of their more prized items.

A sampling should include tender, bone-in rabbit with scallions, peanuts, and a perfect dab of scorching hot peppercorns, cooled down by pickled cabbage bathed in rice wine vinegar and star anise. Dried red chilies are the star in a savory, aromatic composition of crispy fried string beans with tender, flavorful ground pork; while an enormous and cracklin' hot Dungeness crab sautéed with garlic and ginger is festive and very tasty.

Sutro's

A2

1090 Point Lobos Ave. (at Ocean Beach)

Phone: 415-386-3330   Lunch & dinner daily
Web: www.cliffhouse.com
Prices: $$$

Set in the historic Cliff House, perched above the roaring Pacific, Sutro would be worth a trip just for its commanding views of the rugged California coastline. But this SF landmark doesn't rest on its laurels; instead, it serves surprisingly good food.

In season, Dungeness crab is unmissable here, whether in a terrifically colossal crab Louie salad with avocado mousse and hard-boiled eggs, or shatteringly crisp panko-crusted crab cakes over carrot hummus and lemon-tarragon aïoli. The tasty seafood-focused fare goes on to include mussels steamed in Anchor Steam beer and *harissa*; as well as a sautéed red trout sandwich with fennel, cucumber, and yogurt.

After your meal, stroll the beach or visit the windswept ruins of the Sutro Baths next door.

Trattoria da Vittorio

D4

150 W. Portal Ave. (bet. 14th Ave. & Vicente St.)

Phone: 415-742-0300   Lunch & dinner daily
Web: www.trattoriadavittorio.com
Prices: $$

Mamma knows best at this West Portal hot spot, with home cooking imported straight from the kitchen of the owner's Italian mother, Mamma Francesca. One bite of her lasagna, rich with creamy ricotta and hearty Bolognese, will have you cheering "Mamma mia," while oversized portions have some crying "basta!" A semi-open kitchen and cheerful staff add to the sense of homey hospitality. A kids' menu makes it an extra popular choice for families.

Start meals with an immaculately fresh caprese salad, then sample a crisp pie from the Neapolitan wood-burning pizza oven. Don't miss the outstanding tiramisu: ultra-creamy and not overly sweet, these layers of espresso-soaked cake with whipped mascarpone and shaved chocolate won't require coaxing to scrape clean.

Troya 😊

D1

349 Clement St. (at 5th Ave.)

Phone: 415-379-6000
Web: www.troyasf.com
Prices: $$

Lunch & dinner daily

If it weren't for the Asian supermarkets just outside, you could be forgiven for thinking you were in the Mediterranean upon arriving at delightful Troya with its tiled terra-cotta floors and gently worn wooden furniture. Neighborhood regulars are cheerfully greeted by a squadron of swift yet very friendly waiters, who bustle by patrons as the aromas of rich spices fill the room.

The vibrant Turkish food includes tender, almost pearl-like *manti* dressed in paprika-infused yogurt; crisp flatbreads topped with an aromatic blend of ground beef, lamb, and tomato; gently fried zucchini cakes; juicy kebabs; as well as lighter wraps and salads for lunch. Meze like plump dolmas and creamy hummus are a great addition to that late-afternoon glass of wine.

Wako

D1

211 Clement St. (bet. 3rd & 4th Aves.)

Phone: 415-682-4875
Web: www.sushiwakosf.com
Prices: $$$

Dinner Tue – Sun

From the outside, Wako doesn't look like much, but this sushi-centric newcomer holds plenty of surprises within. The dining room exudes a contemporary, Zen-like vibe, with an L-shaped counter, multi-hued wood, and exquisite fresh flower arrangements. The sushi chef and staff are extremely attentive to guests.

While an à la carte menu offers sushi and traditional small plates, many diners opt for the four- or seven-course omakase, which may include items like a whole grilled sweetfish with cucumber salad, *agedashi* tofu, and roasted eggplant in dashi. The highlight, though, is the nigiri, with supremely pristine, Japanese-sourced snow crab, Hokkaido uni, bonito, and *otoro* on excellent rice. A compact selection of sake adds to the authentic experience.

SoMa

Once the city's locus of industry, sprawling SoMa (short for South of Market) has entered a post-industrial era that's as diverse and energetic as San Francisco itself. From its sleek office towers and museums near Market, to the spare converted warehouses that house the city's hottest startups, SoMa teems with vitality, offering memorable experiences around every turn. Tourists may skip it for its lack of Victorians, but SoMa's culinary riches and cultural cachet are of a different, authentically urban kind—the neighborhood equivalent of a treasured flea-market find.

FINE ARTS & EATS

Most visitors to SoMa tend to cluster in the artsy northeast corridor (bordering downtown) for trips to the Museum of Modern Art (now closed for renovations), Yerba Buena Center for the Arts, Contemporary Jewish Museum, and a profusion of other galleries and studios. For a pit stop, join the tech workers snagging a caffeinated "Gibraltar" from local coffee phenomenon **Blue Bottle**, housed in the back of Mint Plaza (there is also a **Mint Plaza Farmer's Market** held on summer Fridays). For a more serene setting, gaze over Yerba Buena Gardens with a cup of rare green tea and spa cuisine at **Samovar Tea Lounge**.

In a city where everyone loves to eat, even the **Westfield San Francisco Centre** mall is a surprisingly strong dining destination, offering cream puffs, fresh fish, and *bi bim bap* in its downstairs food court. Local chain **Buckhorn Grill**, in the Metreon Mall, is another treasure for deliciously marinated, wood-fired tri-tip. A hard day's shopping done, hit happy hour on Yerba Buena Lane with the yupsters fresh from their offices, indulging in a strong margarita at festive Mexican cantina, **Tropisueño**, or a more sedate sip at chic **Press Club**, which focuses on Californian wine and beer. In the midst of it all, the Moscone Center may draw conventioneers to overpriced hotel restaurants and clumsy chains, but the savvier ones beeline to **ThirstyBear Brewing Company**, where classic Spanish tapas and organic brews come without the crowds or crazy prices. Alternatively, stroll over to the Rincon Center for a unique meal at **Amawele's South African Kitchen**, which has won the hearts of local office workers with unique and tasty food like "bunny chow"—a curry-filled bread bowl.

PLAY BALL

SoMa's southeast quarter has undergone a revival in the last decade, with baseball fans flooding AT&T Park to watch the Giants, perennial World Series contenders. The park's food options are equally luring and include craft beer, sushi, and Ghirardelli sundaes. Crabcake sandwiches at **Crazy Crab'z** have a fan club nearly as sizable as the team itself. Off the field, this corridor is dominated by the tech scene, which has transformed the area's former factories and warehouses into humming open-plan offices. An oasis of green amid the corporate environs, South Park is a lovely retreat, particularly with a burrito from cheerful taqueria **Mexico au Parc** in hand. Just outside the park, legions of young engineers in their matching company hoodies form long lines every lunchtime outside **HRD Coffee Shop**—it may look like a greasy spoon but serves tasty Korean-influenced fare like spicy pork and kimchi burritos. Hip graphic designers can be seen speeding their fixed-gear bikes towards Market to pick up desktop fuel from **The Sentinel**, where former Canteen Chef Dennis Leary offers house-roasted coffee in the mornings and excellent corned-beef sandwiches for lunch.

Silicon Valley commuters begin pouring out of the Caltrain station around 5:00 P.M., giving the area's nightlife an extra shot in the arm. **21st Amendment**, a brewpub with

hearty food and popular beers like Back in Black, is a favorite for a relaxed bite; whereas sexy **Supperclub** fuses racy performance art and global cuisine, all served on a bed. For those in need of an understated retreat, the 700-label selection at ripped-out-of-France wine bar, **Terroir**, will enchant natural-wine junkies.

BEST OF THE WEST

SoMa's western half may be grittier, but is still a must for those in search of great eats. After a closure and remodel, Vietnamese standby **Tú Lan** is once again drawing lines of customers for its killer imperial rolls, despite the drug-addled environs of its Sixth Street digs. Crowds also cluster at neighboring **Dottie's True Blue Café**, a gem for all-American breakfasts of blueberry-and-cornmeal pancakes or salsa-drenched Southwestern omelets, served with a side of local characters. Indeed, very little is same old-same old on this side of the city, whether it's the tattooed skateboarders practicing their moves, the omnipresent cranes constructing new condo towers, or the drag performers who entertain bachelorette parties over Asian-fusion fare at bumping nightspot **AsiaSF**. Amidst the edgy bars, kitschy boutiques, and design start-ups of Folsom, **Citizen's Band** turns out seasonal "diner-inspired cuisine" like a killer burger on buns from next-door **Pinkie's Bakery**, while Ethiopian stews on spongy *injera* fuel a booming takeout business at **Moya**. Feast on fragrant Thai curries at **Basil Canteen** in the original Jackson Brewery building. Then hit the 11th Street bars for hours of drinking and dancing, before soaking up all the evening's sins with a rich Nutella-banana triangle from late-night perma-cart, **Crêpes a Go Go**.

SoMa

NOB HILL

A

B

Jackson St.

Washington St.

Jackson St.

CHINATOWN

NOB HILL

California St.

UNION SQUARE

Post UNION SQUARE

Bluestem Brasserie

Powell St

M.Y. China

The Cavalier

OLD MINT

MOSC CENTER

54 Mint

Lu

TENDERLOIN

CIVIC CENTER

ASIAN ART MUSEUM

CITY HALL

UN PLAZA

SF PUBLIC LIBRARY

Civic Center

TBD

AQ

SF WAR MEMORIAL & PERFORMING ARTS CENTER

Van Ness

J
K
B
M
N

Una Pizza Napoletana

1601 Bar & Kitchen

Manora's Thai Cuisine

Bar Agricole

Sushi Zone

Cathead's BBQ

MISSION

136

FINANCIAL DISTRICT

TRANSAMERICA PYRAMID

EMBARCADERO CENTER

Clay St.
Sansome St.
Battery St.
Drumm St.

FERRY BLDG.

SAN FRANCISCO BAY

One Market ☓☓
Steuart St
Boulevard ⊛☓☓

Embarcadero
RINCON CENTER

SAN FRANCISCO-OAKLAND BAY BRIDGE

RINCON PARK

Epic Roasthouse ☓☓
Waterbar ☓☓

Yank Sing ☓☓

RN74 ☓☓

Folsom & Embarcadero

TRANSBAY TRANSIT CENTER (Const.)

Town Hall ☓☓

TEMPORARY BUS TERMINAL

Prospect ☓☓☓

PIER 26

Salt House ☓

New Montgomery St.
2nd St.
Stevenson St.
Mission St.
Howard St.
1st St.
Folsom St.
Tehama St.
Beale St.
Main St.
Spear St.
Fremont St.
Steuart St.

PIER 28

Trou Normand

Ame ☓☓

Minna St.

SF MOMA

RINCON HILL

PIER 30

Essex St.
Harrison St.

PIER 32

YERBA BUENA GARDENS

Benu ●

The Fly Trap ☓☓

Hawthorne St.

Brannan & Embarcadero

Brannan St.
Delancey St.

PIER 36

MOSCONE CENTER

The Embarcadero

PIER 38

Zero Zero ⊛☓☓

SOUTH PARK
S. Park St.

SOUTH BEACH

PIER 40

Le Charm ☓☓

Perry St.
Stillman St.
Rilch St.
Zoe St.

3rd St.

Second St-King St

Saison ⊛☓☓

Fringale ⊛☓☓

4th St.
Freelon St.

Twenty Five Lusk ☓☓☓

Townsend St.

24 Willie Mays Pl.

AT&T PARK

Basin

CHINA BASIN PARK

CALTRAIN STATION

Caltrain Station

China

Terry

PIER 48

Bluxome St.
5th St.

King St.

Berry St.

PIER 50

MISSION BAY

4th
Mission Rock St.
China Basin St.
3rd
Francois St.

PIER 54

MISSION BAY

Mission Bay Blvd.
Mission Bay Blvd.
N.
S.
Blvd.

Owens St.
Nelson Rising Ln.

7th St.
King St.
Berry St.
Townsend St.
Morris St.
Bryant St.

MISSION

137

Ame ⚜

Contemporary ☓☓☓

C2

689 Mission St. (at 3rd St.)

Phone: 415-284-4040   Dinner nightly
Web: www.amerestaurant.com
Prices: $$$

The St. Regis hotel is where Napa-based husband-and-wife team Hiro Sono and Lissa Doumani serve up their distinct creations in the City by the Bay. Ame's look is appropriately slick for its setting on the lobby level of this concrete and glass tower. An eastern vibe accents the sexy space with mesquite wood floors, a red lacquer wall, and smoked glass wine cellar. The sashimi bar is where those raw treats emerge from—think seasonal plates like thinly sliced amberjack ceviche with avocado, slivers of charred Fresno chili, and finger lime dressing.

As at Terra and Bar Terra, influences from Japan, Europe, and America steer this skillfully rendered cuisine. Bruschetta topped with a plump orb of creamy burrata is drizzled with olive oil and arranged with a mélange of brassica and pungent *bagna cauda* vinaigrette. Lobster tail is grilled to sweet and tender perfection then dressed with a lemony butter sauce enriched with sea urchin. The petite "individual" huckleberry pie may get you out of having to share; the crust is flaky, fruit is bright, and it is all lusciously plated with tangy Meyer lemon curd and crème fraîche ice cream.

Casual French sib Urchin Bistrot recently opened in the Mission.

138

AQ

Contemporary ✕✕

B3

1085 Mission St. (bet. 6th & 7th Sts.)

Phone: 415-341-9000   Dinner Tue – Sat
Web: www.aq-sf.com
Prices: $$$

On this edgy block of Mission Street, AQ's elegant exterior stands out immediately. The interior is even more impressive with a soaring loft, exposed brick, and sleek furniture. The décor (like the menu) changes with each season, so a spring visit may reveal sprigs of cherry blossom, hydroponic herbs growing at the wood-topped bar, and bushels of yellow tulips. The beauty extends to superbly arranged contemporary plates like soft-shell crab with dulse *pistou*; or slow-cooked beef tongue, peppery and pastrami-like, with béarnaise and poached egg over tarragon sponge cake. Whether you choose the four-course prix-fixe or tasting menu, the hip staff is friendly and engaging. The outstanding cocktails (fig leaf fizz frothy with egg whites) alone merit a visit.

Bar Agricole

Californian ✕✕

B4

355 11th St. (bet. Folsom & Harrison Sts.)

Phone: 415-355-9400   Lunch Sat – Sun
Web: www.baragricole.com   Dinner Tue – Sun
Prices: $$

Cocktails and conversation are always a pleasure at Bar Agricole, which is known for having one of the city's best drink programs. Its narrow, industrial-modern dining room boasts soaring ceilings from which huge acrylic sculptures hang, while mod concrete booths line the side wall. An outdoor patio, with plant beds and a trickling fountain, is particularly popular for brunch.

The menu is thoroughly Californian and loaded with the season's best, showcased in dishes like a frisée, arugula, and radish salad with a *citronette* dressing; halibut *brandade* with asparagus; as well as roast pork leg and belly with Canario beans, greens, and horseradish. At brunch, opt for flavorful, tender, and homemade lamb sausage served over fried eggs and wilted kale.

Benu ✿✿✿

Contemporary 🍴🍴🍴

C2

22 Hawthorne St. (bet. Folsom & Howard Sts.)

Phone: 415-685-4860   Dinner Tue – Sat
Web: www.benusf.com
Prices: $$$$

Don't miss the street views directly into this kitchen as you enter—these chefs are preparing a masterpiece. Outside in the modern courtyard, benches are exactly the kind of place to linger peacefully. The interior is awash in earthy colors covering sleek banquettes and oversized cushions. The slate-gray dining room is serene with clean lines drawing the eye across the meticulous design, while staff are impressively warm and relaxed for a restaurant of this caliber.

Chef Corey Lee's nightly tasting menu is a truly unique marriage of contemporary American and Korean influences. Dishes promise a fascinating interplay of flavors, as in the cooked romaine hearts bathed in caramelized anchovy, chili, and cilantro. Find subtlety and elegance in the wild bamboo fungi and shoots with chicken and cabbage in a lush broth. A silky custard with Jinhua ham, Dungeness crab, and flecks of gold leaf and truffle is royally decadent. Duck reaches a height of technical complexity when prepared with turnips, lam kok olives, dandelion, and hot mustard.

A spectacular dessert composed of luscious fresh yuba skin surrounding creamy almond custard with dried yuba and white chocolate will have you seeing stars.

Bluestem Brasserie

American ✕✕

B2

1 Yerba Buena Ln. (at Market St.)

Phone: 415-547-1111   Lunch & dinner daily
Web: www.bluestembrasserie.com
Prices: $$

Bluestem Brasserie is a pleasant haunt that welcomes both locals and passersby from nearby Market Street. The voluminous space features loft-like ceilings, a sweeping staircase, and a lounge frequented for after-work cocktails.

The somewhat bumbling service doesn't quite match the classy ambience, but it's nothing that a menu rife with the best of Californian ingredients can't fix. Start with an arugula salad with grilled sweet corn, fresh apricots, and goat's milk cheese, tossed in a Meyer lemon *citronette*. Barbecue-spiced chicken is super juicy bathed in a fragrant garlic-rosemary jus; while dessert is a successful pairing of butterscotch-tapioca pudding with a salty-smoky bacon butter cookie shaped like a...you guessed it...pig!

Cathead's BBQ

Barbecue ✕

A4

1665 Folsom St. (bet. 12th & 13th Sts.)

Phone: 415-861-4242   Lunch & dinner Wed – Mon
Web: www.catheadsbbq.com
Prices: ☜☜

A bright red building as bold as its barbecue and as fiery as its habanero sauce could only be Cathead's. This hot spot has already generated quite a buzz, so expect to wait in line. After ordering and paying, take a seat—preferably at the counter which offers the best views of the brick smokers. The space is tiny, making takeout big business here.

The menu features smoldering delights, plus locally inspired items like cornmeal-crusted tofu, or a dandelion-and-potato salad. But really, you're here for the meat combo starring St. Louis ribs, slow-smoked pulled pork, delicious sweet tea barbecue chicken, and Coca-Cola-smoked brisket. Sides (purple cabbage-habanero slaw or pimento mac and cheese) are so delish you'll wish they were a meal on their own.

Boulevard ✿

Californian ✗✗

D1

1 Mission St. (at Steuart St.)

Phone: 415-543-6084
Web: www.boulevardrestaurant.com
Prices: $$$

Lunch Mon – Fri
Dinner nightly

At this lovely corner where Mission Street meets the Embarcadero is Boulevard—an easy yet timeless spot with prime views of the Bay and its bridge. The ambience exudes historic charm and the crowd is composed of power suits brokering business deals. Lunch also sees a blend of families and tourists seated in the lively dining room; solo diners make a beeline for the counter lining the open kitchen.

Service is on the ball without ever seeming overbearing. Combined with Chef Nancy Oakes' careful, never fussy, and ever-classic Californian cuisine, Boulevard is a home run. Amid vaulted ceilings and rose-colored sconces, nibble your way through sea scallop crudo crowned by a cucumber and radish salad tossed in an insanely delicious ginger, soy, and chili dressing. Local petrale sole, cooked *a la plancha* until perfectly tender beneath a lovely crust, is set upon Hollandaise-kissed asparagus for a fine pairing. Elegant composition and excellent product are the watchwords at dessert, whether it's a butterscotch pudding with dark chocolate Bavarian crème and vanilla chantilly, or spongy Meyer lemon cakes with a luscious scoop of black pepper-olive oil ice cream. They are—simply put—sheer bliss.

The Cavalier

Gastropub XX

B2

360 Jessie St. (at 5th St.)

Phone: 415-321-6000   Lunch & dinner daily
Web: www.thecavaliersf.com
Prices: **$$**

One of the city's high-profile openings, this is the third effort from the team behind Marlowe and Park Tavern. Everything here has a British bent, echoed in the hunting-lodge-gone-sophisticated décor with red-and-blue walls accented by taxidermied trophies and tufted banquettes. Across-the-pond classics have Californian twists like a deep-fried Scotch duck egg wrapped in truffled duck rillettes. The restaurant has quickly become a see-and-be-seen haunt of the tech oligarchy (complete with a private club). However, the food is comforting and homey as seen in a caramelized roast chicken set atop horseradish mash.

Though reservations are a must, its location in Hotel Zetta means service runs from morning to night, giving diners plenty of options.

Epic Roasthouse

Steakhouse XX

D1

369 The Embarcadero (at Folsom St.)

Phone: 415-369-9955   Lunch Wed – Sun
Web: www.epicroasthousesf.com   Dinner nightly
Prices: **$$$**

A meal at Epic is a ticket to a wondrous view: the Bay Bridge arching over gentle water with Treasure Island across the way, plus the twinkle of lights in the evening. It's so pretty that you might struggle to keep your eyes on the plate. This roast house's surroundings are no slouch either, with a smart, clubby, leather-clad dining room leading to a terrace designed for sunny afternoons.

As the name promises, meat is the big draw here, with juicy, tender cuts of everything from American prime beef to Japanese Wagyu. An old-school shrimp cocktail, fish dishes, and even venison round out the kitchen's offerings, and a wine list full of bold reds complements the cooking. Like most steakhouses, prices can get high; consider lunch for a more affordable visit.

San Francisco ▶ SoMa

143

54 Mint

B2

16 Mint Plaza (at Jessie St.)

Phone: 415-543-5100
Web: www.54mint.com
Prices: $$

Lunch Mon – Fri
Dinner Mon – Sat

Though several of its compatriots in Mint Plaza have gone under, this contemporary trattoria remains strong, with passionately made, authentic Italian fare. From house-cured *salumi* to asparagus topped with burrata and truffle oil, a meal could be made out of starters alone. However, that would mean missing delicious entrées like pillowy gnocchi with rich oxtail ragù and grilled octopus with fingerling potatoes.

Original brick walls, cream leather bar stools, and polished concrete floors give 54 Mint a contemporary, industrial feel that's heightened by the shelves of balsamic vinegar, pasta, and other Italian pantry staples available for purchase. Alfresco dining on the plaza is also a must, whether for warm evenings or sunny $16 prix-fixe lunches.

Fly Trap

C2

606 Folsom St. (bet. 2nd & 3rd Sts.)

Phone: 415-243-0580
Web: www.zareflytrap.com
Prices: $$

Dinner Mon – Sat

This contemporary Middle Eastern restaurant is definitely a trap for corporate folk from neighboring offices, who often end up turning "just one" delicious after-work cocktail into a meal inside this warm and inviting dining room. Here, old architectural and botanical sketches as well as vintage maps abound; and the staff is attentive, efficient and kind, never fussy or intrusive.

The unique food has a strong Persian influence that is showcased in tender meatballs with *harissa*, pomegranate, and pistachios. But even the more contemporary fare boasts a nuanced blend of spices, like the black cardamom in a braised short rib with quinoa, cranberry beans, and salsa verde. A tangy goat cheesecake with eggplant jam may sound strange, but is utterly satisfying.

Fringale 🐵

French ✗✗

C3

570 4th St. (bet. Brannan & Bryant Sts.)

Phone: 415-543-0573	Lunch Tue – Fri
Web: www.fringalesf.com	Dinner nightly
Prices: $$	

This tech-centric corner of SoMa has seen booms and busts aplenty since the restaurant's opening in 1991, but Fringale has held strong, with a loyal squad of regulars who come for a taste of its Basque-inflected French cooking. The timeless décor starring clean wood furnishings and soft lighting is ideal for a business lunch or date night.

Start with the tasty calamari *à la plancha*—its topping of briny black olives and sliced jalapeños clearly differentiates Fringale from its tired bistro competition. After the mostly French staff recommends a wine, dive into the juicy roasted chicken breast over fluffy Israeli couscous and crunchy fennel. Finish with a creamy, nutty hazelnut-and-roasted almond mousse cake, drizzled with rich dark chocolate, of course!

Le Charm

French ✗✗

C3

315 5th St. (bet. Folsom & Shipley Sts.)

Phone: 415-546-6128	Dinner Tue – Sat
Web: www.lecharm.com	
Prices: $$	

Le Charm is indeed a *très* charming *boîte*. Closely spaced tables topped with bistro paper cluster together in the persimmon-hued dining room rife with wood floors and illuminated by pretty lamp sconces. A petite bar upfront offers an ideal respite to the likes of expats on a budget or novices to the cuisine.

The open kitchen resides next to this bar and turns out a tandem of venerable French classics like excellently seasoned chicken liver salad drizzled with tart sherry vinegar; followed by supremely tender osso buco fortified by Porto, grapes, and gnocchi *à la Parisienne* flavored with garlic and parsley. The staff is happy to converse *en français*, likely about the richness behind a warm, whipped cream-crowned apple tarte Tatin.

Luce ✿

Contemporary ✕✕✕

B3

888 Howard St. (at 5th St.)

Phone: 415-616-6566
Web: www.lucewinerestaurant.com
Prices: $$$

Lunch & dinner daily

Standing in its own modern glass glory at the base of the Intercontinental Hotel, Luce is rightly known as much more than some hotel restaurant. Inside, find floor-to-ceiling windows shimmering with voile, heavily upholstered banquettes, and huge globe fixtures casting a gentle, purple sort of glow across the room—perhaps making that glass-walled wine display all the more appealing.

Despite its endearing energy and busy music, weekends can be quieter as the corporate crowds die down. Clear and refined seasonally driven flavors are the hallmarks of Chef Daniel Corey's cuisine. While lunch is a simpler affair, the kitchen shines at dinner with meals that open with warm, near-Proustian madeleines, light yet rich with the savory taste of Parmesan. Heartier courses feature a generous lamb loin with morsels of crunchy-golden and sweet belly meat, served beside fried kale, creamy celery purée, a scattering of tiny pioppini mushrooms, and pan juices finished with tangerine segments.

Desserts are beautifully crafted and delicious—end with bars of *muscavado* cake alongside pieces of lightly charred pineapple, sweet pineapple conserve, crème fraîche ice cream, and an ultra-fine brown sugar tuile.

Manora's Thai Cuisine

Thai 🍴

A4

1600 Folsom St. (at 12th St.)

Phone: 415-861-6224
Web: www.manorathai.com
Prices: 💵💵

Lunch Mon – Fri
Dinner Mon – Sat

A firmly rooted dining destination in this otherwise underdeveloped part of town, Manora's has been a source for authentic Thai dishes since the '80s. Crowds flock here for the affordable lunch specials, which include gems like pad Thai topped with plump shrimp and a golden fried egg, fragrant lemon chicken soup, and moist, perfectly charred satay skewers surrounded by fresh vegetables.

The pace at dinner is more relaxed, with endearing service that makes customers truly feel at home amid the wood carvings of the dining room. The fresh, zingy flavors of dishes like spicy green papaya salad draw diners through the well-aged wooden door again and again. Meals are all the better when cooled off with a creamy cold coffee or sweet Thai iced tea.

M. Y. China 😊

Chinese 🍴🍴

B2

845 Market St. (bet. 4th & 5th Sts.)

Phone: 415-580-3001
Web: www.tastemychina.com
Prices: $$

Lunch & dinner daily

Martin Yan's China is a glitzy showstopper set under the dome of the Westfield shopping center. Glossy wood panels separate the sprawling series of rooms, dominated by a marble and white-tiled open kitchen where one can watch as dough is pulled, twisted, and cut into noodles.

The famed chef honors his menu with focus and clarity. Try the wild boar dumplings—presented in a bamboo steamer and cradled in a ceramic spoon. Stuffed with a luscious meatball and afloat in hot broth, these parcels are wrapped in a delicate casing and accompanied by slivered ginger in red vinegar. Beijing knife-cut noodles are equally memorable, served as a hearty bowl of toothsome wheat flour strands topped with diced tofu in hoisin vinaigrette, cool veggies, and micro basil.

One Market

C1

1 Market St. (at Steuart St.)

Phone: 415-777-5577
Web: www.onemarket.com
Prices: $$

Lunch Mon – Fri
Dinner Mon – Sat

Located at the very end of Market Street facing the Ferry Building, this perennial power-lunch spot draws crowds for its bright, bustling vibe and Bay views. High ceilings and a busy open kitchen catch the eye, while efficient bow-tied waiters attend to the booths and banquettes.

Chef Mark Dommen's contemporary Californian food is fresh and seasonal, starting with Nantucket Bay scallops sautéed in brown butter with baby mustard greens in a pool of fermented black bean sauce, garnished with apple and puffed rice. This might lead to a colorful composition of seared flounder over flavorful black-eyed peas with smoky bacon and tart *sofrito* vinaigrette. Traditional desserts like pear galette are sized as "traditional" or "singular" (half) portions.

Prospect

D1

300 Spear St. (at Folsom St.)

Phone: 415-247-7770
Web: www.prospectsf.com
Prices: $$$

Lunch Mon – Fri
Dinner Mon – Sat

Prospect is still living up to all the hype. Its large bar and lounge is always humming with well-dressed, young-professional clusters; the dining room attracts power brokers; while the private room is forever hosting a fête. The restaurant is as sophisticated and stylish as the food, so dress suitably.

Interpretations of American dishes are prepared with skill and may reveal perfectly seasoned fried green tomatoes served with frisée, plump white prawns, and a streak of red pepper aïoli. A crisp-skinned roasted chicken breast and confit thigh placed over a bed of farro dotted with crunchy cauliflower florets is stunningly trailed by an elegant version of strawberry shortcake—buttery, thin biscuits sandwiched with jam and tangy Greek yogurt.

RN74

Californian ✗✗

C1

301 Mission St. (at Beale St.)

Phone: 415-543-7474
Web: www.rn74.com
Prices: $$$

Lunch Mon – Fri
Dinner nightly

Named for the Burgundy region "Route Nationale 74" in France, RN74 is part restaurant and part wine bar. At the base of the Millennium Tower, set amidst office buildings, it draws a large corporate crowd, particularly for lunch and after-work drinks. Architectural basics like high ceilings and concrete pillars are balanced with unique design elements like train station-style boards that list available wine bottles.

There is also a large bar-lounge area, but most flock here for the Californian menu infused with French accents. Expect such flavorful and harmonious preparations as *garganelli* tossed with artichoke hearts, peas, and wild nettles; and supremely moist fried chicken paired with foraged mushrooms—a dish as solid and stylish as the place itself.

Salt House

American ✗

C2

545 Mission St. (bet. 1st & 2nd Sts.)

Phone: 415-543-8900
Web: www.salthousesf.com
Prices: $$

Lunch Mon – Fri
Dinner nightly

Housed on the ground floor of a former printing warehouse, this industrial but comfortable spot is a refuge in the sea of glass-fronted skyscrapers that surround it. The owners, who are also behind nearby Town Hall and Anchor & Hope, know exactly what diners want. Inside, the atmosphere is quiet and business-friendly at lunchtime, but amplifies when the after-work crowd streams in.

The food also reflects a duality between bolder, more ambitious dinners and simple, elegant lunchtime salads, tossing earthy and sweet beets with creamy goat cheese and crunchy pistachios; or sandwiches like the succulent Waldorf chicken on a crusty roll. Inventive desserts, like a grapefruit cake with semifreddo and pink peppercorn meringue, are also not to be missed.

Saison ✿✿✿

D3

Californian 𝕏𝕏𝕏

178 Townsend St. (bet. 2nd & 3rd Sts.)

Phone: 415-828-7990   Dinner Tue – Sat
Web: www.saisonsf.com
Prices: $$$$

No expense has ever been spared in this massive wow-inducing space. There are enough shining copper pots to supply a village of restaurants in France; wood tables, smart chairs, and faux-fur rugs mean that someone has recently been to Scandinavia. There are also no barriers between the kitchen and dining areas—underscored by the chefs' visits to each table, personally presenting and describing dishes.

Dining here is gorgeous yet polarizing with most reactions being love or hate. Is the staff warm and convivial or somewhat pompous? Did the chef just interrupt you to present the next course? Fan of the classic 80s soundtrack?

One thing that is undeniable is the level of extraordinary skill and detail that Chef Joshua Skenes uses to craft each dish on his spontaneous menu. Meals begin with a dazzling parade of sea creatures (some sourced by their privately-commissioned fishing boat), which are undeniably exceptional. Artichoke hearts may be served with a gentle crunch, while firm, fresh scallops are brought to an entirely new dimension with sauce *barigoule*. Thick batons of toast are soaked in a complex soy mixture and topped with a lush lobe of uni displaying the essence of culinary brilliance here.

1601 Bar & Kitchen ☺

Sri Lankan ✗✗

A4

1601 Howard St. (at 12th St.)

Phone: 415-552-1601   Dinner Tue – Sat
Web: www.1601sf.com
Prices: $$

♿ The flavors of India and Asia infuse the creative dishes at this
quiet winner, which blends Eastern and Western ingredients
to arrive at its very own delicious concoctions. A decidedly
untraditional *lamprais* might stuff a classically French bacon-
wrapped rabbit loin, toasted buckwheat, and eggplant curry
into a banana leaf. Meanwhile, the halibut "ceviche" is more
like a flavored sashimi, with hints of coconut milk and rings
of serrano chilies.

The sleek, contemporary space with its wraparound
windows, lovely art, and slate walls, is a perfect showcase for
the food. Dine solo at the bar with a bittersweet Dubonnet
sangria, or come with a group to share dishes and bottles of
wine at the communal table—the polished staff makes either
experience enjoyable.

Sushi Zone

Japanese ✗

A4

1815 Market St. (at Pearl St.)

Phone: 415-621-1114   Dinner Mon – Sat
Web: N/A
Prices: $$

[S] Sushi snobs may stay away from this cash-only, no reservations
favorite—situated at a corner where SoMa, the Mission, and
Hayes Valley collide—but that doesn't mean it's wanting for
popularity. The tiny space offers seating at just a handful of
tables and a chrome stool-lined counter, and locals pack in
like sardines. When the room is full, as it usually is, you can
expect your meal to go at the pace of the *itamae* (in other
words, slowly).

Cooked items include baked mussels capped by caramelized
mayo, whereas raw fare brings pleasing nigiri of halibut,
ocean trout, hamachi, and mackerel that are firm, super-
fresh, and generously cut. And if you like mango and more
spicy mayo, you're in luck as they star in a number of their
creatively rendered maki.

TBD

B3

1077 Mission St. (bet. 6th & 7th Sts.)

Phone: 415-431-1826   Dinner Tue – Sat
Web: www.tbdrestaurant.com
Prices: $$

This hip, casual sequel to AQ shares its big sister's penchant for abbreviation in the name and creativity on the plate. Inventive, vegetable-centric bites are the stars of the show, like roasted cauliflower with a smoky *gribiche*, tender fresh octopus with kohlrabi in a garlic-wasabi broth, and plump, succulent duck sausage over crunchy spinach and a blood-orange *mostarda*.

TBD's fare is all the more impressive given that everything is cooked over a wood hearth, which provides a primal center to the lively room. (It gets warm, though, so the easily overheated may want to sit elsewhere.) Also worthy of attention is their thoughtful drink selection, with a wide range of cask ales, sherries, Rhône-centric wines, and "loophole" aperitif cocktails.

Town Hall

C1

342 Howard St. (at Fremont St.)

Phone: 415-908-3900   Lunch Mon – Fri
Web: www.townhallsf.com   Dinner nightly
Prices: $$

Though the elegant red brick exterior of Town Hall makes it seem like it's been on Howard Street for ages, it's merely a decade old. This is surprising given the deeply satisfying, tried-and-tested Southern flavors on offer. Expect garlic-herb toast topped with barbecue shrimp, St. Louis-style ribs, and spicy shrimp and flounder étouffée. It's all about simple pleasure and hearty portions here.

Given the delicious fare, know that Town Hall is always buzzing, whether it's the office lunch crowd angling for a table or after-work groups of friends hitting the bar for a Vieux Carré cocktail. The outdoor patio provides a quieter experience, and is perfect for savoring every bite of the signature butterscotch-chocolate *pot de crème*—if you still have room.

Trou Normand

C2

140 New Montgomery St. (at Natoma St.)

Phone: 415-975-0876
Web: www.trounormandsf.com
Prices: $$

Lunch & dinner Mon – Fri

Named for the Norman tradition of drinking a glass of Calvados to revive the palate during a heavy meal, Bar Agricole's SoMa sequel shares its predecessor's skill with outstanding cocktails. They're perfect palate-cleansers for the expansive and delightful house charcuterie like rich duck pâté with plum and Armagnac or garlicky *finocchiona* kissed with fennel seeds.

While their *salumi* and selection of spirits are huge draws, Trou Normand is an all-day menu of shareable French- and Italian-leaning plates. Come for pancetta-egg sandwiches with locally roasted coffee in the morning, sausage sandwiches with homemade sauerkraut at lunch, and pastas or roasted meats at dinner.

The large, glamorous space and back patio are favorites among hipster tech types.

Twenty Five Lusk

C3

25 Lusk St. (bet. 3rd & 4th Sts.)

Phone: 415-495-5875
Web: www.25lusk.com
Prices: $$$

Lunch Sun – Fri
Dinner Mon – Sat

As one of the sleekest and chicest respites in town, Twenty Five Lusk is *the* scene for the well-dressed, well-connected, and well-to-do. An after-work cosmo crowd quickly fills in the lower-level bar and lounge decked with rounded settees surrounding hanging fireplace orbs. Upstairs, slick modern surfaces meet brick-and-timber warehouse.

A glassed-in kitchen returns the focal point to cooking which may include dishes like tomato and fennel bisque poured over lobster morsels; grilled prawns posed atop carrot purée and a mound of grits sprinkled with *togarashi*; or a hearty braised pork shoulder served over wilted kale and sided with cornbread and green tomato salsa. Try the classic *baba* inventively soaked in strawberry syrup and coupled with basil sorbet.

Una Pizza Napoletana

Pizza 🍴

A4

210 11th St. (at Howard St.)

Phone: 415-861-3444
Web: www.unapizza.com
Prices: $$

Dinner Wed – Sat

In keeping with owner Anthony Mangieri's monastic devotion to the perfect pie, Una Pizza Napoletana is a spare space, housed in a chilly former garage on an industrial corner of SoMa. The vibe is completely casual yet alluring with crowds riveted by the altar—a tiled turquoise oven, where Mangieri stretches dough and deftly coaxes the crackling wood fire to produce his vegetarian pies. Their blistered and puffy crusts sport a delicious char as well as an addictively chewy texture thanks to tangy fermentation.

Waits are long, but the hassle is well worth it after one bite of the Filetti, slathered with creamy buffalo mozzarella and juicy cherry tomatoes. Mangieri is unquestionably a master of his craft, and his pies are a cut above local competition.

Waterbar

 Seafood 🍴🍴

D1

399 The Embarcadero (bet. Folsom & Harrison Sts.)

Phone: 415-284-9922
Web: www.waterbarsf.com
Prices: $$$

Lunch & dinner daily

Stunning views of the Bay Bridge is the chief draw at this Embarcadero fave for sipping wine on the lovely terrace and slurping oysters at the enormous raw bar. Though the polished, modern dining room can seem serious (as can the expense account-rocking prices), warm and thoughtful service brings things back down to earth.

Seafood-centric entrées make global use of the local waters' bounty including tender squid almost bursting with chorizo alongside candy-like chickpeas. Perfectly crisp pan-roasted striped bass atop flavorful wild rice oozes with delectable flavors and textures; and an Americana-influenced dessert menu (think carrot cake ice-cream sandwiches with rum-raisin sauce) is the final touch in ensuring that Waterbar stays packed to the gills.

Yank Sing

Chinese ✗✗

D1

101 Spear St. (bet. Howard & Mission Sts.)

Phone: 415-781-1111

Web: www.yanksing.com

Prices: $$

Lunch daily

With a higher price tag than the average Chinatown joint, Yank Sing is arguably *the* place in town for dim sum. While peak hours entail a wait, one can be assured of quality and abundant variety from these rolling carts. The signature Peking duck with its lacquered skin and fluffy buns is a memorable treat, as are the equally sweet and salty *char siu bao*. Of course, dumplings here are the true highlight, from plump and fragrant pork *xiao long bao*, to paper-thin *har gao* concealing chunks of fresh, sweet shrimp. Don't see favorites like the flaky egg custard tarts? Just ask the cheerful staff, who'll radio the kitchen for help via headsets.

The upscale setting is cheaper by day, but the zigzagging carts can get hectic; things calm down a bit at dinnertime.

Zero Zero

Pizza ✗✗

C3

826 Folsom St. (bet. 4th & 5th Sts.)

Phone: 415-348-8800

Web: www.zerozerosf.com

Prices: $$

Lunch & dinner daily

Zero Zero may be named for the superlative flour used in its enticingly blistered, thin-crust pies, but this is much more than a pizzeria. While pies like the Geary with chewy clams, caramelized bacon, and Calabrian chilies, are delicious, this casual spot offers much more than a good slice. Absolute knockouts include tomato-braised chickpea bruschetta, oozing with melted burrata; and a salad of smoky grilled radicchio hearts cut by creamy Pt. Reyes blue cheese.

A mix of families, hipsters, and business people fresh from the Moscone Center fill the warm, bi-level space. Group dining is ideal for sharing and sampling more of the menu, and the sizable bar will ensure that everyone's equipped with a terrific cocktail or pint of local draft root beer.

155

East Bay

A signature mash-up of wealthy families, senior bohemians, and college kids, Berkeley is extolled for its liberal politics and lush university campus. Snooty gourmands and reverential foodies consider it to be the Garden of Eden that sprouted American gastronomy's leading purist, Alice Waters. Her Chez Panisse Foundation continues to nurture the **Edible Schoolyard**, an organic garden-cum-kitchen classroom for students. Waters' also founded **Slow Food Nation**, the country's largest celebration of sustainable foods; and her influence can be tasted in numerous establishments serving Californian cuisine.

GOURMET GHETTO

B udget-conscious Berkeleyites needn't look to restaurants alone for pristine, local, and organic food. Their very own **North Shattuck** corridor (also known as the "gourmet ghetto") gratifies with garden-fresh produce as well as takeout from **Grégoire** and **Epicurious**. This stretch is also home to aficionados who frequent co-ops like the **Cheese Board Collective**, **Cheese Board Pizza Collective**, and **Acme Bread Company** for first-rate produce and variety. **The Juice Bar Collective** keeps diet-conscious droves coming back for more; whereas meat addicts can't get enough of Chef Paul Bertolli's **Fra'Mani Salumi**, where traditional Italian flavors mingle with creative techniques. Every Thursday, the **North Shattuck Organic Farmer's Market** draws cooking enthusiasts looking to expand their repertoire with a vast range of regionally sourced produce.

M eanwhile, hungover scholars can't imagine beginning a day without brunch at **La Note**, where the cinnamon-brioche *pain perdu* packs a walloping punch. Too rich? Test the spread at **Tomate Café**, churning out an amazing Cuban breakfast followed by lunch on the pup-friendly patio. Cooks on a mission collect routinely at ingredient-driven **Berkeley Bowl**, a grocery store-farmer's market hybrid, to scan their offering of fresh produce, cooked items, and health foods. Named after a region in Southwest India, **Udupi Palace** is equally revolutionary in concept, with cooking that is wildly popular for that region's delicacies. Sample the likes of *dosas*, packed with spiced mashed potatoes and paired with fiery *sambar*, for an undoubtedly satisfying meal.

OAKLAND

Located across the bridge from the city, Oakland may not exude the same culinary flamboyance. Nevertheless, this earnest and enterprising city has seen a resurgence of its own, thanks to an influx of businesses and residences. With panoramic views of the Bay, terrific restaurants, shops, and a hopping nightlife, Jack London Square is not only a tourist draw but equally revered by locals for sun-soaked docks and a **Sunday Farmer's and Artisan Market**. Routine-loving locals cherish mornings at **La Farine**, a European-style bakery, serving pastries, cakes, and buttery croissants. As noon sets in, downtown crowds nosh on po'boys from **Café 15**. But over in Temescal, **Bakesale Betty** caters to big appetites with bulky chicken sandwiches served atop ironing-board tables. Post-work revelry reaches epic status at the **Trappist**, pouring over 160 Belgian and other specialty beers. However, if dessert is the most divine way to end a day, then convene at **Fentons Creamery**, churning handmade ice creams for over 120 delicious years. Similarly, **Lush Gelato** spotlights homegrown ingredients like Cowgirl Creamery Fromage Blanc or McEvoy Ranch Olive Oil in some of the city's most decadent flavors. **Tara's Organic Ice Cream** continues the craze with unique licks like beet-balsamic in compostable cups.

HOME IS WHERE THE HEART IS

Down-home Mexican food fans get their fiesta on at taco trucks parked along International Boulevard. However, local joints like **Tacos Sinaloa** remain the real deal for these treats. The **Art & Soul Festival** in August brings a buffet of world flavors; and **Chinatown Streetfest** adds to the lure with fragrant curries served alongside flavorful barbecue. Bonus bites await at **Market Hall**, a shopper's paradise presenting fresh, sustainable seafood at **Hapuku Fish Shop**; specialty eats at **Pasta Shop**; and delicious blends from **Highwire Coffee Roasters**. Set between Oakland and Berkeley, Rockridge boasts of plethora of quaint boutiques and tasty eateries—namely **Oaktown Spice Shop** on Grand Avenue, showcasing excellent herbs and exotic spices, available in both small amounts and bulk bags.

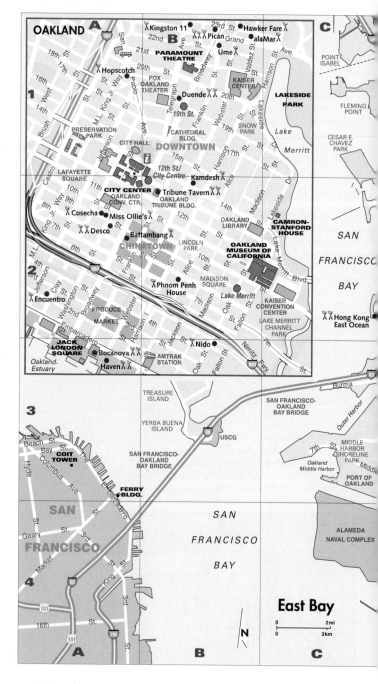

OAKLAND

A   B   C

Kingston 11   23rd St.   Hawker Fare
22nd   Picán   Grand   alaMar
21st   Ume
18th 17th St.   20th   PARAMOUNT THEATRE
16th   Hopscotch
14th West St.   FOX OAKLAND THEATER
M.L. King Jr. Way   Duende   19th St.
Brush   Telegraph   Franklin   Webster
PRESERVATION PARK   CATHEDRAL BLDG.
CITY HALL   DOWNTOWN
LAFAYETTE SQUARE   15th St.   17th
Castro   Jefferson   12th St/ City Centre   Kamdesh
10th   11th   CITY CENTER   Alice
9th Way   Tribune Tavern
8th   OAKLAND CONV. CTR.   OAKLAND TRIBUNE BLDG.
7th   Cosecha   Miss Ollie's   14th
Desco   12th St.   OAKLAND LIBRARY
6th   Battambang   CHINATOWN   LINCOLN PARK
5th   Franklin   10th   OAKLAND MUSEUM OF CALIFORNIA
4th   Phnom Penh House   MADISON SQUARE
Jefferson   Clay   Encuentro   Washington   Broadway   2nd   Madison   Oak   Lake Merritt
PRODUCE MARKET   Webster   4th   KAISER CONVENTION CENTER
Embarcadero   Harrison   Jackson   LAKE MERRITT CHANNEL PARK
JACK LONDON SQUARE   Nido
Oakland Estuary   Bocanova   AMTRAK STATION
Haven   Oak St.   Fallon St.   Nimitz Fwy.

POINT ISABEL
FLEMING POINT
CESAR E. CHAVEZ PARK
KAISER CENTER
LAKESIDE PARK
SNOW PARK
Lake Merritt
Lakeside Dr.
CAMRON-STANFORD HOUSE
SAN FRANCISCO BAY
Hong Kong East Ocean

1
2
3
4

TREASURE ISLAND
YERBA BUENA ISLAND
SAN FRANCISCO-OAKLAND BAY BRIDGE
USCG
SAN FRANCISCO-OAKLAND BAY BRIDGE
Beach St.
Bay St.
COIT TOWER
Columbus Ave.
Hyde
Embarcadero
FERRY BLDG.
SAN
Geary St.
3rd St.
FRANCISCO
Market
King St.
16th St.
101
280
80

Burma
SAN FRANCISCO-OAKLAND BAY BRIDGE
Outer Harbor
7th St.   MIDDLE HARBOR SHORELINE PARK
Oakland Middle Harbor   Middle
PORT OF OAKLAND
ALAMEDA NAVAL COMPLEX

SAN
FRANCISCO
BAY

East Bay

0   2mi
0   3km

N

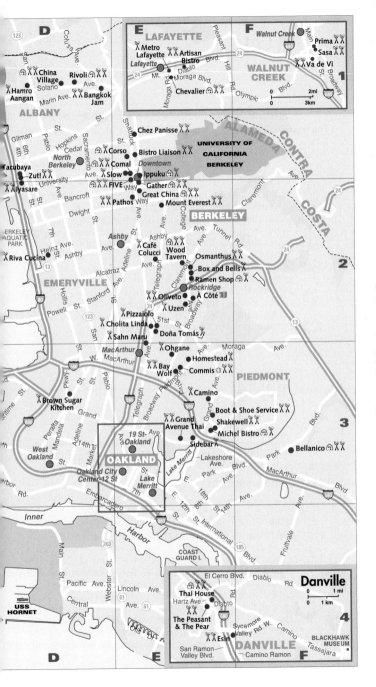

D

(123)
Colusa Ave.

China Village
Hamro Aangan
Rivoli
Solano Ave.
Marin Ave.
Bangkok Jam

ALBANY

St.
St.
Gilman St.
Hopkins St.
Cedar St.
Sacramento St.
Shattuck Ave.

Tacubaya
North Berkeley
Zut!
Iyasare
University Ave.
Bancroft Way
Dwight Way

4th
6th
7th
San Pablo Ave.

BERKELEY AQUATIC PARK
Heinz Ave.
Ashby Ave.

80

Chez Panisse
Corso
Bistro Liaison
Comal
Slow
FIVE
Ippuku
Gather
Great China
Pathos
Mount Everest
Downtown
College Ave.

UNIVERSITY OF CALIFORNIA BERKELEY

ALAMEDA
CONTRA COSTA

24

BERKELEY

Ashby Ave.
Ashby
Café Colucci
Wood Tavern
Osmanthus
Box and Bells
Ramen Shop
Oliveto
Rockridge
À Côté
Uzen
Alcatraz Ave.
Adeline St.
Telegraph Ave.
Claremont Ave.
Tunnel Rd.

EMERYVILLE
Hollis St.
Stanford
Powell St.
(123)
Pizzaiolo
Cholita Linda
Sahn Maru
MacArthur
Doña Tomás
Ohgane
51st
Broadway

Riva Cucina
(13)

San Pablo Ave.
W. MacArthur Blvd.

580

80

Brown Sugar Kitchen

Bay Wolf
Homestead
Commis
Camino
Moraga Ave.
Piedmont Ave.

PIEDMONT

Grand
Peralta St.
Mandela Pkwy.
Adeline St.
14th St.
Market St.

Grand Avenue Thai
Sidebar
Shakewell
Michel Bistro
Boot & Shoe Service
Grand Ave.

580

Bellanico
13

West Oakland

19 St-Oakland
OAKLAND
Oakland City Center-12 St
Lake Merritt
7th St.
Lakeshore Ave.
Park Blvd.
MacArthur Blvd.
18th St.
14th
E. 12th St.
International Blvd.

Inner Harbor
Embarcadero
(260)

COAST GUARD I.
185

Pacific Ave.
Lincoln Ave.
Central Ave.
(61)

USS HORNET

D — — **E**

E — **LAFAYETTE**

Metro Lafayette
Artisan Bistro
Lafayette
Chevalier
Mt. Diablo Blvd.
Moraga Rd.
Moraga Blvd.
24

Pleasant Hill Rd.
Olympic Blvd.

F — Walnut Creek
Prima
Sasa
Va de Vi
Main St.
Broadway
580
24

WALNUT CREEK

0 — 2mi
0 — 3km

Danville

El Cerro Blvd.
Diablo Rd.

Thai House
Hartz Ave.
The Peasant & The Pear
Esin
Diablo Rd.
Sycamore Valley Rd. W.
Camino
San Ramon Valley Blvd.
Camino Ramon
Tassajara

DANVILLE

BLACKHAWK MUSEUM

0 — 1 mi
0 — 1 km

E — — **F**

161

À Côté

E2

5478 College Ave. (bet. Lawton & Taft Aves.), Oakland

Phone: 510-655-6469
Web: www.acoterestaurant.com
Prices: $$

Dinner nightly

A long-running small-plates icon set within the posh stores of Rockridge, À Côté nearly always requires a wait—only a handful of seats are available for reservations. But, after settling into a cozy wood table or perhaps at the granite bar, a lively, very communal vibe will ease any irritation. Forty-plus wines offered by the glass augment the appeal.

The seasonal menu has a French effect, discernable in plump fava bean falafel set atop tart tahini and pickled turnips; or green-garlic soup with a *fromage blanc* crouton. Entrées like seared yellowtail Jack brightened with asparagus, spring onion, and a Meyer lemon-blood orange relish perk up the palate; while a wood-fired oven and heated patio provide comforting warmth for indoor and outdoor meals.

alaMar

B1

100 Grand Ave., Ste. 111 (at Valdez St.), Oakland

Phone: 510-907-7555
Web: www.alamaroakland.com
Prices: $$

Lunch Mon – Fri
Dinner Mon – Sat

While alaMar does a steady business serving sandwiches and salads to downtown Oakland office workers, the food-savvy prefer to dine here at night, when the menu flips to a memorable array of seafood dishes—many offered by the pound in low-country boil style. Golden-brown blue crab poppers boast a punchy anchovy-piquillo aïoli, while a boil of fresh local crawfish is studded with house-made sausage, corn on the cob, and spring garlic.

The space, with aqua-painted walls and rope elements, is tastefully nautical and designed to cater to guests' comfort as they peel apart dinner—there are towels on the tables and a special hand-washing sink. Bring a group to shoot the breeze as you work; then split some beignets with caramel-mocha sauce as a reward.

Artisan Bistro

French

E1

1005 Brown Ave. (at Mt. Diablo Blvd.), Lafayette

Phone: 925-962-0882
Web: www.artisanlafayette.com
Prices: $$

Lunch & dinner Tue – Sun

From the warm welcome to top-notch service, Artisan Bistro's staff makes dining here a genuine pleasure. They're aided by the quaint setting of a Craftsman-style cottage featuring a garden patio, romantic interior, and trickling fountain amongst the flora.

Arrive early to kick things off with a creative cocktail at the tiny front bar, then move to a table to enjoy Chef/owner John Marquez's Cal-French fare. This may reveal a bright Cobb salad draped with delicately poached Maine lobster, or seared John Dory over artichokes, asparagus, and capers. Ladies who lunch swear by the chicken and avocado sandwich, served with shoestring fries. And for a fantastic finish, don't miss the outstanding butterscotch panna cotta with candied lemon and blueberry sauce.

Bangkok Jam

Thai

D1

1892 Solano Ave. (bet. Fresno Ave. & The Alameda), Berkeley

Phone: 510-525-3625
Web: www.bangkokjamberkeley.com
Prices:

Lunch & dinner daily

Do not be deterred by the plain façade sandwiched amid retail stores. Inside, this long and narrow space is contemporary and stylish with glittering chandeliers, dark wood tables, and brick wainscoting. A sweet, attentive staff keeps things casual and kid-friendly.

Whet the appetite with a plate of crispy vegetable spring rolls stuffed with carrots, cabbage, and onion, served with a tangy sweet and sour dipping sauce. Follow this with organic lemongrass chicken breast, tender and smoky, served over rice and complemented by a duo of spicy lime and sweet tamarind sauces. However, curries are the true standout here, with choices ranging from pumpkin to sweet and spicy mango stewed in coconut red curry with cabbage, peas, carrots, bell peppers, and tofu.

Battambang

850 Broadway (bet. 8th & 9th Sts.), Oakland

Phone: 510-839-8815
Web: N/A
Prices: 🐚🐚

Lunch Mon – Sat
Dinner nightly

Embrace the unknown at one of the Bay Area's very few Cambodian restaurants. Though the menu may be unfamiliar to American palates, Battambang boasts warm, hands-on service that will make any diner feel at ease. Don't let its gaudy exterior deter you: the interior is pleasant and tastefully adorned.

The must-order here is the *amok trei*, a hard-to-find dish of catfish steamed in a fragrant banana leaf. Layered with red lemongrass sauce and coconut milk, it's utterly beguiling. Equally good is the spicy-sour *yihoeur char tumpaing*, a stir-fry of calamari and bamboo shoots with lemongrass and ground chili. Adventurous diners should also sample the omelet-like *num banchev*, an eggy rice-flour crêpe with chicken, prawns, sprouts, and strong, funky fish sauce.

Bay Wolf

3853 Piedmont Ave. (at Rio Vista Ave.), Oakland

Phone: 510-655-6004
Web: www.baywolf.com
Prices: $$

Dinner nightly

Bay Wolf has been a Bay Area icon since the mid 1970's. As the restaurant celebrates its 40th birthday, the kitchen is still successfully preparing food the way it always has—excellent ingredients are treated with simplicity and care. True to the local philosophy, this oft-changing menu spotlights seasonal and local ingredients.

Set in a converted house with a small bar and dining rooms on either side, patrons can be seen nibbling on fried ricotta-stuffed squash blossoms before proceeding to a pork loin roulade with toasted pistachios spiraling through it, deliciously paired with wild rice pilaf. But, the real scene is on the front porch where local artists, intellectuals, and retirees spend hours lingering over buttery apricot upside down cake.

Bellanico 😊

F3

Italian ✗✗

4238 Park Blvd. (at Wellington St.), Oakland

Phone: 510-336-1180
Web: www.bellanico.net
Prices: $$

Lunch & dinner daily

Neighborhood favorite Bellanico serves up consistently good, rustic Italian fare. Large windows overlook Park Boulevard, while inside, persimmon-colored walls, wood furnishings, and an open kitchen welcome regulars. Lunches are low-key and frequented by business people. Dinners are filled with local couples and families appreciative of the "bambini" dishes—apropos in a place named for the owners' daughters. Like its sister spot Aperto, the seasonal, ingredient-driven menu focuses on local, organic products. Start with a selection of *cicchetti* and antipasto of cauliflower fritters with garlic *aglioli* before moving on to other items including spicy *tagliolini pepati* with bacon. Smoke fiends adore the grilled pork chop adorned with well-seasoned *brodo*.

Bistro Liaison

E1

French ✗✗

1849 Shattuck Ave. (at Hearst Ave.), Berkeley

Phone: 510-849-2155
Web: www.liaisonbistro.com
Prices: $$

Lunch Sun
Dinner nightly

This slice of Paris in Berkeley, just two blocks from campus, draws regulars with its authentic bistro vibe, complete with closely spaced tables and cheerful yellow walls displaying vintage French posters and artwork. On warm days, diners scramble to score one of the sidewalk tables, though the traffic on busy Shattuck Avenue might dispel any fantasies of the Champs-Élysées.
The fare, like the décor, is classic French, with dishes like escargots in garlic butter and a croque-monsieur oozing with Emmenthaler cheese. At dinner, hearty bœuf bourguignon and steamed mussels in garlic and white wine send diners into Gallic reveries. Finish with a buttery, flaky apple tarte Tatin, drowned in caramel and topped with a scoop of rum-raisin ice cream.

Bocanova

A3

55 Webster St. (at Jack London Sq.), Oakland

Phone: 510-444-1233 Lunch & dinner daily
Web: www.bocanova.com
Prices: $$

Located in lively Jack London Square, everything is big at Bocanova—several dining rooms, a massive (and admired) bar, and the spacious patio overlooking the harbor. The industrial-chic space highlights soaring ceilings, funky light fixtures, and stained glass accents amid fine wood furnishings. Adding to the allure is an open kitchen starring a competent lineup of chefs.

Unlike mere mortals, Bocanova aces the art of compartmentalizing. Whether *From the Pantry, From the Raw Bar,* or *From the Feidora*, dishes are sure to gratify. Expect the likes of a *huarache* topped with crumbled Oaxaca cheese and ghost chili salami; grilled Pacific cod tacos capped with a zesty tomato-avocado relish; and chicken enchiladas smeared with an aromatic tomatillo salsa.

Boot and Shoe Service

E3

3308 Grand Ave. (bet. Lake Park Ave. & Mandana Blvd.), Oakland

Phone: 510-763-2668 Lunch & dinner Tue – Sun
Web: www.bootandshoeservice.com
Prices: $$

Named for its former incarnation as a shoe-repair shop, this very accommodating Grand Avenue standby brings stellar pizzas and a totally relaxed vibe to its hungry neighborhood. The light, bright space suits every configuration, from the solo dining counter to gregarious communal tables and a semi-private room for large groups. Adept servers cater to the whims of hipsters and families alike.

Dig into blistered Californian pies like wild nettle and *ricotta salata*; or try bacon, Calabrian chili, and cream. Other menu offerings should also be explored, especially the chili-inflected heirloom bean ragù with a velvety soft-cooked egg, smoky from the wood-fired oven. Healthier options feature a nutty farro salad with tender marinated beets and fresh herbs.

Box and Bells

Gastropub ✗

E2

5912 College Ave. (bet. Harwood Ave. & Chabot Rd.), Oakland

Phone: 510-923-2000
Web: www.boxandbells.com
Prices: $$

Lunch Sun
Dinner Tue – Sun

Dine as the chefs do at this popular venture from James Syhabout (Commis, Hawker Fare), who themed the menu around what cooks like to eat on their nights off. Bold, rich flavors predominate, from a Gruyère-topped burger on a buttery pretzel bun, to creamy deviled eggs topped with crispy shallots. Seared trout with peas and clam vinaigrette is a lighter alternative.

The concrete-and-wood dining room has a cool industrial feel, and the muted lighting, high decibel levels, and bustling bar counter are unmistakable signs of a youthful hot spot. Boxing gloves and portraits of boxer dogs bedeck the walls, but boozehounds are more likely to salivate over the appealing cocktail list—not to mention a back bar jam-packed with single-malt, bourbon, and rum.

Brown Sugar Kitchen

American ✗

D3

2534 Mandela Pkwy. (at 26th St.), Oakland

Phone: 510-839-7685
Web: www.brownsugarkitchen.com
Prices: 🥜🥜

Lunch Tue – Sun

Its industrial West Oakland locale is far from a restaurant row, but visitors to this soul-food palace (open for breakfast and lunch only) will find plenty of company—mostly ahead of them in line. Over the years, Chef/owner Tanya Holland has built a loyal following of families and foodies who arrive early to avoid long waits for tender, flaky biscuits and signature buttermilk fried chicken with a cornmeal waffle. Others go for the juicy jerk chicken with a kick of heat, cooled by mashed yams and pineapple-red onion salsa. The earthy, well-seasoned black-eyed pea salad is another favorite and fittingly so.

Casual and welcoming with a chill vibe and colorful look, BSK may be a crowd magnet, but it's earned the hype. Also try nearby sib, B-Side BBQ.

Café Colucci

E2   Ethiopian ✗

6427 Telegraph Ave. (at 65th St.), Oakland

Phone: 510-601-7999   Lunch & dinner daily
Web: www.cafecolucci.com
Prices: ෨෨

On a stretch of Telegraph that's something of an Ethiopian
restaurant row, Colucci stands out for its eye-catching décor,
including a plant-laden terrace, fabric-draped ceiling, and
selection of African art. As with all Ethiopian restaurants,
bring clean hands and leave your fork at home: You'll be
dining exclusively with *injera*, the spongy-sour bread that's
traditional to the country.

The menu offers many appealing options to scoop, from
mild *begue tibs* (lamb with onions, garlic, and rosemary), to
spicy eggplant *wot*, stewed in a piquant *berbere* sauce. Fried
potato slices called *dentich tibs* are great on their own, but
extra tasty when paired with *assa tibs*, a whole baked fish.
Save room for a buttery pistachio baklava and house-roasted
Ethiopian coffee.

Camino

E3   Californian ✗

3917 Grand Ave. (bet. Jean St. & Sunny Slope Ave.), Oakland

Phone: 510-547-5035   Lunch Sat – Sun
Web: www.caminorestaurant.com   Wed – Mon dinner only
Prices: $$

With its look of a medieval refectory and that central wood-
burning hearth, Camino can seem like a trip to the days of
yore—but the cool crowd, fun cocktails, and innovative
food are decidedly modern. Take a seat under wrought-iron
chandeliers at one of the long, communal tables (one of them
is cut from a single redwood tree!) and expect to make some
new friends.

Chef-owner Russell Moore worked at Chez Panisse for
many years, and his food is appropriately hyper-seasonal.
An egg baked in the wood oven, its yolk still creamy, is
nestled in leeks, herbs, and cream, while slices of char-grilled
sourdough provide the base for a sandwich of juicy pancetta
and rustic sauerkraut. Moist, sticky Lardy cake is also grilled,
and topped with rich ricotta and honey.

Chevalier

E1

960 Moraga Rd. (at Moraga Blvd.), Lafayette

Phone: 925-385-0793   Dinner Tue – Sun
Web: www.chevalierrestaurant.com
Prices: $$

East Bay

Chevalier radiates French charm from the flowers on its patio to the beautifully manicured hedges. Additionally, the dining room feels wonderfully European with chic inflections like drapes set across walls of windows. Adding to this lure is a cadre of friendly servers—even the chef circulates for a chat with guests, both old and new.

The three-course prix-fixe menu is the only way to go here. *Par exemple*, start with mixed greens topped with a warm, pastry-wrapped square of goat cheese sprinkled with *herbes de Provence* and a lemon-thyme vinaigrette. Next comes *poulet rôti fermier à la Tropézienne*, perfectly seasoned, crispy skinned chicken draped over a ragout of tomato, squash, olives, and rosemary. Finish with a luscious vanilla bean crème brûlée.

Chez Panisse

E1

1517 Shattuck Ave. (bet. Cedar & Vine Sts.), Berkeley

Phone: 510-548-5525   Dinner Mon – Sat
Web: www.chezpanisse.com
Prices: $$$$

A recent fire was no deterrent for this Berkeley legend, which is back in business with a fresh façade and unique decorative touches. Inside, the vibe remains Arts and Crafts-influenced, with wooden walls, copper trim, and eye-catching light fixtures. The tables may be linen-clad, but service is gentle and relaxed, and guests are encouraged to drop into the open-plan kitchen.

A daily set menu (cheaper on Mondays, pricier on weekends) features the best of local products like an asparagus and sweet pea salad with baked ricotta, black truffle and *baccalà* ravioli; followed by perfectly grilled pork loin with fennel, nettles, and crisp potatoes. Outstanding local cheese with fresh bread is an optional add-on, and the wine selection is top-notch.

China Village 😊

D1

1335 Solano Ave. (at Ramona Ave.), Albany

Phone: 510-525-2285   Lunch & dinner daily
Web: www.chinavillagealbany.com
Prices: 😊

It takes a village to feed a big group, and this laid-back spot is a favorite with families. A stylish recent renovation has added a sleek front bar, contemporary chandeliers, and dramatic Chinese art, but one look at the scorching-hot menu options—think spicy Sichuan frog and flaky sautéed fish with pickled chili peppers—confirms the authenticity factor.

Skip the Hunan, Mandarin, and Cantonese offerings in favor of the Sichuan specialties, like dry-fried, bone-in chicken laced with ground chili and numbing peppercorns. And be sure to order the five-spice hot and spicy pork shoulder. A house specialty, the mouthwatering dish is fork- (or chopstick) tender and rests atop a deliciously piquant chili-oil jus with baby bok choy, scallions, and garlic.

Cholita Linda

E2

4923 Telegraph Ave. (bet. 48th & 51st Sts.), Oakland

Phone: 510-594-7610   Lunch & dinner Tue – Sat
Web: www.cholitalinda.com
Prices: 😊

The old Bay Area saw of farm-to-table gets a tasty spin at this purveyor of Latin fare, which transformed from a megapopular farmer's market stand into a packed house of communal tables. Bright, colorfully decorated, and flooded with natural light, it's a casual space where diners order and pay at the counter, then sip drinks from glass Mason jars under the potted palms.

The outstanding Baja fish tacos are the source of Cholita Linda's reputation, but its dishes traverse Latin America, from a hearty Cubano sandwich to a plate of slow-braised, well-seasoned carnitas with black beans and fried plantains. With such reasonable prices, there's no excuse not to order a sweet, smooth mango *agua fresca* to wash down the tender, tangy *pollo al pastor* tacos.

Comal 👻

Mexican XX

2020 Shattuck Ave. (bet. Addison St. & University Ave.), Berkeley

Phone: 510-926-6300   Dinner nightly
Web: www.comalberkeley.com
Prices: $$

The word is out—Comal is excellent and everybody knows it! Jam-packed since day one, the hot spot on this (Berkeley) block serves delicious Mexican dishes in an industrial space fitted with soaring ceilings. Within this lofty lair, the dress is casual and the staff gracious.

The regional food (mostly small plates) is elevated by seasonal Californian ingredients and is great to share. The menu may change frequently, but flavors are consistently spectacular in fresh, tangy, and zesty halibut ceviche; tender corn tortillas filled with wood-grilled rock cod, spicy pickled cabbage, and avocado aïoli; or rich duck enchiladas smothered with delicious *mole coloradito*. Every item is made from scratch—from the griddled tortillas to the wonderful *moles* and salsas.

Corso 👻

Italian X

1788 Shattuck Ave. (bet. Delaware & Francisco Sts.), Berkeley

Phone: 510-704-8004   Dinner nightly
Web: www.corsoberkeley.com
Prices: $$

A Tuscan follow-up from the couple behind nearby Rivoli, Corso is every bit the equal of its big sister, thanks to generous, Florentine-inspired dishes like a roasted squid panzanella with torn flatbread, buttery white beans, and bright dashes of lemon juice and chili oil. Pasta fiends will swoon for house-made tagliatelle in a meaty beef and pork sugo, while butter-roasted chicken boasts juicy meat, golden-brown skin, and fresh peas and asparagus alongside.

Soul-warming in its hospitality, Corso is the kind of place where servers will bring complimentary pistachio biscotti simply because they're "so good when they're warm." It's no surprise that the tiny trattoria is a favorite among new couples, so be sure to reserve in advance and come hungry.

Commis

E3

Contemporary XX

3859 Piedmont Ave. (at Rio Vista Ave.), Oakland

Phone:	510-653-3902	Dinner Wed – Sun
Web:	www.commisrestaurant.com	
Prices:	$$$$	

A quiet, serious retreat on a busy Oakland thoroughfare, Commis is a destination for those seeking thoughtful and refined cuisine in the East Bay. Though Chef/owner James Syhabout has opened multiple casual follow-ups, it remains his flagship—with a long, narrow room that draws the eye to the calm, methodical team working diligently to the strains of '80s pop in the open kitchen. Don't fret if you get assigned a counter seat—they're the rare kind that are actually comfortable enough for a long meal.

At $95, the 10-course tasting menu is one of the Bay Area's most affordable, with strong kitchen chops demonstrated in dishes like gently smoked scallops twirled with tart rhubarb and peppery radish, or tender asparagus topped with creamy trout mousse. A pungent tisane of button mushrooms will whet your appetite for the beautifully cooked lamb saddle with crunchy grains and Brussels sprout purée. The wine list emphasizes pinot noir and riesling, fine pairings for the path-breaking food.

Dessert saves some of the best courses for last: both the vanilla ice with Meyer lemon and orange foam and the creamy parsnip pudding with crisp sour apples and sweet caramel sauce will linger in the memory.

Cosecha

Mexican ✗

A2

907 Washington St. (at 9th St.), Oakland

Phone: 510-452-5900   Lunch & dinner Mon – Sat
Web: www.cosechacafe.com
Prices: 🅿️

This Mexican café is housed in Old Oakland's historic Swan's Market, a great spot for die-hard food fans. Guests order at the counter and sit at one of the communal tables in the warehouse-like space. Note that they serve dinner but close early, so arrive in time to nibble your way through a menu featuring local ingredients infused into flavorsome Mexican fare.
Everything is homemade including the tortillas and *horchata*. Discover a quesadilla filled with sweet yam and Oaxaca cheese, served with a wonderfully zesty salsa verde. Both achiote-marinated chicken and braised pork tacos are explosively flavorful, topped with pickled onion and cilantro, but save room for *mole verde con pollo*—chicken breast steeped in a delish pumpkin seed-green chile *mole*.

Desco

Italian ✗✗

A2

499 9th St. (at Washington St.), Oakland

Phone: 510-663-9000   Lunch Mon – Fri
Web: www.descooakland.com   Dinner nightly
Prices: $$

After a tumultuous series of turnovers, this beautiful Old Oakland space has found a solid owner in Donato Scotti (of Redwood City's Donato Enoteca), who's given it an Italian spin. Inside, the exposed brick walls, copper-topped bar, wood-burning oven, and mosaic floors in the 1870s-era building are as captivating as the food is delicious.
Desco's simple offerings are full of flavor, from a house-made charcuterie board of smoked duck, roasted *porchetta*, and rabbit terrine to golden pappardelle bathed in a thick lamb, red onion, and tomato *sugo*. For dessert, the pear-almond torta with hazelnut gelato is a must. The wine list boasts 50 Italian selections, half of which are available by the glass—no wonder the bar is so popular for happy hour.

Doña Tomás

East Bay

E2

5004 Telegraph Ave. (bet. 49th & 51st Sts.), Oakland

Phone: 510-450-0522
Web: www.donatomas.com
Prices: $$

Lunch Sat – Sun
Dinner Tue – Sat

Fresh, seasonal, organic ingredients from the Bay Area are fused with Mexican flavors and preparations resulting in a successful hybrid at Doña Tomás. The restaurant has two dining areas and a bar frequented by locals who come to chat with the friendly bartenders, mingle with friends, and dive into the flavorful Cal-Mex food.

Speaking of which, expect dishes like corn tortilla chips with well-seasoned guacamole; followed by slow-roasted pork layered in soft, delicate tacos and matched with *pico de gallo*, pinto beans, and red rice. Pan-fried petrale sole joined with luscious corn and zucchini pudding keeps fish fans elated.

The happy hour set return time and again for discounted drinks featuring a good selection of Mexican tequila, mezcal, and cerveza.

Duende

B1

Spanish ✗✗

468 19th St. (bet. Broadway & Telegraph Ave.), Oakland

Phone: 510-893-0174
Web: www.duendeoakland.com
Prices: $$$

Dinner Wed – Mon

Savor the flavors and sounds of Spain at this novel restaurant in developing Uptown Oakland, where Chef Paul Canales turns out everything from *pintxos* to paella. The voluminous bi-level space set in the historic Floral Depot is packed with large windows, exposed brick, and colorful murals which contribute a fun vibe attracting groups of hip, urban types.

The food is authentic with seasonal accents and has included rabbit and lobster sausage with blistered Padrón peppers; and seafood-studded *arroz negro*, thick with rockfish, scallops, cherry tomatoes, and garlic aïoli. The crowd is loud and festive, especially when one of the rotating local musicians hits the stage for a set. Like the food and ambience, the music lends Duende a casual, warm energy.

Encuentro

Vegetarian ✗

A2

550 2nd St. (at Clay St.), Oakland

Phone: 510-832-9463

Dinner Tue – Sat

Web: www.encuentrooakland.com

Prices: $$

Recently relocated, Encuentro is now sitting pretty in an industrial-chic space fitted with large windows, lofty ceilings, and an easy-breezy front bar. Though it's minimal in a California-meets-Manhattan way, the kitchen promises maximum satisfaction via its haute (read: heavenly) take on vegan treats. Avocado bruschetta drizzled with olive oil and chili jam entices with a kick of spice, while baby kale and roasted veggies are enriched with toasted quinoa and a lemon-tahini dressing.

Here, each menu item is so carefully composed and appetizingly prepared (think of empanadas stuffed with pumpkin seed *piccadillo* served atop pinto beans with cashew *crema*) that you won't miss the meat—which explains why the dining room is peppered with carnivores.

Esin

Mediterranean ✗✗

E4

750 Camino Ramon (at Sycamore Valley Rd.), Danville

Phone: 925-314-0974

Lunch & dinner daily

Web: www.esinrestaurant.com

Prices: $$

Esin brings tasty Mediterranean and American inspiration to this boutique-filled Danville shopping complex. The spacious restaurant outfitted with a front bar combines several dining areas trimmed in dark wood, nicely contrasted with soft beige walls and bright windows. Lunchtime service efficiently accommodates groups of area business people, while evenings draw locals who soak in the ambience.

Meals here might begin with a hearty Tuscan-style kale and white bean soup flavored with oregano and garlic, liberally sprinkled with Parmesan cheese. Then, sample the tender pot roast in reduced jus over a generous mound of garlicky mashed potatoes and roasted root vegetables. Homemade dessert specials are sure to beckon, as in the warm fig and almond galette.

175

FIVE

American 🍴🍴

E2

2086 Allston Way (at Shattuck Ave.), Berkeley

Phone: 510-225-6055
Web: www.five-berkeley.com
Prices: $$

Lunch & dinner daily

Set on the main level of the Shattuck Plaza, FIVE caters to hotel guests and stylish suits. Yet, it is an equally cherished destination among locals and families too. The boldly patterned walls and massive chandelier lend a sense of drama, while service is welcoming and friendly.

The menu of well-prepared American fare is as wonderful as the décor itself. Expect items where every element oozes deliciousness as in rich duck confit enchiladas crowned with tangy salsa verde, avocado purée, lime crème fraîche, and *queso fresco*. Add to it an elegant side of "mac" and cheese (piping-hot orzo with smoked Gouda and tangy organic tomato jam), and finish with an excellent butterscotch pudding with peanut brittle and whipped cream that simply must *not* be missed.

Gather

Californian 🍴🍴

E2

2200 Oxford St. (at Allston Way.), Berkeley

Phone: 510-809-0400
Web: www.gatherrestaurant.com
Prices: $$

Lunch & dinner daily

With its heavily vegetarian bill of fare, reclaimed and repurposed décor, and local Berkeley crowd, Gather is a must for mostly-meatless diners of all ages. This aptly-named hit offers a relaxed vibe for a light lunch, cocktails at the bar, dinner on the patio, and everything in between.

Surprisingly hearty dishes like chicory salad tossed with sliced fennel and fines herbes vinaigrette won't leave you craving meat, nor will the gourmet Wagon Wheel grilled cheese with braised greens and chanterelle mushrooms. Dinner is more complex, with ambitious offerings like the vegan "charcuterie," a platter of four delicious vegetable preparations. Should you venture into San Francisco City, be sure to visit its new—and already acclaimed—sister restaurant, Verbena.

Grand Avenue Thai

Thai XX

E3

384 Grand Ave. (bet. Perkins St. & Staten Ave.), Oakland

Phone: 510-444-1507
Web: www.grandavethai.net
Prices: ⊜⊗

Lunch Mon – Sat
Dinner nightly

Thanks to its charming décor, friendly service, and flavorful cuisine, Grand Avenue Thai is a winning standout—just one block from picturesque Lake Merritt. The space is small with bright walls, fresh flowers, and colorful local artwork. Service is prompt even with a steady to-go business.

Be sure to try one of the house favorites like the sweet and fragrant coconut curry with chunks of pumpkin, eggplant, broccoli, and string beans. The summer rolls neatly wrap up fresh veggies and garlicky rice noodles for a dip in peanut-chili sauce. The ever-popular pad Thai combines plump prawns stir-fried with egg, bean sprouts, scallions, and peanuts in a tasty tamarind-Thai fish sauce. Spice can be tame, but the kitchen is happy to indulge the fire fiends.

Great China ⊛

Chinese XX

E2

2190 Bancroft Way (at Fulton St.), Berkeley

Phone: 510-843-7996
Web: www.greatchinaberkeley.com
Prices: $$

Lunch & dinner Wed – Mon

Great China may have moved a block away following a catastrophic fire, but that hasn't dimmed its appeal. Chic enough for the style-savvy, cheap enough for Cal students, and authentic enough for local Chinese families, it's one of the few local restaurants everyone can—and does—agree on.

Fresh and flavorful meat and produce set Great China's food apart. And while it's not super-spicy, it's also not reliant on chili oil and Sichuan peppercorns to mask low-quality ingredients. Bring a group and savor it all: tender and aromatic twice-cooked pork, piquant *mapo* tofu, beautifully lacquered tea-smoked duck with fluffy steamed buns, and tender-crisp *ong choy* (water spinach) with fermented tofu paste. Generous portions and ample seating seal this savory deal.

Hamro Aangan

Nepali ✗

D1

856 San Pablo Ave. (bet. Solano & Washington Aves.), Albany

Phone: 510-524-2220   Lunch & dinner daily
Web: www.hamroaangan.com
Prices: ⊜⊜

Nepali restaurants have proliferated in the East Bay of late, but Hamro Aangan remains at the top of the heap thanks to its rustic, flavorful, generously portioned fare. The handmade *momos* (steamed dumplings filled with spiced cabbage, carrot, and onion) are accompanied by a garlicky, curried sauce, while the fluffy, layered chicken biryani is rich with caramelized onions and ground cardamom. Goat stew with tomato and an intensely-spiced gravy is another delicious option.

Located on busy San Pablo Avenue, Hamro is low-key, with red, rose, and copper décor and a beautiful mural from a local Nepali artist on the wall. It attracts a steady stream of regulars, particularly families, making it an excellent choice for a casual meal with kids in tow.

Haven

Contemporary ✗✗

A3

44 Webster St. (at Jack London Sq.), Oakland

Phone: 510-663-4440   Lunch Sat – Sun
Web: www.havenoakland.com   Dinner nightly
Prices: $$

Part of the Daniel Patterson Group, Haven has seen a few chef changes, but locals continue to rely on it for good food and a sleek, industrial-chic setting in prime Jack London Square. With windows facing the Square and counter seats offering great views into the open kitchen, it's hard to pick a perch; in either case, kick things off with one of the intriguing barrel-aged cocktails.

The food is contemporary and seasonal, with exquisite ingredients in dishes like roasted Monterey squid with smoked fingerling potatoes, chorizo, and green olives, or lamb roulade with warm lentils and roasted fennel. For dessert, cinnamon churros with caramelized peaches and nasturtium whipped cream are a delight. And be sure to reserve ahead for their praise-worthy brunch.

Hawker Fare

Asian 🍴

B1

2300 Webster St. (at 23rd St.), Oakland

Phone: 510-832-8896
Web: www.hawkerfare.com
Prices: 💲

Lunch Mon – Fri
Dinner Tue – Sat

East Bay

Those hawker stalls across Southeast Asia may not qualify as trendy, but here in uptown Oakland, hipsters in oversized eyeglasses and skinny jeans clamor for humble and tasty (if toned-down) street food. Groups of hard-drinking twenty- and thirty-something's are everywhere at Hawker Fare, sharing plates, perusing the faux-graffiti on the walls, and bobbing their heads to the beat of their own soundtrack.

They come for well-made Thai dishes like peppery arugula salad with lotus root, jicama, and Chinese sausage; or spicy red *gang dang* tofu curry with chunks of pumpkin over steamed rice. Indeed, rice is everywhere on the menu, from lunchtime bowl combos to a creamy coconut pudding with banana jam and sesame—a treat that merits the frequently long waits.

Homestead

American 🍴

E3

4029 Piedmont Ave. (bet. 40th & 41st Sts.), Oakland

Phone: 510-420-6962
Web: www.homesteadoakland.com
Prices: **$$**

Dinner Tue – Sun

If it wasn't housed in a beautiful Julia Morgan-designed building, this farm-to-table jewel would be defined by the enticing smells that waft in upon entrance. It's a rustic space, full of large windows peering onto Piedmont Avenue, and the jars of dry ingredients, pickling vegetables, and Julia Child cookbooks on the counter create an upscale country-kitchen vibe.

The menu focuses on the best and freshest of local produce such as a panzanella salad with shaved carrot and crunchy asparagus. Braised octopus with Marcona almonds is light and fresh, allowing room for the star of the show: incredible wood-roasted pork, tender and moist, with potato gratin alongside. For a bright breakfast, look no further than the house-baked pastries and quiche.

Hong Kong East Ocean

C2

3199 Powell St. (at Emeryville Marina), Emeryville

Phone: 510-655-3388 Lunch & dinner daily
Web: N/A
Prices:

Primo panoramic views of the Bay Bridge and cityscape give this two-story favorite well-deserved attention. The spacious dining rooms may appear slightly dated, but who cares, given the stunning waterfront scene?

Lunchtime here at Hong Kong East Ocean is a dim sum affair. The place is packed with business folks savoring their *xiao long bao* (ground pork soup dumplings with fragrant, ginger-infused pork broth); fluffy pork buns; delicious sticky-rice-noodle crêpes filled with garlicky beef and cilantro; or steamed vegetable rolls, stuffed with sautéed mushrooms and wrapped in tofu. Nights draw a large crowd of local families who show up for seafood offerings such as wok-fried Dungeness crab with spicy herbs, or rock cod with ginger and scallions.

Hopscotch

A1

1915 San Pablo Ave. (at 19th St.), Oakland

Phone: 510-788-6217 Lunch & dinner daily
Web: www.hopscotchoakland.com
Prices: **$$**

A stone's throw from the heart of transitioning (read: gentrifying) uptown Oakland, Hopscotch's kick-starter buzz may have died down, but its small size means that reservations are a must. Checkered floors and red-and-chrome chairs lend a retro diner vibe, but you'd be hard-pressed to find cocktails as intriguing as a Domino (combining Scotch, amaro, blackberry, and jalapeño) at some local greasy spoon. The winning American fare boasts subtle Japanese influences like the kabocha pumpkin cake with fresh pomegranate seeds. In the same vein, a tangy and bright pomegranate-and-sunchoke salad offers a refreshing counterpoint to heartier options like the cheekily named "first base" burger topped with sesame aïoli and griddled beef tongue.

Ippuku 😊

Japanese   ✗

E1

2130 Center St. (bet. Oxford St. & Shattuck Ave.), Berkeley

Phone: 510-665-1969   Dinner nightly
Web: www.ippukuberkeley.com
Prices: $$

Ippuku is not just tasty but a wholly fun experience. The hidden gem, just steps from UC Berkley, thrives in a strip of restaurants and bars. Its traditional entrance leads to the slim room outfitted with low tables over floor cut-outs, booths, and a dining counter situated before a grill in the back. However, the front is really where the chefs meticulously work their magic.

The décor is a stunning display of urban Japan with wood and cement accents. Ippuku is also an ace date place, secreted away from the bustle outside even though it sees a routine roster of students and locals. Sake bottle lamps cast a gentle glow upon plates of yuba dolloped with wasabi; *tsukune* with *yakitori* sauce; and skewered Brussels sprouts with *shichimi*-Kewpie mayo.

Iyasare 😊

Japanese   ✗✗

D2

1830 4th St. (bet. Hearst Ave. & Virginia St.), Berkeley

Phone: 510-845-8100   Lunch & dinner Wed – Mon
Web: www.iyasare-berkeley.com
Prices: $$

Beautiful and innovative Japanese food draws smartly dressed couples to this Fourth Street newcomer—casual yet stylish with its dark wood furnishings, cushioned banquettes, and exhibition kitchen. The many hard surfaces can make things noisy, so opt for the spacious, heated front patio if conversation is a priority; it's also a nice place for a sun-drenched lunch.

The menu of small plates is dizzyingly delicious, from an opener of compressed monkfish liver in tangy ponzu sauce, to silky fried *agedashi* tofu in an umami-rich soy-bonito broth. Tender roasted duck breast with nutty *hachiyo*-miso paste and pickled cucumber, or silky, ultra-fresh hamachi carpaccio are memorable. Finish with a parfait of matcha ice cream with mochi balls and *azuki* bean paste.

Kamdesh

Afghan   %

B2

346 14th St. (at Webster St.), Oakland

Phone: 510-286-1900   Lunch & dinner daily
Web: N/A
Prices:

Cheerfully perched on a commercial corner in downtown Oakland, Kamdesh's sunny yellow façade is a welcome sight. Expect to find business folks at lunch, locals at dinner, and a take-out clientele all day long.

Afghan *kababs* are all the rage here—perfectly seasoned, marinated, charbroiled, and absolutely mouthwatering. Try the lamb *tikka kabab*, moist and smoky with cumin, piled over fluffy *pallow* (brown basmati rice) infused with lamb jus and completed with a spicy cilantro chutney and salad. Other delicious options include tender *mantoo* dumplings stuffed with seasoned ground beef and onions, then drizzled with tangy yogurt sauce; or the flavorful charbroiled chicken wrap with yogurt, cucumber, tomato, mint, and red onion in a chewy, thick *naan*.

Kingston 11

Caribbean   %

B1

2270 Telegraph Ave. (bet. 23rd St. & Grand Ave.), Oakland

Phone: 510-465-2558   Lunch Tue – Fri & Sun
Web: www.kingston11eats.com   Dinner Tue – Sat
Prices: $$

Thanks to this lively Jamaican pop-up gone permanent, authentic island flavors have arrived in uptown Oakland. Its environs remain a bit dicey, but once inside, the smiling servers, boisterous crowds of families and friends, and reggae beats will transport you to the Caribbean—with a dose of California-chic from the modern interior design.

Boldly flavored fare includes tender, smoky jerk chicken with an intense and peppery spice rub, and a milder (but wildly delicious) curried goat stew with potato, carrots, and onion. Crisp and flaky salt-fish fritters are mouthwateringly delicious, and ideal for dunking in an herbaceous *chimichurri*. Skip the forgettable desserts and save your calories for a refreshing rum cocktail at the Fern Gully bar.

Metro Lafayette

Californian ✗

E1

3524 Mt. Diablo Blvd. (bet. 1st St. & Oak Hill Rd.), Lafayette

Phone: 925-284-4422   Lunch & dinner daily
Web: www.metrolafayette.com
Prices: $$

East Bay

The signs and framed vintage map hint of the Paris Metro, but this longtime hot spot could be renamed "The Patio." Both cuisine and dining are decidedly Californian and that means enjoying this flavor-packed fare out on the patio, or inside the sophisticated space fitted with a bar and sunroom overlooking local scenesters dining alfresco.

The oft-changing menu embraces global flavors, so a meal might start with a surprisingly light and complex rendition of onion soup that is perfectly seasoned, silky from a dash of cream, and presented with Parmesan toast. Follow this with two tacos loaded with tender grilled fish, salsa verde, avocado, drizzles of lime *crema*, and fresh tomato salsa. Seasonal desserts may reveal a warm organic plum crisp.

Michel Bistro 😊

French ✗

E3

3343 Lakeshore Ave. (at Trestle Glen Rd.), Oakland

Phone: 510-836-8737   Lunch Sat – Sun
Web: www.michelbistro.com   Dinner Tue – Sun
Prices: $$

A slice of France on a prime block of Lakeshore Avenue, this bistro boasts a heavily Gallic waitstaff and clientele chatting away in their native tongue. With its exposed brick, soaring ceilings, and cute touches like an excerpt from a Marcel Pagnol play inscribed on the wall, it's a simple but pleasant spot to enjoy a delicious, low-key meal.

The food is authentic, with some modern touches like the green almonds in a trout *amandine* with Lyonnaise-style potato salad, or the bison in a tartare with a quail egg. Brunch is a highlight with a gourmet eggs Benedict over artisan *levain* and butter-basted asparagus that steals the show. At either meal, the vanilla crème brûlée is a rich treasure—too often jumbled on other menus, it's perfectly rendered here.

183

Miss Ollie's

Caribbean ✗

A2

901 Washington St. (at 9th St.), Oakland

Phone: 510-285-6188   Lunch & dinner Tue – Sat
Web: www.missolliesoakland.com
Prices: $$

Raised in Barbados, Chef/owner Sarah Kirnon brings a taste of the Caribbean to her novel home in Old Oakland. Named after her grandmother, Miss Ollie's features an utilitarian-chic space, enlivened by corner windows, cheerful paintings, and deep orange bottles of house-made habanero sauce. Watch out—it rings with spice and packs a punch.

Callaloo, ackee, chow chow, and *giromon* may not be words in the average foodie's vernacular, but Chef Kirnon presents them here, as part of a pleasing roster of dishes like *phulourie*—crisp *garam masala*-tinged split-pea fritters served with *shado beni* or tamarind chutney—washed down with sorrel, a sweet hibiscus punch. But, it's that familiar, moist, crispy fried chicken that takes the crown, so grab it if available.

Mount Everest

Nepali ✗✗

E2

2598 Telegraph Ave. (at Parker St.), Berkeley

Phone: 510-843-3951   Lunch & dinner daily
Web: www.themounteverestrestaurant.com
Prices:

Lured by the wafting scents of spices just a few blocks south of UC Berkeley's campus, students, professors, and local business people flock to Mount Everest. The corner spot has plenty of light, cheery yellow walls, friendly service, and a relaxed atmosphere. Overflow crowds settle on the balcony. The menu offers Indian cuisine, but specializes in traditional Nepalese dishes like steamed *momos* filled with minced cabbage, carrot, and onion, with a deeply spiced dipping sauce of sesame, turmeric, and ginger. The earthy *channa masala* or chickpea stew with distinct seasoning; and chicken *tikka masala* featuring creamy tomato sauce infused with pungent spices, both beg to be sopped up with naan and rice. Students appreciate the inexpensive *thali* at lunch.

Nido

Mexican ✗

B3

444 Oak St. (at 5th St.), Oakland

Phone: 510-444-6436
Web: www.nidooakland.com
Prices: $$

Lunch Tue – Sun
Dinner Tue – Sat

The industrial area west of the I-880 freeway doesn't boast many good restaurants, but this hidden Mexican gem is an exception. Complete with hip reclaimed-wood décor and a local clientele of business people and trendy foodies, it's definitely a cut above a taqueria in terms of quality and price, with fresher, lighter food in smaller—but by no means stingy—portions.

At lunch, a trio of tacos includes moist pork *adobado* with a sweet-and-spicy pineapple salsa, grilled chicken with *chamoy* glaze, and smoky beef *barbacoa* with caramelized onions. Dinner brings pozole with chicken and *chile negro*, and a grilled pork chop with braised greens and almond *mole*. With a truly relaxed vibe and home cooked feel to the food, it's worth the extra effort to drop by.

Ohgane

Korean ✗

E3

3915 Broadway (bet. 38th & 40th Sts.), Oakland

Phone: 510-594-8300
Web: www.ohgane.com
Prices: ⊖⊖

Lunch & dinner daily

Ohgane still beats out the local Korean competition thanks to its delicious food, contemporary dining rooms, and private parking lot (huge bonus in this area!). Business crowds appreciate the all-you-can-eat lunch buffet. At night, Korean families gather beneath the ventilation hoods for tabletop mesquite grilling (*soot-bool*)—a specialty that is absolutely the way to go for dinner. During lunch, have the kitchen grill it for you and still enjoy the likes of smoky and tender *galbee*—beef short ribs marinated for 72 hours in garlic, soy, and sesame oil.

First, meals here start with an assortment of *banchan*— sixteen small bites including spicy kimchi, glazed sweet yam, and mild egg cake. Other kitchen-prepared dishes include *mandoo* and *dolsot bibimbap*.

Oliveto

Italian XX

E2

5655 College Ave. (at Shafter Ave.), Oakland

Phone:	510-547-5356	Lunch Mon – Fri
Web:	www.oliveto.com	Dinner nightly
Prices:	**$$$**	

Its memorable location in a prime corner of Rockridge is only the first hint of Oliveto's good looks: diners enter through a delightful mini-market and café—selling everything from pasta to Maine lobster—before climbing the spiral staircase into this elegant dining room, where a huge wood-burning oven, linen-topped tables, and bunches of fresh flowers delight the eye.

Nothing about Oliveto screams "Italian," from the décor to the all-American staff; yet its menu is completely authentic. Crisp, pan-roasted chicken breast rests on juicy herbed barley and asparagus, while charred Brussels sprouts get a kick from sweet saba and chopped walnuts. Barbaresco and Barolo, perfect with the strong selection of pastas and roasted meats, dominate the wine list.

Osmanthus

Asian XX

E2

6048 College Ave. (bet. Florio St. & Harwood Ave.), Oakland

Phone:	510-923-1233	Lunch & dinner daily
Web:	www.osmanthusrestaurant.com	
Prices:	**$$**	

Chef-owner Julia Klein has brought her cooking experience at Napa's Terra to bear on this "modern-classic Asian" restaurant. Osmanthus offers some fun bites that recall the '80s heyday of Asian fusion (shrimp toast or ginger-soy tuna tartare with avocado, maybe?) and some with more current touches like the *sriracha*-honey glaze served atop superlative fried Brussels sprouts with bacon. Sichuan influences abound, but chili-hounds beware: the cooking is more about flavor than fire.

Inside, the former Nan Yang has been updated with a serene look, boasting a dark tiled floor, colorful paper lanterns, and colonial-style revolving fans. Drinkers should sample the signature house cocktail, while teetotalers enjoy a Thai iced tea—in regular or crème brûlée form.

Pathos

Greek ✗✗

E2

2430 Shattuck Ave. (bet. Channing Way & Haste St.), Berkeley

Phone: 510-981-8339	Lunch Sat – Sun
Web: www.pathosrestaurant.com	Dinner Wed – Sun
Prices: $$	

Forget the flaming *saganaki* and cries of "Opa!"; Pathos is a sophisticated newcomer that will dispel any tired conceptions of Greek food. You'll want to dress up and bring a date to match its stylish décor, all hammered copper bar, oversized framed windows, and patterned banquettes.

Most dishes come straight from the wood-fired oven, including a lighter take on moussaka, with nutmeg-infused Greek yogurt béchamel baked over ground beef and eggplant; or a roasted red bell pepper stuffed with ground beef and rice. The *htapodi*, tenderly grilled octopus over shaved red onion and fried capers, is another hit for its full, smoky flavor. Turn to the friendly staff for help in selecting from among the many Greek wines, or try an ouzo or *metaxa*-centric cocktail.

Phnom Penh House

Cambodian ✗

B2

251 8th St. (bet. Alice & Harrison Sts.), Oakland

Phone: 510-893-3825	Lunch & dinner Mon – Sat
Web: www.phnompenhhouse.com	
Prices:	

Devotees in the know pray to the parking gods and push through Oakland's Chinatown crowds to get to one of the best Cambodian restaurants in the Bay Area. While the outside appears unassuming, the interior is a calm respite with colorful, native artwork and temple tiles. Expect a warm welcome from the family who runs this simple but pleasant place.

The menu is full of flavorful, fragrant, and fresh dishes such as a vibrant salad of shredded green papaya, carrots, and delicious herbs tossed in a garlicky house-made vinaigrette. The spicy flavors of lemongrass permeate tofu cubes sautéed with onion, button mushrooms, and red bell pepper; and infuse the *sach chhrouk ann kreun*—charboiled and glazed pork with crunchy, tangy pickled vegetables.

Picán

Southern XXX

B1

2295 Broadway (at 23rd St.), Oakland

Phone: 510-834-1000   Lunch & dinner daily
Web: www.picanrestaurant.com
Prices: $$

Picán is all business in Oakland—jamming with a corporate set at lunch and after-work cocktail clusters at dusk. The large space flaunts a bar and lounge (where you can order off the menu), and elegant dining areas with soaring ceilings and stately columns. The team of servers are friendly if a bit scattered during busy meal times.

While the chef change may have brought a few bumps in the road at times, the dishes turned out by the kitchen now are smoothing out nicely. Look for braised pork belly with buttery white beans and thick toast; the signature buttermilk fried chicken with decadent smoked Gouda mac 'n cheese and a side of cabbage- and pickled red onion-slaw; or hushpuppies with mustard dipping sauce. Don't miss their fantastic bourbon selection.

Pizzaiolo

Pizza

E2

5008 Telegraph Ave. (bet. 49th & 51st Sts.), Oakland

Phone: 510-652-4888   Dinner Mon – Sat
Web: www.pizzaiolooakland.com
Prices: $$

Lines are still a given at Temescal's pizza palace. In fact, find eager patrons arriving before the doors even open. A smattering of entrées and hearty plates like king salmon baked on a fig leaf with asparagus and mint yogurt evoke spring on a plate. But, crowds are here for their pies, crisp from the wood-burning oven and topped with the finest and freshest of ingredients like tangy tomato sauce, house-made sausage, and decadent *panna*.

The large dining room with handsome plank floors and dark wood tables centers around the exhibition kitchen lined with bowls of pristine local produce. Couples and groups gather at tables or pack the polished wood bar. Add on a rich caramel *pot de crème* and the endless queues will start to make sense.

Prima

Italian ✕✕

F1

1522 N. Main St. (bet. Bonanza St. & Lincoln Ave.), Walnut Creek

Phone: 925-935-7780
Web: www.primawine.com
Prices: $$$

Lunch Mon – Sat
Dinner nightly

With a premier location amid high-end boutiques, this contemporary Italian Romeo is a draw for business folk and local shoppers alike. The spacious interior wears a contemporary style accentuated by smart tables.

There are three distinct seating areas: a glass-enclosed porch framed in dark wood, a front room with views of the wood-fired oven, and another dining haven just past the bar with a fireplace and vaulted ceilings. The food is authentically Italian, from a refreshing panzanella salad tossed with sweet basil and ripe heirloom tomatoes; to al dente *tagliatelle* swirled with a meaty ragù. Considering the hefty prices, service may be lacking. But, all blemishes quickly fade away thanks to their distinguished atmosphere and notable food.

Ramen Shop 🐾

Japanese ✕

E2

5812 College Ave. (bet. Chabot Rd. & Oak Grove Ave.), Oakland

Phone: 510-788-6370
Web: www.ramenshop.com
Prices: 🪙🪙

Dinner Wed – Mon

A trio of Chez Panisse buddies have brought their innovative take on ramen to this quaint stretch of Rockridge. The slender shop has been a winner since day one and seats local residents plus visitors at a Douglas fir counter. Beyond, find the talented brigade hard at work in the steaming kitchen accented with jade green tiles. Tables are a more child-friendly seating option.

Ingredient-driven goodness is revealed in each bowl. Take for example the *shoyu* Meyer lemon ramen with its amber, pork-infused broth afloat with droplets of melted fat, plunged with distinctly straight, thin, house-made noodles and luscious *chasu* bobbing with a soft-boiled egg and chewy Mendocino nori. A sprinkling of fragrant citrus zest offers that oh-so-Californian flourish.

Riva Cucina

Italian ✗

D2

800 Heinz Ave. (at 7th St.), Berkeley

Phone: 510-841-7482
Web: www.rivacucina.com
Prices: **$$**

Lunch Tue – Fri
Dinner Tue – Sat

Riva Cucina has all of the charm you'd expect from a restaurant specializing in what is ostensibly Italy's culinary soul—Emilia Romagna, where Chef Massimiliano Boldrini hails from. Most of the kitchen action is on view from the tables or bar in the airy room, but for a private repast make your way behind those red velvet panels. The walls are bare, but the colors are deep and warm.

Locals are lucky to partake in this regional cooking. From a small but appealing menu, pick an artichoke soup before moving on to cloud-light knobs of gnocchi in a creamy sauce of smoked salmon. Finish with an excellent pork loin scaloppini trickled with capers and verdant spinach. With just one bite of the *torta della nonna* you'll notice the kitchen's attention to detail.

Rivoli

D1

1539 Solano Ave. (bet. Neilson St. & Peralta Ave.), Berkeley

Phone: 510-526-2542
Web: www.rivolirestaurant.com
Prices: **$$**

Dinner nightly

Northern Californian cooking with a trace of Italian flavor is the main draw at this lush charmer on the Albany-Berkeley border, serving up delectable and seasonal dishes. Rivoli is always popular and a winner among its patrons, who come here to savor undeniably excellent items like a crisp endive salad tossing peppery arugula, sweet plums, and blue cheese. Tender braised lamb-stuffed ravioli topped with tomato sauce, spiced chickpeas, and garlic-mint yogurt is another jewel.

Set in an adorable cottage, the dining room also features enormous picture windows overlooking a lush "secret" garden blooming with tender fronds and climbing ivy. The greenery is a stunning contrast to the crisp, white-linen tables, smartly serviced by an engaging waitstaff.

Sahn Maru

E2

4315 Telegraph Ave. (bet. 43rd & 44th Sts.), Oakland

Phone: 510-653-3366   Lunch & dinner Wed – Mon
Web: www.sahnmarukoreanbbq.com
Prices: $$

As one of East Bay's top Korean restaurants, Sahn Maru's name (which translates as "top of the mountain") is perfectly fitting. Its casual vibe, large size, and friendly service makes it a good choice for groups. Never mind the wainscoting and country-quaint chairs that juxtapose walls covered with pictures of Korean dishes—this is a place for authentic food. Meals start with barley tea and tasty *banchan* like daikon kimchi, bean sprout salad in sesame oil, and fish cakes, alongside a bowl of delicately flavored kelp and daikon soup. Lunchtime might feature a deliciously unexpected combination of beef *bulgogi* stir-fried with *jap chae*. While the spot earns raves for Korean barbecue, the kitchen prepares it for you, as there are no tabletop grills.

Sasa

F1

1432 N. Main St. (bet. Cypress St. & Lincoln Ave.), Walnut Creek

Phone: 925-210-0188   Lunch & dinner daily
Web: www.sasawc.com
Prices: $$

For a stylish, contemporary Japanese retreat in the heart of Walnut Creek, Sasa is a true find. Sleek furnishings, stone accents, water streams, and a lovely garden patio give this respite its flair and feel. Not to be outdone, the crowd here is as chic as the space itself and gathers for delicious sake sips alongside small plates of modern Japanese fare.

While avid Japanophiles and purists might cry foul, the rest of us can enjoy the creative interpretations of traditional ingredients and flavors, evident in such sushi and *makimono* as the N. Main filled with tuna, crab, and a spicy aïoli. Other dishes might include smoky kalbi beef lettuce wraps crested with *sukemono* or fluffy popcorn chicken *kara-age* finished with sea salt and lemon juice.

Shakewell

E3

3407 Lakeshore Dr. (bet. Longridge & Trestle Glen Rds.), Oakland

Phone: 510-251-0329   Dinner Tue – Sun
Web: www.shakewelloakland.com
Prices: $$

This trendy eatery, the brainchild of *Top Chef* alums Jennifer Biesty and Tim Nugent, was made for sipping and supping. Donning a bar up front and several dining nooks on either side of a central walkway, Shakewell keeps things Medichic with Moorish accents, reclaimed wood, and organic elements.

Service is particularly warm, and an even warmer teal-green wood-fired oven in the back turns out deliciously smoked items like crisp falafel topped with chorizo aïoli. A summer squash salad with heirloom tomatoes, fried bread, and feta offers an inspired blend of Greek and Tuscan flavors, and Bomba rice with braised fennel, *piperade*, chicken, and prawns is a fluffy take on paella. For a party in your mouth, finish with the caramel syrup-spiked flan Catalan.

Sidebar

E3

542 Grand Ave. (bet. Euclid Ave. & MacArthur Blvd.), Oakland

Phone: 510-452-9500   Lunch Mon – Fri
Web: www.sidebar-oaktown.com   Dinner Mon – Sat
Prices: $$

A loyal crowd of regulars flocks to this lively Oakland gastropub, located right across Grand Avenue from Lake Merritt. Though it offers only a handful of tables, Sidebar makes eating at the spacious rectangular bar a delight, with attentive servers and a view of the action in the semi-open kitchen.

The cuisine is hearty and varied with starters like a chopped romaine salad with fennel salami and creamy garlic-herb dressing; braised chicken thighs with curried coconut-lime cream; and deviled eggs with smoky bacon and cheddar. Themed evenings include Mussel Madness Mondays and Goat Cheese Soufflé Wednesdays, but there's no shame in sticking to the excellent Niman Ranch burger, with house-pickled onions and chipotle Thousand Island dressing.

Slow

Californian ✗

E1

1966 University Ave. (bet. Martin Luther King Jr. Way & Milvia St.), Berkeley

Phone: 510-647-3663
Web: www.slowberkeley.com
Prices: 🜚🜚

Lunch Mon – Sat
Dinner Tue – Sat

Slow lives up to its credo of presenting gourmet food crafted from local ingredients at judicious prices. Once inside this slightly sized refuge, place your order at the counter, and then take a seat among a handful of tables in the jovial, yellow-walled front area featuring an open kitchen. Note—for those looking to linger, dine out back in the pretty rose garden.

The roster of Californian dishes spins to the season and expectedly gushes with flavor. While some may start with a chilled beet and savoy salad tossed with tangy goat cheese and a refreshing Meyer lemon *citronette*; others may opt to dive straight into meaty oxtail braised until falling off the bone, coupled with caramelized pieces of sunchoke, heirloom carrots, and cauliflower.

Tacubaya

Mexican ✗

D1

1788 4th St. (bet. Hearst Ave. & Virginia St.), Berkeley

Phone: 510-525-5160
Web: www.tacubaya.net
Prices: 🜚🜚

Lunch & dinner daily

Megapopular Oakland Mexican restaurant Doña Tomas is reincarnated in taqueria form at this Berkeley shopping complex, where families grab a bite before or after errands: A line of people extends out the door from morning until night, ordering tangy limeade at the counter and claiming seats in the festive pink-and-orange dining room or on the sunny front patio.

The crowds come for *chilaquiles* and churros at breakfast, then transition into flavorful chorizo-and-potato *sopes* with black bean purée at lunch. Moist, well-seasoned beef enchiladas are doused in a smoky, tangy *guajillo*-tomatillo sauce and covered with melted cheese. For a sweet finish, tamales filled with cranberry jam and drizzled with goat-milk caramel are both beguiling and unusual.

Thai House 🐷

E4

254 Rose Ave. (bet. Diablo Rd. & Linda Mesa Ave.), Danville

Phone: 925-820-0635 Lunch Mon – Fri
Web: www.thaihousedanville.net Dinner nightly
Prices: 🍜

On a quiet, tree-lined street just off of the main road, flower beds and large umbrellas surround this charming bungalow. Inside, cozy nooks accommodate work lunches or families dining amid ornate Thai art, carvings, and tapestries. Embroidered fabrics cover the tables and complement the pretty blue-and-white pottery.

The menu is just as impressive, offering authentic dishes made from fresh ingredients with explosive flavor (heat levels are adjusted per your request). The red curry with moist, tender chicken, perfectly cooked vegetables, and basil served with jasmine rice is a delectable balance of creamy, sweet, spicy, and tangy essences. Silky yet crisp cubes of tofu *pad kra-prow* infused with fantastic red-chili heat are sure to delight.

The Peasant & The Pear

E4

267 Hartz Ave. (at Linda Mesa Ave.), Danville

Phone: 925-820-6611 Lunch & dinner daily
Web: www.thepeasantandthepear.com
Prices: $$

Peasants are hard to come by at this upscale Danville bistro, which draws ladies who lunch for leisurely meals in its cozy environs. But despite its wealthy clientele, this spot isn't the least bit stuffy, thanks to a friendly staff in the dining room and a relaxed California spirit in the kitchen.

Named for a nearby pear orchard that was once the world's largest, this restaurant features numerous pear dishes, like a grilled double-cut Sonoma pork chop with sweet potato-and-pear gratin. Chef/owner Rodney Worth, who trained under Loretta Keller, offers a playful and eclectic menu, from creamy burrata in a toasted baguette sandwich with pear-honey compote to Kentucky bourbon crème fraîche atop a velvety butternut squash soup.

Tribune Tavern

Gastropub ✗✗

B2

401 13th St. (at Franklin St.), Oakland

Phone: 510-452-8742   Lunch & dinner daily
Web: www.tribunetavern.com
Prices: $$

The team behind foodie-mobbed Chop Bar resurrected an Oakland landmark for their latest project: the former newsroom of the iconic *Tribune* building. And baby boy is quite the looker, featuring luxe leather sofas, wine barrels, and stained glass casting an elegant light onto the horseshoe-shaped bar.

Corporate types pack the bar for hearty, English-inspired items like a whole rabbit cooked down and presented as a jar of spreadable delight; Shepherd's pie bubbling with ground meat and topped with Parmesan-potato mash; and a strawberry trifle sundae. Happy hour brings bites such as house pickled vegetables, smoked pork belly-stuffed dates, or the Tavern burger. Cocktails are stellar, while teetotalers are kept happy with house-made sodas.

Ume

Japanese ✗

B1

2214 Broadway (at Grand Ave.), Oakland

Phone: 510-444-7586   Lunch Mon – Fri
Web: www.umeoakland.com   Dinner Tue – Sat
Prices: $$

The name Ume (Japanese for plum) is not the only thing that is translated here—this inventive kitchen recasts traditional small plates with contemporary Californian flair. Its casual nature makes this an ideal alternative to highfalutin sibling restaurants Coi and Haven; the sleek yet laid-back setting is perfect for families and small groups who are eager to share a tasty, fuss-free yet very fine meal. The back dining counter was made for foodies trying to get a glimpse of the action.

Sample an array of Cal-Japanese dishes like fresh English and sliced snap peas in a nutty miso dressing topped with fragrant purple shiso chiffonade. Tender, smoky morsels of grilled chicken rubbed with spicy fermented *yuzu kosho* will keep you coming back for more.

Uzen

Japanese 🍴

E2

5415 College Ave. (bet. Hudson St. & Kales Ave.), Oakland

Phone: 510-654-7753
Web: N/A
Prices: $$

Lunch Mon – Fri
Dinner Mon – Sat

Small Uzen may have a blink-and-you-missed-it façade, but really, you wouldn't want to pass up this popular sushi restaurant. There isn't much in terms of décor, but the space gets flooded with natural light from a front wall of windows. The best seats in the house are at the sushi bar where you can chat with the friendly chefs who will share their recommendations.

The à la carte menu is ideal for less exploratory palates, but the best way to enjoy Uzen is via their list of fresh nigiri personally handled by the *itamae*. Traditional flavors come alive in a crispy vegetable roll with toasted nori; firm slices of albacore tuna, rich silky slivers of mackerel, and tender fresh water eel, each presented over neat mounds of sushi rice. It's all so *oishi-so*!

Va de Vi

Fusion 🍴🍴

F1

1511 Mt. Diablo Blvd. (near Main St.), Walnut Creek

Phone: 925-979-0100
Web: www.vadevi.com
Prices: $$

Lunch & dinner daily

"Va de vi" is a Catalan phrase that roughly means "It's all about wine." Here you'll find no dissent from the moneyed locals who gather for flights with such cheeky names as "There's No Place Like Rhone." The fountain-enhanced, bucolic patio is a treasured sipping destination, as is the L-shaped counter with a view of the open kitchen set amid rich polished woods.

Good wine demands good food, and the global menu offered here entices with ultra-fresh choices like ahi tuna tartare topped with wasabi tobiko; or roasted asparagus in romesco, crowned with baked prosciutto chips. Asian influences abound particularly in soy-glazed black cod; or pork belly with sticky rice and a chili glaze. Add on a sweet staff and easy vibe—no wonder it's such a hit.

Wood Tavern ☺

Californian ✗✗

E2

6317 College Ave. (bet. Alcatraz Ave. & 63rd St.), Oakland

Phone: 510-654-6607
Web: www.woodtavern.net
Prices: $$

Lunch Mon – Sat
Dinner nightly

Wood Tavern borders Oakland and Berkeley on a stretch of College Avenue full of little shops and cafés. Surrounded by pale green walls, wood joists, and wine racks, locals gather at the happening bar or catch up with friends over a meal. It's the idyllic, casual, neighborhood spot.

The butcher-block charcuterie and cheese board selections are popular starts. Then, move on to the black mission fig tart on puff pastry with onion jam and blue cheese foam, accompanied by a watercress salad with prosciutto. Linger over perfectly seasoned burgers topped with oozing cheddar and homemade pickles on crusty baguettes, served with mounds of crisp shoestring fries. Save room for the chocolate brownie in a pool of salted caramel with a scoop of malt ice cream.

Zut!

Mediterranean ✗✗

D1

1820 4th St. (bet. Hearst Ave & Virginia St.), Berkeley

Phone: 510-644-0444
Web: www.zutonfourth.com
Prices: $$

Lunch & dinner daily

Though it translates to the rough French equivalent of "Darn it!" Zut! needn't be perturbed: It boasts a loyal crowd of regulars who fill the place during lunchtime, shopping breaks, and for long, wine-fueled dinners. The bistro-like setting is a big draw, with a colorful mural, doors that open onto the front patio on warm nights, and waiting patrons spilling onto busy Fourth Street.

The Mediterranean-meets-American menu has something for everyone, from a light, lemony pea and pancetta risotto to a hearty burger. Local ingredients abound, like the Frog Hollow Farms pears, Pt. Reyes blue cheese, and winter chicories in a sweet and tangy salad. Don't miss the moist, custardy bread pudding, made with Acme *pain au levain*, dark chocolate, and bourbon caramel.

Marin

Marin

Meandering Marin is located north of the Golden Gate Bridge and draped along breathtaking Highway 1. Coastal climates shower this county with abounding agricultural advantages, which in turn become abundantly apparent as you snake your way through its food oases, always filled with fresh, luscious seafood, slurpable oysters, and cold beer. Farm-to-table cuisine is de rigueur in this liberal-leaning and affluent county, boasting an avalanche of local food suppliers. One of the most celebrated purveyors is the quaint and rustic **Cowgirl Creamery**, whose "cowgirls" are charged with churning out delicious, distinctive, and hand-

crafted cheeses. By specializing in farmstead cheeses alone, they have refined the process of artisan cheese-making, and garnered national respect along the way. Continue exploring these fromageries at **Point Reyes Farmstead Cheese Co.**, a popular destination among natives for the "Original Blue" and its famously lush and heady satisfaction. Thanks to such driven, enterprising cheese-makers (who live by terroir or taste of the earth), surrounding restaurants follow the European standard by offering cheese before or in lieu of a dessert course. After such a savory spread, get your candy crush going at **Munchies of Sausalito**; or opt for a more creamy scoop at **Noci Gelato**.

If cheese and meat are a match made in heaven, then North Bay must be a thriving intermediary with its myriad ranches. At the crest is **Marin Sun Farms**, a glorified and dedicated butcher

shop whose heart and soul lies in the production of locally raised, natural-fed meats for fine restaurants, small-scale grocers, and everything in between. Championing local eating is **Mill Valley Market**, a can't-miss commitment among gourmands for top-quality foods, deli items, and other organic goods.

STOP, SIP & SAVOR

To gratify those inevitable pangs of hunger after miles of scenic driving complete with ocean breezes, **The Pelican Inn** makes for an ideal retreat. Serving hearty English country cooking and a range of brews from the classic "bar," this nostalgic and ever-charming rest stop will leave you yearning for more. Continue your hiatus by strolling into **Spanish Table**, a shopper's paradise settled in Mill Valley, only to find foodies reveling in unique Spanish cookbooks, cookware, specialty foods, and drool-worthy wines. Peckish travelers should swing by **Three Twins Ice Cream** for organically produced creamy goodness that leaves an everlasting memory.

201

Waters off the coast here provide divers with exceptional hunting ground, and restaurants throughout Marin count on supremely fresh oysters, plump clams, and meaty mussels. The difficulty in (legally) sourcing these large, savory mollusks makes red abalone a treasured species in area Asian establishments, though seafood does seem to be the accepted norm among restaurants in this town. If fish doesn't float your boat, **Fred's Coffee Shop** in Sausalito is a no-frills find for outrageously fulfilling breakfast signatures like deep-fried French toast with a side of calorie-heavy, crazy-good caramelized 'Millionaire's bacon.' Carb addicts routinely pay their respects at **M.H. Bread & Butter**, said to be the best bakery in the area. Their crusty loaves make for fantastic sandwiches, but are equally divine just slathered with butter. If that's too tame for your tastes, enticing Puerto Rican flavors and *especiales* abound at **Sol Food**, settled in San Rafael. While this fertile county's regional and natural ingredients are sold in countless farmers' markets, its most renowned celebration of food and wine may be found at Sausalito's own **Tomato Festival**—held every August. Given its culinary chops and panoramic views, Marin is one of the most sought after stops for celebrities and visitors alike. True, some places can seem crowded or touristy; however, its area chefs and restaurants are lauded for good reason, and know how to make the most of their choice homegrown produce and food purveyors.

Arti

Indian ✕

A1

7282 Sir Francis Drake Blvd. (at Cintura Ave.), Lagunitas

Lunch & dinner daily

Phone: 415-488-4700
Web: www.articafe.com
Prices: ⊜⊜

If Indian cuisine is about aromas, flavors, and textures, then Arti is an idyllic incarnation. Settled in a surreptitious shopping center in sleepy 'lil Lagunitas, this *desi* den is all charm and cheer—a yellow dining room is propitiously chaperoned by vases of fresh flowers. Befitting its delicate disposition, a handful of tables spaced along wood benches are embellished with colorful fabric pillows.

Arti tantalizes all callers with her inventive food. Tour your way through the fiery south with tangy Goan shrimp *vindaloo*. Then journey north for beautifully spiced and creamy chicken *tikka masala*. If fish and fowl don't fit the bill, tender lamb cubes in a rich cashew-coconut *korma* served with fragrant basmati rice are bound to hit the spot.

Arun

Thai ✕

C1

385 Bel Marin Keys Blvd. (near Hamilton Dr.), Novato

Lunch Tue – Fri
Dinner Tue – Sat

Phone: 415-883-8017
Web: www.arunnovato.com
Prices: ⊜⊜

Don't be fooled by its location in an industrial park: this Thai restaurant is completely transporting, thanks to the small, well-tended garden in front, bubbling fountain, colorful walls, and dark wood tables. Dinner is more formal than lunch, but either service offers a calming air.

The standards are all present and accounted for: satays, curries (like a delicious, mildly spiced red curry with prawns, squash, and bell pepper), and heaps of fragrant jasmine rice. At dinner, Thai barbecue is king and unveils an appealing Islamic lamb dish. Vibrant in appearance and fresh in flavor, all items are strong, but the moneybag-like curry pouches are particularly memorable, thanks to their golden exterior, tie of leek at the top, and rich ground chicken filling.

Bar Bocce

A3

Pizza ✗

1250 Bridgeway (bet. Pine & Turney Sts.), Sausalito

Phone: 415-331-0555   Lunch & dinner daily
Web: www.barbocce.com
Prices: **$$**

As chill a hangout spot as they come, Bar Bocce is seemingly designed to while away the hours with its pretty view of the water, namesake bocce courts, and roaring fire pit. Friendly and casual, it's a place where an afternoon glass of wine can easily fade into a multi-hour dinner, shared with a group of friends on the heated patio overlooking Sausalito's harbor.

Wood-fired sourdough pizzas, like a marble potato pie with fontina, bacon, and a fresh farm egg, are the heart of the menu, accented by antipasti such as shaved Brussels sprouts and pecorino salad or golden cod *brandade* fritters with a tangy citrus aïoli. Cheerful servers are always happy to recommend a bottle of *vino* (or three) to keep the festivities humming in the inviting little bungalow.

Barrel House Tavern

A3

Californian ✗✗

660 Bridgeway (at Princess St.), Sausalito

Phone: 415-729-9593   Lunch & dinner daily
Web: www.barrelhousetavern.com
Prices: **$$**

The former San Francisco-Sausalito ferry terminal has found new life as this lovely Californian restaurant, which gets its name from its barrel-like arched wood ceiling. A front lounge with a crackling fireplace and well-stocked bar is popular with locals, while tourists can't resist the expansive dining room and back deck, which boasts spectacular views of the Bay.

The cocktail and wine offerings are strong, as is the house-made soda program, which produces intriguing, never-too-sweet combinations like yellow peach, basil, and ginger. These pair beautifully with meaty Dungeness crab sliders coupled with watermelon-jicama slaw; though they might be too tasty to keep around by the time grilled swordfish and pork belly with white beans hit the table.

Brick & Bottle 🐶

American ✗✗

C2

55 Tamal Vista Blvd. (bet. Madera Blvd. & Wornum Dr.), Corte Madera

Phone: 415-924-3366   Dinner nightly
Web: www.brickandbottle.com
Prices: **$$**

Discover a world of comfort going on behind the door to Brick & Bottle. This may seem like just a marketplace bar with happy hour from 4:30-7:00 P.M. every day and TV's screening football, but in the back, diners are snuggled into booths tucking into American classics with a distinct Californian twist.

The pizzas and sandwiches take center stage, as in a pulled pork sandwich with cider vinegar-barbecue sauce. Dinners may include Maine diver scallops with herb-flecked risotto, or Petrale sole with Dungeness crab and Yukon potato purée. Don't miss the noteworthy side of orzo mac and local goat cheese with tomato jam, or grandmother's lovely recipe for butterscotch pudding. It may not seem like the trendiest spot, but the food here is all-American good.

Buckeye Roadhouse

American ✗✗

A2

15 Shoreline Hwy. (off Hwy. 101), Mill Valley

Phone: 415-331-2600   Lunch & dinner daily
Web: www.buckeyeroadhouse.com
Prices: **$$**

This Marin hideout has welcomed generations of locals through its doors since 1937, even as its location on Highway 1 gave way to the more bustling 101. Enter the whitewashed craftsman building, and you'll be given your choice of dining in either the clubby bar or their grand dining room (complete with wood-paneled walls, red leather banquettes, and a tall fireplace).

The food here is classical but never dull, with a simple menu of salads, sandwiches, barbecue, and meat from the wood grill. A brunchtime meal of eggs Benedict boasts tender rosemary ham and rich potato croquettes, while plump asparagus ravioli with lemon olive oil stars in the evening. Finish up with a slice of pie—the famous s'mores version or a tart Key lime are both winners.

Bungalow 44

B2

44 E. Blithedale Ave. (at Sunnyside Ave.), Mill Valley

Phone: 415-381-2500   Dinner nightly
Web: www.bungalow44.com
Prices: $$

Nestled amid the fancy stores of quaint Mill Valley, vibrant Bungalow 44 draws a varied crew to its casual, contemporary environs. It's always busy at the bustling bar and slightly more subdued dining room, so for some peace and quiet, retire to the tented outer room with its glowing fireplace. Some prefer the counter to soak up the sizzle from the open kitchen.

Playful American cuisine is their dictum which shines through in tuna carpaccio—an homage to Italian antipasto—here starring tissue-thin slices of tuna served with citrusy *mizuna* and creamy mustard sauce. The whiff of cayenne from kickin' fried chicken is as tempting as the juicy meat—add the rich mashed potatoes. Local draft wines paired with pillowy-soft beignets make for a rewarding finish.

Copita

Mexican ✗✗

A3

739 Bridgeway (at Anchor St.), Sausalito

Phone: 415-331-7400   Lunch & dinner daily
Web: www.copitarestaurant.com
Prices: $$

One of Sausalito's newest additions is this easy breezy Bridgeway bar and kitchen owned by cookbook author, Joanne Weir. The congenially attended room is a lovely spot to while away a lazy afternoon amidst sienna-glazed walls and vivid tile accents. A wall of tequila bottles behind the bar and a prominently positioned wood-burning rotisserie arouse the desire to drink, eat, and relax.

Copita's expert kitchen produces sumptous south-of-the-border fare dressed with a distinctly Californian sensibility. Munch on crisp jicama batons sprinkled with chili, lime, and salt before delving into a bowlful of tart halibut ceviche studded with bits of ripe mango; or house-made tortillas stuffed with plump shrimp, strips of roasted poblano, and early corn.

El Huarache Loco

Mexican 🍴

C2

1803 Larkspur Landing Circle (off Sir Francis Drake Blvd.), Larkspur

Lunch & dinner daily

Phone: 415-925-1403
Web: www.huaracheloco.com
Prices: 🪙🪙

What started as a food truck now occupies a spot in the Marin County Mart. But it's a far cry from an urban taqueria as denizens peck away on laptops after ordering at the counter. Inside, bright natural light flows through and framed photos provide a crash course on important terminology pertaining to organic and sustainable permaculture.

Here, atop a decorative tiled floor, patrons peruse a menu focused on the delicious street fare of Mexico City. Start with crispy fried chicken *taquitos* topped with guacamole and *queso fresco*, or mini *sopes* overflowing with potatoes and chorizo. Try a *huarache* in one of eight versions—perhaps steak or smoky chorizo—crowned with salsas (from a station that covers every level of heat) and nirvana will follow.

El Paseo

Steakhouse 🍴🍴

B2

17 Throckmorton Ave. (at Blithedale Ave.), Mill Valley

Dinner nightly

Phone: 415-388-0741
Web: www.elpaseomillvalley.com
Prices: $$$

"Rockstar chef" is a term that often gets tossed around, but it's all too true at this rustic steakhouse, co-owned by celebrity toque Tyler Florence and rocker Sammy Hagar. Hidden down an alley off the shopping arcade of Mill Valley, El Paseo reeks of old-world charm with rustic wood-beamed ceilings and brick walls. Adding a dose of romance are cool high-backed leather chairs warmed up by a live fireplace.

Once seated, the tuxedoed staff will present a cast iron tray of roasted bone marrow topped with a mild horseradish crust and turnip marmalade. A Heritage pork chop is grilled to smoky perfection and coddled with pea purée; while the béarnaise burger makes for a primally satisfying meal, especially if paired with a Napa red from the cavernous cellar.

Fish

A3

350 Harbor Dr. (off Bridgeway), Sausalito

Phone: 415-331-3474
Web: www.331fish.com
Prices: $$

Lunch & dinner daily

Casual and family-friendly, this Sausalito seafood spot offers diners the choice of a bright and airy dining room with simple wood furnishings or an alfresco picnic table, both with great views of the harbor. If you dine outdoors, watch out for the local seagulls and crows, who are always ready to snag a snack from your plate (but provide great entertainment for the younger set).

The cooking is fresh and flavorful, from a Dungeness crab roll with butter and chives to crisp Anchor Steam-battered halibut served with house-made wedge fries and tartar sauce. Check the chalkboard for the latest specials, like mussels with chorizo and fennel or grilled Monterey sardines. After dining, visit the raw seafood counter for a selection of items to cook at home.

Frantoio

A2

Italian ✗✗

152 Shoreline Hwy. (off Hwy. 101), Mill Valley

Phone: 415-289-5777
Web: www.frantoio.com
Prices: $$

Dinner nightly

Named after the olive press used in olive oil production throughout Italy, Frantoio is distinguished by its own house-made olive oil, cold-pressed in a hefty granite contraption displayed just off the dining room. Bottled and sold on-site, this stellar product beams atop shavings of *Prosciutto di Parma* with arugula and *mozzarella di Bufala*. Baked sea bass fillets are spread with an herbaceous horseradish crust—big on flavor but gentle on garnishes like chive-infused olive oil.

Though its proximity to Highway 101 and roadside hotels isn't pleasant, an orange-and-charcoal color scheme and lofty ceilings ensure that the surrounds become a quickly fading memory. Also of assistance: perfectly crisp Neapolitan pizzas, quenched by some fine wines.

Insalata's ⊕

Mediterranean ✗✗

B2

120 Sir Francis Drake Blvd. (at Barber Ave.), San Anselmo

Phone: 415-457-7700
Web: www.insalatas.com
Prices: $$

Lunch & dinner daily

San Anselmo restaurateur Chef Heidi Krahling honors her late father, Italo Insalata, at this crowd-pleasing Marin hangout. The *zucca*-orange stucco exterior alludes to the Mediterranean air within. Insalata's upscale setting is framed by lemon-yellow walls hung with grand depictions of nature's bounty setting the scene for the array of fresh and flavorful cuisine to come.

Sparked by Middle Eastern flavors, Insalata's specialties include velvety smooth potato-leek soup made brilliantly green from watercress purée. Also sample grilled lamb skewers drizzled with cumin-yogurt atop crunchy salad and flatbread. The takeout area in the back is stocked with salads, sides, and sandwiches made with house-baked bread. Boxed lunches are a fun, tasty convenience.

Left Bank

French ✗✗

B2

507 Magnolia Ave. (at Ward St.), Larkspur

Phone: 415-927-3331
Web: www.leftbank.com
Prices: $$

Lunch & dinner daily

Sparkling California sunshine and idyllic Marin County setting aside, this French brasserie gets high marks for authenticity. The menu reads like a greatest hits list of classic cuisine, and includes smooth, rich mousse *de foie de volailles* (chicken liver mousse) capped in black truffle aspic with the classic accouterments: baguette croutons, cornichons, grainy mustard, and red onion jam. Steak frites is another timeless treat, best tailed by crème brulée, profiteroles, and oh my, *tarte au citron*—dessert is worth every calorie.

Yellow walls bearing vintage French posters, linen-draped tables, and a stone fireplace warm the inviting interior. The wraparound porch is *the* place to be for soaking up rays while digging into duck *à l'orange*, alfresco.

Le Garage

A3

85 Liberty Ship Way, Ste.109 (off Marinship Way), Sausalito

Phone: 415-332-5625
Web: www.legaragebistrosausalito.com
Prices: $$

Lunch daily
Dinner Mon – Sat

Cultivated French technique meets bold California flavor at this petite canteen, which, as advertised, is housed in a former garage (complete with roll-up doors). Flavorful bouillabaisse packed with fresh dorade, plump scallops, and local shellfish; a beet-and-apple salad with mandarinquats and goat cheese; sealed by a tangy, buttery lemon tart are only some of the appealing menu options.

Le Garage's building was used to construct World War II battleships, but these days, it's more likely to house well-dressed sailors fresh off their yachts in the harbor, as well as lunching locals from the neighboring businesses. With coffee and croissants each morning, brunch on the weekends, and a thoughtful Cal-French wine list, it's a standby at any time of day.

Marché aux Fleurs

B2

23 Ross Common (off Lagunitas Rd.), Ross

Phone: 415-925-9200
Web: www.marcheauxfleursrestaurant.com
Prices: $$

Dinner Tue – Sat

Its dark wood dining room is charming, but Marché aux Fleurs truly comes alive on warm spring and summer evenings, when Marin residents flock to the picturesque hamlet of Ross to enjoy a meal on its front patio. Mediterranean-inspired eats with a California twist are what these patrons are after—imagine soft gnocchi with corn and chanterelles or squash blossom tempura with fresh ricotta and you will start to grasp the picture.

Local couples love it here and though many are regulars, even first-timers receive a friendly welcome from the engaging staff. Groups are everywhere and their smiles omniscient as they savor bacon-wrapped king salmon over sweet corn and green garbanzo succotash; or split bites of warm chocolate cake with vanilla bean ice cream.

Marinitas

Latin American ✗✗

B2

218 Sir Francis Drake Blvd. (at Bank St.), San Anselmo

Lunch & dinner daily

Phone: 415-454-8900
Web: www.marinitas.net
Prices: $$

Thanks to its audible buzz and crowds spilling out onto the placid sidewalks of San Anselmo, this vast cantina can be spotted from a block away. Diners come in big groups to feast on Mexican and Latin cooking, aided by freshly squeezed margaritas and 101 tequilas. The décor is comfortable, with booths that boast a view of Marinitas' fun knickknacks and huge angled mirrors donning the walls.

Considering the crowds, the food here is still made with great care, from that cocktail glass of creamy Peruvian-style salmon ceviche with *aji amarillo* and citrus, to tender braised pork *tinga* over sweet corn polenta. Many items pack a surprising kick, so be sure to have a bowl of guacamole on hand. The moist *tres leches* cake with mango offers a delectable finish.

Molina

Californian ✗✗

B2

17 Madrona St. (bet. Lovell & Throckmorton Aves.), Mill Valley

Dinner nightly

Phone: 415-383-4200
Web: www.molinarestaurant.com
Prices: $$

Small and deeply personal, this Mill Valley newbie is a showcase for Chef Todd Shoberg, who simultaneously mans the wood-fired oven and flips vinyl records that provide the soundtrack (and double as art). With a funky design full of wood and texture, it's almost like eating in the home of a friend—albeit one with great taste in music who really knows his way around the kitchen.

The best of Marin produce stars on the ever-changing menu, which might include gold rice with prawns, pork belly, and a green tomato gazpacho; or tender, crisp-skinned game hen over a Waldorf-esque salad of romaine, blue cheese, walnuts, and Bing cherries. From the wine to the bread, everything is local, yet inventive and compelling: it's a gift both to and from the community.

Nick's Cove

American 🍴🍴

A1

American 🍴🍴

23240 Hwy. 1, Marshall

Phone: 415-663-1033
Web: www.nickscove.com
Prices: $$

Lunch & dinner daily

It's hard not to fall for this sweet waterside retreat in adorable Tomales Bay, which has served as a refuge for city-dwellers for decades. The vintage fuel pump outside is just for looks in this era of hybrid cars, and the updated interior has a lodge-like feel complete with vaulted ceilings, wood-paneled walls, a fireplace, and smattering of hunting trophies.

Unsurprisingly for northern California's oyster capital, the menu is heavy on seafood, from bivalves both raw and grilled to golden-brown Dungeness crab cakes. The white shrimp enchiladas with *salsa roja* and cilantro cream are soft and succulent. Longing for more even after you've finished your meal? Stay the night on their grounds in one of several cozy cottages with a wood-burning stove.

Osteria Stellina

A1

Italian 🍴🍴

11285 Hwy. 1 (at 3rd St.), Point Reyes Station

Phone: 415-663-9988
Web: www.osteriastellina.com
Prices: $$$

Lunch & dinner daily

Point Reyes Station feels like a mythical Western town with barns, weathered clapboards, and the wholesomeness of an area dominated by cheese-making farms. It's all very restful and sitting on a prominent corner is Stellina. This "little star" sports a lively room where easygoing patrons enjoy wonderful artwork and tables graced with tiny vases of fresh flowers.

The impressive menu lists the sources of its various ingredients, which (as expected) are top-notch and bursting with flavor. Let the informed staff guide you toward an enjoyable penne mingled with cannellini beans and braised greens; or delicate petrale sole laced with fingerling potatoes and sweet baby carrots. Seal this unforgettable meal with a velvety milk chocolate panna cotta.

Picco

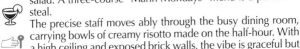

Italian ✗✗

B2

320 Magnolia Ave. (at King St.), Larkspur

Phone: 415-924-0300

Web: www.restaurantpicco.com

Prices: $$

Dinner nightly

Picco is Italian for "summit," and this charming Larkspur hilltop home has long been a beacon among Marin county diners. Chef/owner Bruce Hill is a true local-food devotee; his Italian-influenced fare heaps on Marin ingredients like the fresh turnips that dot his silky-smooth duck *tortelli*; or the Meyer lemon yogurt and beets that sit atop a nourishing kale salad. A three-course "Marin Mondays" menu is a particular steal.

The precise staff moves ably through the busy dining room, carrying bowls of creamy risotto made on the half-hour. With a high ceiling and exposed brick walls, the vibe is graceful but never fussy, making this the perfect setting for couples and groups of friends who congregate here.

Also check out Pizzeria Picco next door.

Pizzalina

Pizza ✗

B2

914 Sir Francis Drake Blvd. (at Sunny Hills Dr.), San Anselmo

Phone: 415-256-9780

Web: www.pizzalina.com

Prices: $$

Lunch & dinner daily

Buried in a corner of the Red Hill Shopping Center, this rustic, casual, yet very comfy pizzeria oozes *molto* charm via distressed wood walls and a marble dining counter. An open kitchen keeps all eyes at the hopping communal tables focused on the eye-catching wood-burning oven. The nose will follow once it catches a whiff of pies, spread with mozzarella, olive oil, meats, and vegetables from local producers, and named after old Marin railroad stops—who wants the Baltimore Park?

A versatile wine medley, much of it on tap, arrives in cute glass beakers, adding to the warm, classy vibe. For extra bliss, pair this with a roasted pear, *burrata*, and arugula salad; then dive into a seasonal pizza; and finish with rich and hearty house-made meatballs.

Marin

Poggio

A3

Italian ✗✗

777 Bridgeway (at Bay St.), Sausalito

Phone: 415-332-7771

Web: www.poggiotrattoria.com

Prices: $$

Lunch & dinner daily

Situated along Sausalito's main drag at the base of the Casa Madrona hotel, Poggio will be celebrating over a decade in business. And yet, its wide-ranging Italian menu is far from tired. The dining room is plush with mahogany-lined archways and lavish booths, but the most desirable seats are out on the front terrace with views of the quaint harbor and yacht club. Sunny by day and heated at night, it's a great place to savor a crisp pizza, bottle of wine, and watch the world go by.

A meal at this upscale trattoria might include sautéed day boat scallops with sunchoke purée and pancetta; trailed by braised veal tortellini in a nutty *Parmigiano* broth. Roasted halibut with seared artichokes (sourced from the restaurant's own garden) is an all-time delight.

R'Noh Thai

B2

Thai ✗✗

1000 Magnolia Ave. (bet. Frances & Murray Aves.), Larkspur

Phone: 415-925-0599

Web: www.rnohthai.com

Prices:

Lunch Mon – Sat
Dinner nightly

Generous portions and thoughtful preparations are the key ingredients at this Thai restaurant, which occupies a long wooden building overlooking a small creek. The interior is warm and inviting, with bright skylights, oil paintings of water lilies, and a fireplace crackling away.

R'Noh's popularity is most evident at lunch, when local business people drop in for the daily special of a light curry with salad and rice. Ginger chicken, packed with mushrooms and tender meat, is a more mild but still flavorful option. The menu expands slightly at dinner, offering delicious plates like a crispy shrimp roll filled with plump prawns. Highly attentive servers can recommend a wine from the short list, or try their supremely thirst-quenching homemade lemonade.

Sir and Star 😊

American ✗✗

A1

10000 Sir Francis Drake Blvd. (at Hwy. 1), Olema

Dinner Wed – Sun

Phone: 415-663-1034
Web: www.sirandstar.com
Prices: $$

The dynamic duo of Chef/owners Daniel DeLong and Margaret Gradé have been missed in Marin's culinary scene since their previous restaurant, Manka's Inverness Lodge, was destroyed in a fire. Now, they're cooking again in this quaint yet quirky dining room, this time situated in the historic Olema Inn. It's a roadhouse, but a very quiet one—so don't bring your rowdy pals.

Simplicity and hyper-local fare are the focus here with dishes like Tomales Bay oyster shooters with wee ribbons of kohlrabi; spring onion soup with *gougères*; or luscious pork tenderloin with Bolinas beets and artichokes. A medieval fireplace (in winter) or tree-shaded patio (in summer) provides a romantic setting to unplug and relax over a wine list dominated by Marin grapes.

Sushi Ran 😊

Japanese ✗✗

A3

107 Caledonia St. (bet. Pine & Turney Sts.), Sausalito

Lunch Mon – Fri
Dinner nightly

Phone: 415-332-3620
Web: www.sushiran.com
Prices: $$

Sushi fans have long flocked to Sausalito to dine at this pleasant, if sparsely appointed, Japanese room armed with genuine warmth. A mixed crowd fills the packed-together tables, murmuring gently over sips of green tea in ceramic mugs or the impressive variety of sake and wine. Despite a prime location on Caledonia, the city's main shopping street, the vibe here is quiet and never boisterous.

At Sushi Ran the fish is as pristine as the execution, which may reveal smoked trout salad, sweet with carrots yet punchy with yuzu and miso. Prices are elevated but so is the freshness in sushi like *ana ebi*, *kani*, and crab; or hamachi and *maguro* sashimi. In light of *aji nori* potatoes hit perfectly with salt and truffle oil, the inept service is pardoned.

Peninsula

Peninsula

A COLLISION OF CULTURES

Situated to the south of the city, the San Francisco Peninsula separates the Bay from the expansive Pacific Ocean. While it may not be known across the globe for stellar chefs and pioneering Californian cooking, the Peninsula boasts an incredibly diverse and rich Asian culture. Area eateries and numerous markets reflect this region's melting-pot and continue to draw locals for authentic international cuisines. Those in need of a taste from the East should join Korean natives at **Kukje Super Market** as they scoop up fresh seafood, links of *longaniza*, and a host of other prepared delicacies. Or practice the art of chopstick wielding at one of the many Japanese sushi bars, ramen houses, and *izakayas*. Filipino foodies tickle their fancy with an impressive selection of traditional breads and pastries at **Valerio's Tropical Bake Shop** in Daly City. Fittingly set in a Filipino-dominated quarter referred to as "**Little Manila**," Valerio's is famously revered as *the* best bakery around. Beyond the Far East, sugar junkies of the Western variety savor classic Danish pastries at Burlingame's **Copenhagen Bakery**, also applauded for creamy special occasion cakes. Over in San Mateo, Italians can't miss a stop

at **Pasta Pasta** for freshly made shapes, homemade sauces, and salads that are both fulfilling and easy to put together at home. If your domestic skills leave much to be desired, charming **La Biscotteria** has premium, hand-crafted Italian pastries and cookies, including cannoli, *amaretti*, *sfogliatelle*, and biscotti in an assortment of flavors. This precious gem in Redwood City also sells beautiful hand-painted Deruta ceramics imported from Umbria.

The Peninsula is also home to a large Mexican-American population. Their taste for home can be gratified at such authentic taquerias as **El Grullense** in Redwood City; **El Palenque** in San Mateo; and **Mexcal Taqueria** in Menlo Park. Just as **Gabriel & Daniel's Mexican Grill** in the Burlingame Golf Center clubhouse is an ideal place to unwind after playing a round out on the plush course, dive-y **Back A Yard** in Menlo Park is forever popular among foodies craving flavorful Caribbean cuisine. Pescetarians know that **Barbara's Fish Trap** in Princeton by the Sea is a sought-after "catch" for fish 'n chips by the harbor, whereas pig trumps fish at **Gorilla Barbeque**. Here, fat-frilled pork ribs are all the rage, especially when served out of an orange railroad car parked on Cabrillo Highway in Pacifica.

SUMMER'S BOUNTY

In addition to harboring some of the Bay Area's most authentic Cantonese dens and dim sum houses, Millbrae is a lovely spot to raise one last toast to summer. In fact, **The Millbrae Art & Wine Festival** is a profusion of wicked fairground eats—from meltingly tender cheesesteaks and Cajun-style corndogs, to fennel-infused sausages and everything in between. Motivated home chefs head to **Draeger's Market** in San Mateo to pick up some wine and cheese for dinner, and perhaps even sign up for cooking classes in a range of basic to highly specialized subjects. When in this 'hood, be sure to revel in a riot of Japanese goods at **Suruki Market**. Half Moon Bay is a coastal city big on sustainable produce; and in keeping with this philosophy, residents prepare for cozy evenings indoors by loading up on local fruits and vegetables from one of the many roadside stands on Route 92. Find them also scanning the bounty at **Coastside Farmer's Market**, known to unveil such Pescadero treasures as Harley Farms goat cheese and organic eggs from **Early Bird Ranch**.

Peninsula

219

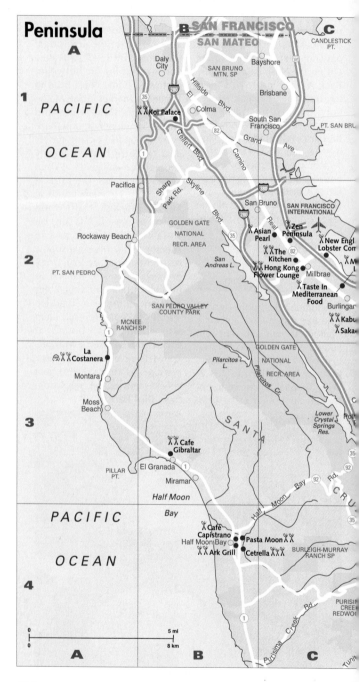

Peninsula

A

B SAN FRANCISCO

SAN MATEO

C

PACIFIC

OCEAN

CANDLESTICK PT.

Daly City

SAN BRUNO MTN. SP

Bayshore

Brisbane

Koi Palace

Colma

South San Francisco

PT. SAN BRU.

Grand Ave

Pacifica

Sharp Park Rd.

Skyline Blvd.

San Bruno

SAN FRANCISCO INTERNATIONAL

GOLDEN GATE NATIONAL RECR. AREA

Zen Peninsula

Asian Pearl

New Engl Lobster Con

Rockaway Beach

PT. SAN PEDRO

San Andreas L.

The Kitchen

M L

Hong Kong Flower Lounge

Millbrae

Taste In Mediterranean Food

SAN PEDRO VALLEY COUNTY PARK

MCNEE RANCH SP

Burlingar

Kabu

Saka

La Costanera

GOLDEN GATE NATIONAL RECR. AREA

Pilarcitos L.

Pilarcitos Cr.

Montara

Moss Beach

SANTA

Lower Crystal Springs Res.

Roll

PILLAR PT.

Cafe Gibraltar

El Granada

Miramar

Half Moon

Bay

Half Moon Bay

92

Rd.

CRU

Café Capistrano

PACIFIC

Pasta Moon

OCEAN

Ark Grill

Cetrella

BURLEIGH-MURRAY RANCH SP

PURISIM CREE REDWO

Purisima Creek Rd.

0   5 mi

0   8 km

A

B

C

220

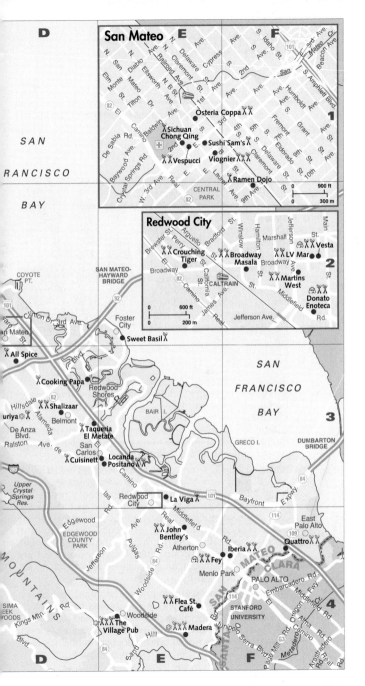

All Spice ⁕

Californian 🍴🍴

D3

1602 El Camino Real (bet. Barneson & Borel Aves.), San Mateo

Phone: 650-627-4303   Dinner Tue – Sat
Web: www.allspicerestaurant.com
Prices: $$

This quaint, two-story Victorian with burgundy trim is tucked back from El Camino Real, so pay attention or completely miss the almost hidden entrance. After a warm greeting, you will be led to a seat in one of their cozy interconnecting rooms. Then take the time to peruse Chef Sachin Chopra's superb carte of California-centric Indian fare.

A roaring fireplace, soft colors, and modern art are an idyllic backdrop for tasty starters like an oblong, golden-brown bread fritter wrapped around spiced potatoes, cheese, and mushrooms, offered with mint chutney for an authentically light and cooling union. Main courses shine, as in tender, well-seasoned duck breast artistically arranged with chestnut purée, deep green dollops of nasturtium leaf coulis, and *berbere*-spiced potato gratin. Each element is not just delicious, but a thoughtful and sublime balance of smoky, sweet, and salty flavors.

End with the chef's tropically inspired treats, including a glass "snowglobe" of airy lemongrass cake, mango custard, and coconut sorbet, all sealed beneath a white chocolate lid—until it is melted tableside when the server pours a rich orange- lemongrass- and white chocolate-sauce. It's date-night certified!

Ark Grill

Indian ✗✗

B4

724 Main St. (bet. Correas & Filbert St.), Half Moon Bay

Phone: 650-560-8152
Web: www.arkgrill.com
Prices: $$

Lunch Fri – Sun
Dinner Tue – Sun

This North Indian spot offers a lunch buffet and à la carte dinner experience that is worth the trek to Half Moon Bay. Set in a converted old house that has a front bay window and small porch, Ark Grill is flooded with natural light and exudes a homey ambience.

In fact, you may as well be sitting in your *nani*'s kitchen with their roster of boldly spiced and flavored fare. Begin with tasty and crispy-fried samosas stuffed with spiced potatoes and peas, before moving on to entrées like plump, succulent prawns and potatoes stewed in a well-spiced *vindaloo*; or tender chunks of marinated chicken in a creamy *tikka masala*—both the perfect foil for a charred and chewy garlic-cilantro *naan*. Need to turn the heat down? Check in with the obliging staff.

Asian Pearl

Chinese ✗

C2

1671 El Camino Real (at Park Pl.), Millbrae

Phone: 650-616-8288
Web: N/A
Prices: ☙

Lunch & dinner daily

Asian Pearl is lauded for its dim sum, but the dinner menu of mostly Cantonese-style dishes is really where the restaurant shines. The large banquet tables are perfect for groups, while smaller rooms can be portioned off for private parties. The staff is curt, but the food is worth it. A back wall lined with tanks full of crustaceans, fish, and mollusks will get your appetite going.

Start with a superbly crisp and crackly-skinned duck that was brined before roasting; then a clay pot filled with tender slices of braised beef in a thick soy- and oyster-sauce—enoki mushrooms are tossed in tableside as if to further tease your taste buds. Too full to move? No worries. Tender pumpkin and taro root simmered in coconut milk are also served over the burner.

Broadway Masala

F2

Indian ✗✗

2397 Broadway (at Winslow St.), Redwood City

Phone: 650-369-9000
Web: www.broadwaymasala.net
Prices: $$

Lunch & dinner daily

Indian food gets its name in lights at Broadway Masala, offering both traditional and modern interpretations of the country's cuisine. The kitchen serves up a fine chicken biryani, full of flavorful spices, tender chicken, and fluffy rice; and the spicy lamb *rogan josh* is equally sumptuous. The modern menu is full of quirky twists: think Cajun chicken *tikka*, spinach-tofu *kofta*, and a smoky *kulcha* filled with finely chopped aplewood-smoked bacon.

The long, narrow space boasts a stylish décor, with contemporary light fixtures, stacked stone pillars, and decorative wine barrels here and there. A side bar offers a solid selection of draft beer and wines, and when the sun is shining, a few tables out front offer people-watching on the namesake thoroughfare.

Café Capistrano

B4

Mexican ✗

523 Church St. (at Miramontes St.), Half Moon Bay

Phone: 650-726-7699
Web: N/A
Prices: ⊜⊜

Lunch & dinner daily

Chef/owner Arturo Mul grew up on the Yucatán peninsula, and the traditional Mayan dishes of his youth are now the backbone of this cute café in the heart of Half Moon Bay. Housed in an older home surrounded by gardens and a small side deck, the spot is warm, homey, and, to the delight of local families, off most tourists' radars.

Start with a Yucatecan appetizer plate of *salbutes* (fried tortillas topped with grilled chicken, pickled onion, and cabbage slaw) and empanadas. Then dig into the smoky pork enchiladas, crowned with cheese and garlicky red chili sauce, or the tender grilled chicken adobo. Be cautious with the house-made habanero hot sauce: its Mayan name, *xni-pec*, means "dog nose" and it'll have yours running if you exceed a few drops.

Cafe Gibraltar

Mediterranean ✗✗

425 Avenue Alhambra (at Palma St.), El Granada

Phone: 650-560-9039
Web: www.cafegibraltar.com
Prices: $$$

Lunch Sun
Dinner Tue – Sun

All the exquisite flavors of the Mediterranean come together at this local favorite in the sleepy coastal town of El Granada, from Spanish and Moroccan to Persian and Greek. Work up an appetite with a pre-dinner stroll along the water's edge, then watch the sun set over the Pacific from a table up front— or slip off your shoes and lounge on cushions at the tented platform in the rear. The rustic décor includes a roaring wood-fired oven, copper pots, and herb bouquets.

Garlic, olives, lemon, and couscous are recurring menu players in dishes like braised chicken with green olives and preserved lemon over fluffy couscous, or house-made flatbread with an assortment of dips (hummus, tzatziki, piquillo pepper *ensaladita*, and savory tomato jam among them).

Cetrella

Mediterranean ✗✗✗

845 Main St. (at Spruce St.), Half Moon Bay

Phone: 650-726-4090
Web: www.cetrella.com
Prices: $$$

Lunch Sun
Dinner Tue – Sun

In the beach town of Half Moon Bay lives stylish and sophisticated Cetrella. Decorated like a Mediterranean villa with stucco walls and vaulted ceilings, there is even a temperature-controlled cheese room bound to gratify those dairy fanatics. The best seats in the house are those in the private wine cellar or around the roaring fireplace in the main dining room, making this a beloved destination for celebrations, groups, and date-night.

The enticing *carte du jour* is produced with skill, and may reveal such delights as a velvety green garlic soup, enriched with cream and delicately garnished with a prosciutto chip; or a braised lamb shank with tender root vegetables. Cardamom panna cotta with strawberry salad is the best way to seal this lovely meal.

Cooking Papa

D3

Chinese ✕

949 Edgewater Blvd., Ste. A (at Beach Park Blvd.), Foster City

Phone: 650-577-1830   Lunch & dinner daily
Web: www.mycookingpapa.com
Prices:

Cantonese and Hong Kong-style dishes draw weekend crowds to the sleek and minimally adorned Cooking Papa, set back in a shopping center alongside one of the Foster City canals. Inside, find expats clustered around faux-granite tables armed with dark wood chairs and framed by a wall of windows running the length of the space—every seat has a glorious water view.

A vast menu features all types of dishes, from simple yet heart-warming *congee* and soft tofu braised with vegetables, to sweet and salty barbecued pork—honey glazed and intensely moist. Americanized standards like hot-and-sour soup may disappoint, so it's best to think outside the box and get the crispy, beignet-like egg puffs for dessert: they're perfect with strong black tea.

Crouching Tiger

E2

Chinese ✕✕

2644 Broadway St. (bet. El Camino Real & Perry St.), Redwood City

Phone: 650-298-8881   Lunch & dinner daily
Web: www.crouchingtigerrestaurant.com
Prices:

The heat is on at Redwood City's palace of Sichuan fare, where spice-hounds come for a dose of the chili-packed Chongqing chicken, *mapo* tofu, and other regional specialties. Sure, there may be blander options, but steaming platters of green chili-topped, richly flavored cumin lamb or plump prawns and crisp sautéed vegetables in hot garlic sauce are enough to induce a love of spice.

Crouching Tiger's midday crowd can be its own fire-breathing dragon, with droves of local workers packing the tables for reasonably priced lunch specials with soup, salad, and rice. Large, round tables are great for big groups (kids too). The chic interior with its dark wood furnishings, art, and drum lanterns, is definitely a step up from the standard Chinese joint.

Cuisinett

French 🍴

1105 San Carlos Ave. (at El Camino Real), San Carlos

Phone: 650-453-3390
Web: www.cuisinett.com
Prices: $$

Lunch daily
Dinner Mon – Sat

French restaurants aren't often known for their chill vibe or affordability, but this casual counter-service charmer proves otherwise, with comforting quiches, salads, and plats at down-to-earth prices. Diners customize with mix-and-match sauces like Dijon mustard or Cognac black pepper to pair with a steak and choice of sides.

Families, kids, and those with dogs in tow can be seen noshing on a refreshing beet-and-endive salad with blue cheese and walnut vinaigrette; or the perfectly cooked roasted chicken with red wine sauce and herbed peas and carrots, all skillfully prepared with the French chef's authentic hand. Note: there will be butter.

Save room for the luscious, flaky *tarte au citron*, or beautiful raspberry and salted caramel macarons.

Donato Enoteca 😊

Italian 🍴🍴

1041 Middlefield Rd. (bet. Jefferson Ave. & Main St.), Redwood City

Phone: 650-701-1000
Web: www.donatoenoteca.com
Prices: $$

Lunch & dinner daily

Donato Enoteca, settled in the heart of Redwood City and just steps away from City Hall, oozes with rustic ambience, from its wood-beamed dining room to the counter facing the busy open kitchen. The latter is perfect for solo diners or those who wish to watch the cooks up close.

The seasonally inspired menu might begin with such wonderfully simple pasta courses as *spaghetti alle vongole* tossed with spicy Calabrian chilies. Expect mains like *controfiletto scalogno*—tender sirloin steak served with roasted scallions and fresh rosemary—and sides of organic *fagiolini* flavored with caramelized *guanciale*. Tiramisu layered with espresso-soaked ladyfingers makes for a luscious finale; and the wine list features a good selection of Italian varietals.

Fey 😊

E4

Chinese ✗✗

1368 El Camino Real (bet. Glenwood & Oak Grove Aves.), Menlo Park

Phone: 650-324-8888   Lunch & dinner daily
Web: www.feyrestaurant.com
Prices: $$

30 Rock comediennes are nowhere to be found at this elegant, upscale Chinese restaurant, but you'll grin all the same once you taste their outstanding tea-smoked duck, roasted to order with meltingly tender meat and shatteringly crisp skin. It's the first of many Sichuan delights to be had, from fiery *mapo* tofu to whole fish piled with hot peppers, numbing peppercorns, and fragrant chili oil. For the best in food, stick to the Sichuan menu; Americanized orders can be met with indifference.

The contemporary dining room features chrome orb lights, cushioned booths, and large tables with built-in heating elements for their signature hot pot offerings. A private room lures Silicon Valley businessmen and big tables in the back cradle families and groups.

Flea St. Café

E4

Californian ✗✗

3607 Alameda de las Pulgas (at Avy Ave.), Menlo Park

Phone: 650-854-1226   Dinner Tue – Sun
Web: www.cooleatz.com
Prices: $$$

Beloved Flea St. Café in Menlo Park fills up early and stays packed until closing time with professor-types and well-to-do couples dressed up for date-night. Located on a sloping hill, the homey bungalow features tiered dining areas, pastel walls, white moldings, and cozy candlelit tables. One of the few bar tables may be open, but reservations are necessary for the dining room.

Flea St. delivers in-season, local, and sustainable ingredients, as in a smooth and earthy roasted pumpkin soup topped with pork belly. Expect the professional service staff to bring the likes of Dungeness crab and sweet potato cake; pan-roasted black cod with nutty wild rice, butternut squash, and crispy leeks; or honey-sweet and gently floral lavender panna cotta.

Hong Kong Flower Lounge

C2

Chinese ✕✕

51 Millbrae Ave. (at El Camino Real), Millbrae

Phone: 650-692-6666   Lunch & dinner daily
Web: www.mayflower-seafood.com
Prices: $$

An iconic presence in Millbrae, the Flower Lounge's pink exterior and green pagoda-style roof are hard to miss—not that the generations of locals who have been coming here for decades have any trouble finding it. At 500 seats, weekend dim sum can be a zoo with long waits, noisy groups, and carts zooming everywhere. The crowds come for reliable favorites like moist barbecue pork buns with a sticky-sweet filling, tender turnip cakes with fluffy eggs and spicy-garlicky XO chili sauce, as well as juicy roasted duck with perfectly crisp skin. Don't see desired dishes like the flaky warm egg tarts on the carts? Just ask, and they will arrive.

Cantonese-style dinner service is quieter, but be sure to call ahead as the restaurant often hosts private events.

Iberia

F4

Spanish ✕✕

1026 Alma St. (at Ravenswood Ave.), Menlo Park

Phone: 650-325-8981   Lunch Mon – Sat
Web: www.iberiarestaurant.com   Dinner nightly
Prices: $$

Spain has landed in Menlo Park, in the form of a fetching brick bungalow on Alma Street. It's a bonanza of bona fide Spanish heart and soul here at Iberia, where traditional tapas, a homey interior, and adjacent food and import shop delight in all things *Español*. Seating options range from a gorgeous garden patio; sun-drenched dining room decked in artwork and linen-topped tables; or the impossibly adorable bar set atop hard wood floors.

Beneath the glow of an intricate wine cellar (that hangs overhead), tables are awash with the likes of *tortilla de patatas*, mini pan-fried potato "omelets;" crispy-fried Dungeness crab fritters; or smoky-sweet chorizo-stuffed dates wrapped in bacon. Not feeling the tapas? Go for the seafood and chicken paella instead.

229

John Bentley's

E4

2915 El Camino Real (bet. Berkshire Ave. & E. Selby Ln.), Redwood City

Phone: 650-365-7777
Web: www.johnbentleys.com
Prices: $$

Lunch Mon – Fri
Dinner Mon – Sat

Set on a quiet stretch of El Camino Real, a vine-covered trellis walkway leads to the stately John Bentley's. A squad of date-night duos and locals from around the way seeking contemporary American cooking have found a fine refuge in this quaint, very classic tavern, whose dark wood wainscoting and oil paintings recall an earlier era of power-lunching. But now along with those wealthy retirees, lunching ladies and even families with well-behaved children come to savor simple, well-executed dishes like flaky broiled Loch Duart salmon set over sautéed spinach drizzled with basil oil.
Arched banquettes make for the best seats in the house and are ideal for savoring each bite of the grilled watermelon Napoleon, sandwiched with Dungeness crab and avocado.

Kabul

C2

1101 Burlingame Ave. (at California Dr.), Burlingame

Phone: 650-343-2075
Web: www.kabulcuisine.com
Prices: $$

Lunch & dinner daily

Though it's settled on a hopping corner in Burlingame's main shopping district and steps from the Caltrain station, this bright, light-filled spot transports diners to Afghanistan with tasty and unique offerings. Hearty *sambosa-e-goushti* (fried dough pockets filled with lamb and chickpeas); *kabab-e-murgh* (tender-charred chicken skewers atop *pallaw*); or sautéed pumpkin with a rich yogurt sauce draws business types at lunch and local families for dinner.
Irrespective of time, service is always casual, despite the white tablecloths. Diners must exercise care not to load up on the fluffy flatbread with a green chili-and-herb chutney that's served at first, lest they miss out on a final course of syrup-soaked baklava studded with chopped walnuts.

The Kitchen

C2

Chinese ✕✕

279 El Camino Real (at La Cruz Ave.), Millbrae

Phone: 650-692-9688 Lunch & dinner daily
Web: www.thekitchenmillbrae.com
Prices: 🪙🪙

Brimming with Chinese diners and clans of corporate types, this chic Millbrae joint entices those hankering for tasty and heart-warming dim sum. While the décor may boast only a few frills (banquet-style tables, bright lights, and white walls with grey wainscoting), the menu is replete with specialties starring fresh seafood—note the wall of fish and crustacean tanks.

Once inside the airy space, start demolishing sure bets like caramelized, crispy roasted duck folded into steamed *bao* with hoisin; or spareribs glazed in a Sichuan chili sauce. But we suggest taking a hint from the crowd and digging into some dim sum. Try the cold jelly fish and seaweed salad tossed in a rice wine dressing; or go for golden perfection in crispy pork dumplings.

Koi Palace

B1

Chinese ✕✕

365 Gellert Blvd. (bet. Hickey & Serramonte Blvds.), Daly City

Phone: 650-992-9000 Lunch & dinner daily
Web: www.koipalace.com
Prices: $$

Long regarded as one of the Bay Area's best spots for dim sum, Koi Palace continues to earn its serious waits (guaranteed on weekends, and common at weekday lunch). The dining room is a step up from its competition, with shallow koi ponds weaving between tables, high ceilings, and huge tables to accommodate the Chinese-American families celebrating big occasions.

They come to share plates of perfectly lacquered, smoky-salty roasted suckling pig or sticky rice noodle rolls encasing plump shrimp, sesame oil, and minced ginger. Not far behind, find lotus leaves stuffed with glutinous rice, dried scallop, and roast pork, as well as big pots of jasmine tea. Save room for desserts like the fluffy almond cream steamed buns and flaky, caramelized custard tarts.

La Costanera 🐷

Peruvian ✗✗

A3

8150 Cabrillo Hwy. (bet. 1st & 2nd Sts.), Montara

Phone: 650-728-1600   Dinner Tue – Sun
Web: www.lacostanerarestaurant.com
Prices: $$

Set atop one of the most beautiful perches in the entire Bay Area, La Costanera affords diners stunning panoramas of the pristine northern California coastline and the Pacific Ocean. It's appropriately walled with windows, and the two-tiered contemporary dining room ensures every table in the large space has a view. A lovely patio is an option on warmer days. La Costanera offers an extensive collection of Peruvian dishes with an emphasis on seafood, ranging from *causas* (round balls of potato purée topped with Dungeness crab, seared scallops, and bold, delicious sauces) to paella filled with fresh shrimp and calamari, sliced peppers, and Peruvian cheese. Be sure to sample the creative cocktails, which nicely utilize Peruvian liquors and juices.

La Viga

Mexican ✗

E3

1772 Broadway (bet. Beech & Maple Sts.), Redwood City

Phone: 650-679-8141   Lunch & dinner Tue – Sun
Web: www.lavigarestaurant.com
Prices: 💲💲

Named after Mexico City's massive seafood market, La Viga is a Redwood City favorite for oceanic fare with a Latin twist. Wedged between an industrial area and downtown, the basic but cheerful dining room draws both blue- and white-collar workers for heaping tacos—soft white corn tortillas stuffed with fried snapper fillet, cabbage, and chipotle *crema*; or crisp prawns with tomatillo-garlic sauce and *pico de gallo*. At the dinner hour, local residents stream in for the famed *camarones picantes*, a sizable mound of al dente *fideos* studded with plump prawns bathed in a spicy tomato sauce. With such fresh ingredients and bold flavors, the low prices and generous portions are particularly pleasing—and allow room for a creamy, delicate flan to finish.

Locanda Positano

E3

Italian ✗✗

617 Laurel St. (bet. Cherry St. & San Carlos Ave.), San Carlos

Phone: 650-591-5700
Web: www.locanda-positano.com
Prices: $$

Lunch & dinner daily

Take a trip to Napoli with a casual Italian meal along the quaint San Carlos strip. Owned by a native and staffed mostly by Italians, it's a perennial favorite among locals for savoring seasonal starters like peaches with burrata, then digging into Neapolitan-style pies like the *pizza con uovo* with salty pancetta, earthy wild mushrooms, and a luscious slow-cooked egg.

Toothsome *scialatelli* pasta with tender clams and cherry tomatoes in a white wine sauce is another simple yet tasty choice. Desserts shouldn't be missed, especially Mamma's tiramisu and the traditional ricotta cheesecake. The *bambini* are courted with their own menu of mini pizzas and simple pastas.

The sleek space with contemporary furnishings is grown-up, but not overly upscale.

LV Mar

F2

Latin American ✗✗

2042 Broadway (bet. Jefferson & Main Sts.), Redwood City

Phone: 650-241-3111
Web: www.lvmar.com
Prices: $$

Lunch & dinner Mon – Sat

Located just a few blocks from its casual cousin La Viga, LV Mar is worlds away in terms of cuisine, offering sophisticated contemporary Latin American fare. The space is appropriately stylish, with slate floors, high ceilings, and paintings of ingredients on the walls. Business lunchers fill the tables by day, giving way to couples and families in the evening.

Local produce shines in dishes like the *pescado con pepitas*, a flaky sea bass fillet encrusted in pumpkin seeds and served over buttery *huitlacoche*-potato purée. The *gordita de pato* encases rich duck meat in a golden puff pastry with port and dried cherries, while caramelized Brussels sprouts boast a Manchego-and-*arbol chile* vinaigrette. For the time-pressed, tortas are available at lunch.

Madera ✿

E4

2825 Sand Hill Rd. (at I-280), Menlo Park

Phone: 650-561-1540
Web: www.maderasandhill.com
Prices: $$$$

Lunch & dinner daily

Built to impress, the Rosewood Sand Hill hotel is a Silicon Valley stunner where panoramic views of the Santa Cruz mountains are in spectacular abundance. Madera's terrace overlooking the pool and gardens is a popular scene at lunch. Come sunset, the vibe revs up as tech titans arrive to claim their spot in this lodge-chic room replete with a toasty fireplace to counter the evening's chill. Vaulted ceilings and an exhibition kitchen maximize the stylish layout.

Dinner best showcases this kitchen's chops, when elevated cooking incorporates all the traits of contemporary cuisine. Rich duck tortellini is a smart choice off the focused menu, arriving dressed with plump morels and truffle-heady pecorino tartufo. Seared halibut shows up on a pool of chlorophyll-vivid, dandelion greens purée along with roasted cauliflower and sweet mussels. A silken browned butter sauce poured over this flaky fish makes for a fantastic finishing touch.

Fresh talent in the pastry department ensures that a meal here ends on a high note. Compositions may read as ambitious, but proof is in the pudding, or rather the toasted anise seed- and dark chocolate mousse-topped hazelnut praline with ginger beer-citron sorbet.

Magda Luna

C2

Mexican 🍴

1199 Broadway, Ste. 2 (bet. Chula Vista & Laguna Aves.), Burlingame

Phone: 650-393-4207   Lunch & dinner Tue – Sun
Web: www.magdalunacafe.com
Prices: 🐝

"Mexican food with a conscience" is on the menu at this newish café in Burlingame, which prides itself on vegetable-heavy, oil-light dishes made with hormone-free, sustainably raised meats. Located on the busy main drag, the restaurant is full of vibrant color and authentic details like decorative murals of Dia de los Muertos-style skulls.

Though healthy, the food here doesn't skimp on flavor. Start with a bowl of warm tortilla chips and a duo of salsas, then dive into a selection of tacos, burritos, and quesadillas. Entrées include *enchiladas Michoacanas* in a spicy-smoky *guajillo* chile sauce, which pair nicely with a fruity house-made *agua fresca*. A welcoming staff and a special menu for *los niños* also make it a great choice for families.

Martins West

F2

Gastropub 🍴🍴

831 Main St. (bet. Broadway & Stambaugh St.), Redwood City

Phone: 650-366-4366   Lunch & dinner Mon – Sat
Web: www.martinswestgp.com
Prices: $$

This gastropub brings old-world charm to Redwood City with a rich wood bar, wax-dripped candelabras, and exposed brick walls. Yet it shines with new-world edge through brushed aluminum chairs, exposed steel beams, and reclaimed materials.

This is all reflected in a kitchen dedicated to contemporary interpretations of pub classics—think golden-fried Scotch quail eggs, their velvety yolks infused with garlic, fennel, and a touch of pepper. Served with updated farm-to-table fashion, "rarebit" becomes thick slices of toasted artisanal bread with savory fenugreek béchamel and tomato-mozzarella salad.

A subdued lunch crowd walks in from the nearby courthouse and city offices. Cocktail hour and dinner have that deliciously rambunctious vibe, befitting a pub.

New England Lobster Company

Seafood ✗

C2

824 Cowan Rd. (off Old Bayshore Hwy.), Burlingame

Phone: 650-443-1559
Web: www.newenglandlobster.net
Prices: $$

Lunch & dinner daily

A wholesale supplier of lobster, crab, and other seafood to the Bay Area since 1986, this semi-industrial complex now offers irreproachably fresh, Californian-influenced fare. The freeway-adjacent space is enormous, with tanks of crabs and lobsters, oysters and clams for shucking, and picnic tables both inside and out.

Begin with house-made potato chip "nachos" heaped with fresh crab meat, black beans, and Monterey Jack cheese. Or, just dive into a pitch-perfect lobster roll accented by creamy avocado and crumbled bacon. New England classics include silky, smoky lobster corn chowder and fluffy whoopie pies.

Be sure to check out the flat-screen TV, broadcasting their seafood as it arrives in the huge central holding tanks, just outside.

Osteria Coppa

Italian ✗✗

E1

139 S. B St. (bet. 1st & 2nd Aves.), San Mateo

Phone: 650-579-6021
Web: www.osteriacoppa.com
Prices: $$

Lunch & dinner daily

In a sea of San Mateo restaurants, Osteria Coppa's skillfully prepared, rustic, and seasonally influenced Italian cooking stands above the pack. Filled with corporate sorts at lunchtime and families for casual dinners or brunch, the wood space is rustic and always flooded with natural light. The back hallway brings glimpses into the kitchen, where blistered, chewy pies topped with garlicky housemade pork sausage, smoky speck, and earthy crimini mushrooms are emerging. While wood-fired pizzas are popular here, also try pastas like house-made *tagliolini* full of chopped Early Girl tomatoes, olive oil, garlic, and basil.

An L-shaped bar is a nice perch to dine solo with a glass of wine, or savor a dessert like the mascarpone-rich butterscotch *budino*.

Pasta Moon

B4

Italian ✗✗

315 Main St. (at Mill St.), Half Moon Bay

Phone: 650-726-5125   Lunch & dinner daily
Web: www.pastamoon.com
Prices: $$

It's definitely *amore* when this (Pasta) moon hits your eye. Located on the main drag in charming Half Moon Bay, Pasta Moon is a sure bet for—yup, you guessed it—pasta!
Its design can feel like a haphazard and half-finished mix of spaces that afford views of pasta-making during trips to the restrooms; but after a few bites, you won't care that the owner needs to find an architect—stat. Dreamy pastas along with homemade pizzas and breads are divine. You can't go wrong with anything on this Californian-Italian menu. The lasagna strays from grandma's standard with impressive results and is packed with rich, creamy flavor; while crispy *fritto misto* and a Brussels sprout salad tossed with pancetta and cannellini beans are beloved at all times.

Quattro

F4

Italian ✗✗

2050 University Ave. (at I-101), East Palo Alto

Phone: 650-470-2889   Lunch & dinner daily
Web: www.quattrorestaurant.com
Prices: $$$

Whether or not you're staying at the Four Seasons, swing by this swanky lair, just off of the hotel's lobby. Its airy atmosphere is marked by a sleek design, natural light, and stone walls displaying a collection of fascinating sculptures.
Quattro's contemporary Italian cuisine is served as a four-course menu (antipasti, primi, secondi, dolci) with an option to mix and match dishes depending on appetite level. Sample the gem lettuce salad with smoked *ricotta salata*, shaved baby carrots, summer squash, and pea tendrils. The outstanding ribeye is a must—grilled and served with black pepper beef jus, caramelized onions, and shishito peppers. The warm *bombolini* are heavenly, dusted with sugar and paired with chocolate-Guinness and salted caramel sauces.

Ramen Dojo

F2

✗

805 S. B St. (bet. 8th & 9th Aves.), San Mateo

Phone:	650-401-6568	Lunch & dinner Wed – Mon
Web:	N/A	
Prices:	🍜	

The two-hour lines may have died down, but a 40-minute wait on the sidewalk is still standard at this noodle hot spot. The interior, when you finally reach it, is utterly spare—the better to showcase steaming bowls of tasty and satisfying soup. Customize your broth (soy sauce, garlic pork, soybean), spiciness, and toppings (like spicy cod roe and kikurage mushrooms), then dive in.

The ramen arrives in minutes, loaded with the standard fried garlic cloves, hard-boiled quail egg, scallion, chili, and two slices of roast pork. Your job is to slurp the chewy, delicious noodles (and maybe some seaweed salad or edamame), then hit the road—the hyper-efficient staff needs to keep the line moving, after all. But for one of the best bowls in town, it's worth it.

Sakae

C2

✗

243 California Dr. (at Highland Ave.), Burlingame

Phone:	650-348-4064	Lunch Mon – Sat
Web:	www.sakaesushi.com	Dinner nightly
Prices:	$$	

Its glory days of crowds packed to the rafters have passed, but Sakae is still a solid option for elegant sushi and other Japanese specialties. Adjacent to downtown Burlingame and the Caltrain station, this is a sleek space clad in varying shades of wood, Japanese pottery, and fresh flowers. Local families enjoy sitting at the bar, where a friendly and engaging sushi chef is a hit with kids.

Skip the specialty rolls and stick to fresh and neat nigiri topped with the likes of albacore, yellowtail, crab, salmon, or daily featured fish. Otherwise, go for the whiteboard's changing specials like maitake mushroom tempura or grilled baby octopus.

Be sure to order a pot of *hoji cha*, a roasted green tea that nicely complements their impressive range of fish.

Shalizaar

Persian 🍴🍴

D3

300 El Camino Real (bet. Anita & Belmont Aves.), Belmont

Phone: 650-596-9000
Web: www.shalizaar.com
Prices: **$$**

Lunch & dinner daily

A perennial favorite for Persian flavors, Shalizaar is friendly, charming, and authentic. Lunchtime draws a large business crowd, while dinners cater to couples on dates. The upscale space features chandeliers, linen-topped tables, Persian carpets, and walls of framed windows that flood everything with light.

Meals here are always a pleasure, thanks to the high quality of every ingredient. Try the signature *koobideh*, smoky ground beef and chicken kebabs served with char-broiled whole tomatoes and rice. Or, tuck into *baghali polo*, a fork-tender lamb shank over bright green rice full of dill and young fava beans. For dessert, take the friendly servers' advice and order the *zoolbia barnieh*, sticky-crisp squiggles of fried cake soaked in rosewater syrup.

Sichuan Chong Qing

Chinese 🍴

E1

211 S. San Mateo Dr. (at 2nd Ave.), San Mateo

Phone: 650-343-1144
Web: N/A
Prices: **$$**

Lunch & dinner Tue – Sun

The medical staff at the Mills Health Center take plenty of heat in an average day, but that doesn't stop them from piling into this compact neighboring Sichuan restaurant for their fix of spicy chili oil and numbing peppercorns. Both ingredients are featured in the crispy Chong Qing chicken and shrimp, each laden with chili peppers (be sure to watch out for shards of bone in the cleaver-chopped chicken).

Skip the mild Mandarin dishes and stick to the house's fiery specialties, like the nutty, smoky cumin lamb with sliced onion and still more chilies and chili oil. Aside from a few contemporary touches, the décor isn't newsworthy and the staff is more efficient than engaging—but you'll likely be too busy enjoying the flavor-packed fare to mind.

Sushi Sam's

Japanese   ✗

E1

218 E. 3rd Ave. (bet. B St. & Ellsworth Ave.), San Mateo

Phone: 650-344-0888   Lunch & dinner Tue – Sat
Web: www.sushisams.com
Prices: **$$**

Fresh sushi in San Mateo means a trip to Sushi Sam's, which is no secret among connoisseurs and neighborhood folk who regularly flock here the moment it opens to avoid a wait. Service is fast and efficient, though stark white walls, Formica tables, and simple wood chairs do little for the no-frills décor. Check the daily specials on the board for the best and freshest fish, which are mostly from Japan. Selections might include silky salmon placed atop neat mounds of rice with a light grating of wasabi; rich, firm mackerel brushed with a dab of ponzu; and buttery toro lightly seared and unembellished to enhance the delicate flavor. The spicy pickled ginger is house-made. For those who don't feel like choosing, order one of the chef's menus.

Sweet Basil

Thai   ✗

E2

1473 Beach Park Blvd. (at Marlin Ave.), Foster City

Phone: 650-212-5788   Lunch & dinner daily
Web: www.sweetbasilfoster.com
Prices: **$$**

Set near a charming bayside walking and biking trail on Foster City's perimeter, Sweet Basil makes for a great meal after a stroll or ride. The snazzy space is contemporary with bamboo floors and rustic tables, but the vibe is casual with the staff hustling to serve the daytime rush of office workers and families for dinner.
Though you may have to wait for a table, the signature kabocha pumpkin and beef in red curry will merit your patience. Other faves include well-marinated chicken *satay*; spicy tofu stir-fried with bell peppers, garlic, and basil; and sticky rice topped with mango. You can choose your own spice level, but watch out—when they say hot, they mean it. Vegetarians should visit sister restaurant Thai Idea next door for extra gratification.

Taqueria El Metate

Mexican 🍴

D3

120 Harbor Blvd. (at Hwy. 101), Belmont

Phone:	650-595-1110	Lunch & dinner daily
Web:	N/A	
Prices:	💰	

Industrial and no-frills, El Metate isn't a looker—but taqueria connoisseurs know it's the place to go for a great meal. Sidle up to the counter and order a round of street-style tacos, topped with well-seasoned carne asada or piquant shredded chicken, then crowned with onions and cilantro. Or go big with an enormous super burrito, stuffed with caramelized, pineapple-studded *al pastor*, fluffy rice, pinto beans, avocado, cheese, sour cream, and *pico de gallo*.

Located right off the 101, the restaurant's minimal room has lines of both white- and blue-collar lunchtime workers streaming out the door, and crowds of Mexican families on weekends (kids adore it). A well-stocked salsa bar, crisp chips, and a refreshing melon *agua fresca* help ease the wait.

Taste In Mediterranean Food

Mediterranean 🍴

C2

1199 Broadway, Ste. 1 (bet. Chula Vista & Laguna Aves.), Burlingame

Phone:	650-348-3097	Lunch & dinner daily
Web:	www.tasteinbroadway.com	
Prices:	💰	

Taste In Mediterranean Food could easily get lost along Broadway's blocks of cafés and boutiques, but this tiny restaurant is truly not to be missed. Beyond the deli cases of baklava and salads, find the open kitchen where rotating lamb, chicken, and beef slowly turn and roast to become gyros, shawarma platters, and wraps.

About half of the guests grab take out; the others sit in the small dining room to enjoy the likes of combo platters spanning the Mediterranean from Greece to Lebanon. Chewy pita bread scoops up nutty hummus, smoky-garlicky baba ghanoush, and herbaceous Moroccan eggplant salad. Or try thin slices of lamb shawarma in a pita wrap with homemade garlic sauce, cabbage, and fried potatoes. Don't forget the baklava from the counter.

Vespucci

E1

147 E. 3rd St. (bet. Ellsworth Dr. & San Mateo Dr.), San Mateo

Phone:	650-685-6151
Web:	N/A
Prices:	**$$**

Lunch & dinner Tue – Sun

When a Southern Italian couple with extensive restaurant experience moves to the New World, the result is nothing less than promising—it may even become one of the most popular spots in town. Intricate white wainscoting, a gilded ceiling, and travertine floors ensure that Vespucci's interior is as charming and classically Italian as the wonderfully warm and hospitable service.

Start with tasty salads like the caprese, fanning fresh mozzarella with tomatoes. Beautifully composed hand-made pastas may showcase linguine twirled with plump, sweet scallops with cherry tomatoes, garlic, and white wine. Don't miss dessert, particularly a world-class panna cotta perfumed with vanilla bean, topped with tangy raspberry coulis and a dollop of whipped cream.

Vesta

F2

2022 Broadway St. (bet. Jefferson Ave. & Main St.), Redwood City

Phone:	650-362-5052
Web:	www.vestarwc.com
Prices:	**$$**

Lunch & dinner Tue – Sat

In the minds of locals and foodies in-the-know, this outstanding pizzeria in downtown Redwood City serves *the* best pizza south of San Francisco. It draws business lunchers and residents for their smoky, chewy, and blistered wood-fired pies spread with tomato, burrata, and peppery arugula; or potato, rosemary, and caramelized bacon—the latter crowned with a fresh farm egg. Additionally, a handful of small plates like pork meatballs, seasonal salads, and grilled carrots round out the cheesy roster.

The high-ceilinged space with mosaic-tiled floors is especially lovely on warm days, when diners can sit in front of wide-open French doors and linger over creamy gelato. Given their quality of food, waits are inevitable, so consider making a reservation.

The Village Pub ✿

Gastropub ✗✗✗

E4

2967 Woodside Rd. (off Whiskey Hill Rd.), Woodside

Phone: 650-851-9888
Web: www.thevillagepub.net
Prices: $$$

Lunch Sun – Fri
Dinner nightly

Though it has the feel of a chichi private club, this attractive New American restaurant is open to all—provided they can live up to the style standards set by its fan base of well-heeled business types and ladies-who-lunch. Inside, richly upholstered red velvet chairs, a long polished bar, and gently draped windows add to the formal, exclusive vibe.

With that said, the food, though executed at a high level, is surprisingly approachable. A crisp, lunch pizza combines chanterelles, San Marzano tomatoes, crunchy chorizo, and finely grated Parmesan; loaded with flavor, it's all too easy to devour. Equally strong is the tender, succulent pork schnitzel, with a crunchy-crisp exterior brightened by lemon, capers, and rich pan juices.

Service is a priority for The Village Pub's wealthy crowd, and the well-attired staff will attend to every need—even grinding coffee to order as an accompaniment for the flourless chocolate cake with chicory cream and spearmint ice cream. The wine list is similarly designed to court the deepest of pockets, with an outstanding selection of French vintages and aged Bordeaux. On a budget? Aim for lunch, which is lighter not only in approach, but also on the wallet.

Viognier

E1

222 E. 4th Ave. (at B St.), San Mateo

Phone: 650-685-3727   Dinner Mon – Sat
Web: www.viognierrestaurant.com
Prices: $$$

Get gussied up and make your way to this elegant spot, nestled atop Draeger's Market in San Mateo. Spend an afternoon browsing the aisles of the gourmet grocery below, or sneak a peek at the cooking class taught in the kitchen upstairs. It's a full day of foodie heaven! Finally, snag a cushioned banquette next to the fireplace and let the feasting begin.

The menu divides into three- four- or five-course fixed price meals where the following may be featured: a salad of heirloom tomatoes with mozzarella, basil, black olive tapenade, and toasted slices of levain bread; chased down by cuttlefish slices with grilled shrimp posed atop white peaches. Pleasing palates for its unique flavors is grilled Hawaiian walu laid over a square of *pommes fondant*.

Zen Peninsula

C2

1180 El Camino Real (at Center St.), Millbrae

Phone: 650-616-9388   Lunch & dinner daily
Web: www.zenpeninsula.com
Prices: $$

It's a dim sum extravaganza here at Zen Peninsula where delicious, steaming-hot bites served out of traditional rolling carts keep the crowds a coming. Special event menus and à la carte seafood specialties are also on offer, but that's not why you're here. Tightly positioned, banquet-style round tables fill up with large groups devouring the likes of *har gow*—sticky wrappers stuffed with shrimp, ginger, garlic, and sesame oil; or roasted suckling pig in a smoky-sweet five spice glaze.

Be prepared to wait for a table during peak hours or on weekends. Clearly the never-ending crowds can't get enough of lip-smacking ground beef crêpes drizzled with soy and sprinkled with slices of scallion; or fluffy egg custard buns flavored with a hint of coconut.

Wakuriya ✿

D3

115 De Anza Blvd. (at Parrot Dr.), San Mateo

Phone: 650-286-0410   Dinner Wed – Sun
Web: www.wakuriya.com
Prices: $$$$

Quietly hiding in a shopping center, Wakuriya is a Bay Area treasure. It's also a true mom-and-pop restaurant—Chef Katsuhiro Yamasaki cooks while his wife, Mayumi, manages and serves with equal passion and skill. The straightforward setting features stone floors, wood furnishings, and counter seating offering views into the immaculate kitchen and the chance to appreciate the chef's meticulous details and deft skills.

The experience of dining here may seem casual and low-key, but each guest had to work hard to score that reservation. Expect to see plenty of foodies hovering iPhones over every beautiful dish.

Each month, the chef presents his own new kaiseki-style nine-course menu. This may begin with a delicate crystal goblet of vibrant asparagus purée (*suri-nagashi*), topped with succulent lobster tail, garnished with pink peppercorns and a steamed asparagus tip. Following a parade of superb sashimi, sample a springtime offering of cherry leaf-wrapped shrimp cakes that are tempura-fried and served with cherry blossom-infused salt. Desserts may bring fresh fruit suspended in a sweet, crystalline gelée with orbs of strawberry mochi drizzled with excellent vanilla crème anglaise.

South Bay

SAN JOSE

San Jose has for long been revered as the tech capital of the world, but it's really so much more. Combine all that tech money with a diverse, international population and get a very dynamic culinary scene. If that doesn't sound like an outrageously successful formula on its own, think of the area's rich wine culture descending from the Santa Cruz Mountains, where a burgeoning vintner community takes great pride in its work, and realize that the South Bay may as well be sitting on a gold mine. Visitors should be sure to see everything the area has to offer, with a sojourn at **The Mountain Winery** in Saratoga—part-outdoor concert venue, part-event space, and part-winery—that offers stunning views of the vineyards and valley below.

FESTIVALS GALORE

The Valley is proud of its tech-minded reputation, but don't judge this book by its cover as South Bay locals definitely know how to party. In San Jose, celebrations kick off in May at the wildly popular **South Bay Greek Festival** featuring music, eats, drinks, and dancing. With little time to recover, buckets of cornhusks wait to be stuffed and sold at the **Story Road Tamale Festival**, held every June within the gorgeous grounds of Emma Prusch Farm Park. In July, **Japantown** breathes new life for the two-day **Obon/Bazaar**, and come August, the Italian-American Heritage Foundation celebrates its annual **Family Festa**. It's a year-round shindig, and **Santana Row** (a sleek shopping village housing numerous upscale restaurants and a fantastic farmer's market) plays a pivotal role in these festivities. One of San Jose's most notable destinations is **San Pedro Square Market**, whose four walls harbor a spectrum of artisanal merchants at historic Peralta Adobe downtown. Farmers and specialty markets are a way of

life for South Bay residents and these locals cannot imagine living elsewhere.

CULTURAL DYNASTY

As further testimony to its international repute, the capital of Silicon Valley is also a melting pot of global culinary influences. Neighborhood *pho* shops and *bánh mì* hangouts like **Huong Lan**, gratify the growing Vietnamese community. They can also be found gracing the intersection of King and Tully streets (home to some of the city's finest Vietnamese flavors) sampling decadent cream puffs at **Hong-Van Bakery** or crispy green waffles flavored with *pandan* paste at **Century Bakery** just a few blocks away. **Lion Plaza** is yet another hub for bakeries, markets, and canteens paying homage to this eighth most populated Asian country. Neighboring Cambodia makes an appearance through delicious noodle soups like **Nam Vang Restaurant** or **F&D Yummy**. Chinese food makes its formidable presence known at lofty **Dynasty Chinese Seafood Restaurant**. Located on Story Road, this is a popular arena for big parties and favored destination for dim sum. **Nijiya Market** is a Japanese jewel in Mountain View that sparkles with specialty goods, top ingredients, and all things Far East. Long before it was cool to be organic in America, Nijiya was focused on bringing the taste of Japan by way of high-quality, seasonal, and local ingredients to the California coast. Today, it continues to tantalize with some of the area's most pristine seafood and meat, as well as an array of tasty sushi and bento boxes. Also available via their website are sumptuous, homespun recipes for a variety of noodle dishes, fried rice signatures, and other regional specialties. Encompassing the globe and travelling from this Eastern tip to South America, Mexican food enthusiasts in San Jose seem eternally smitten by the still-warm tortillas at **Tropicana**, or the surprisingly delish tacos from one of the area's many **Mi Pueblo Food Centers**.

A STUDENT'S DREAM

And yet there is more to the South Bay than just San Jose. Los Gatos is home to prized patisseries like **Fleur de Cocoa** as well as such historic, continually operating, and specialized wineries like **Testarossa**. Meanwhile, cool and casual Palo Alto is home base for celebrated Stanford University, its countless students, and impressive faculty. Find locals lining up for homemade fresh and frozen yogurt at **Fraîche**. Others fulfill a Korean fantasy in Santa Clara, where these same settlers enjoy a range of authentic nibbles and tasty spreads at food court favorite— **Lawrence Plaza**. Just as foodies favor the *soondubu jjigae* at **SGD Tofu House**, conservative palates have a field day over caramelized and roasted sweet potatoes at **Sweet Potato Stall**, just outside the Galleria. Fill a belly with impeccable produce along El Camino Real near the Lawrence Expressway intersection. Then treat your senses to a feast at nearby **Milk Pail Market**, showcasing over 300 varieties of cheese. Have your pick among such splendid choices as Camembert, Bleu d'Auvergne, Morbier, and Cabriquet, as well as imported Mamie Nova Yogurt.

Despite the fast pace of technology in Silicon Valley, **Slow Food**—the grassroots movement dedicated to local food traditions—has a thriving South Bay chapter. Even Google in Mountain View feeds its large staff three organic, square meals a day. For a wider range of delicacies, they may frequent surrounding eateries or stores selling ethnic eats. Residents of Los Altos have their German food cravings covered between **Esther's German Bakery** and **Dittmer's Gourmet Meats & Wurst-Haus**. In fact, Dittmer's delectable sausages are made extra special when served on a salted pretzel roll from Esther's. **Los Gatos Meats & Smokehouse** is another age-old, culinary stalwart serving these meat-loving mortals an embarrassment of riches. Think poultry, fish, and freshly butchered meat sandwiches presented alongside savory specialties like beef jerky, prime rib roasts, juicy pork loin, beef jerky, corned beef, and of course, bacon...but, wait... did you want it regular, pepper, country-style or Canadian? Pair all these salt licks with a sip from Mountain View's famous **Savvy Cellar Wine Bar & Wine Shop** only to discover that it's a picnic in the making. Smokers looking to wind down in luxury may head to the handsome, upscale, and members-only Los Gatos Cigar Club, where the choices are exceptional and conversation, intriguing.

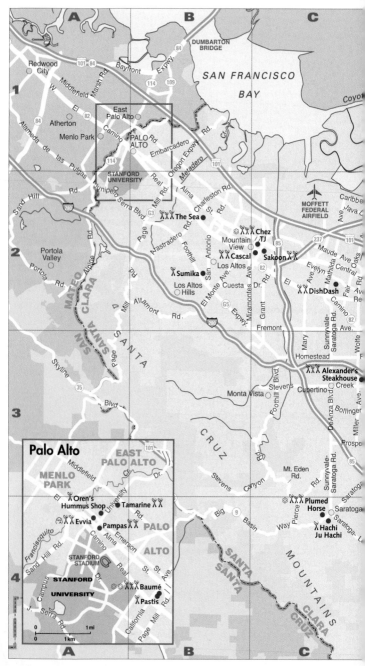

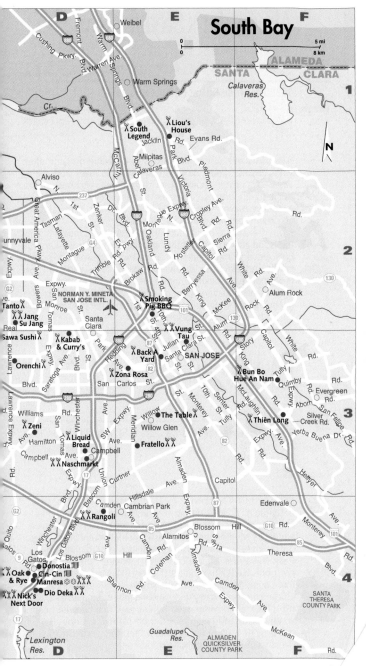

South Bay

0   5 mi

0   8 km

D

Weibel

Cushing Pkwy.

Fremont Blvd.

880

Warren Ave.

Warm Springs

Cr.

Alviso

N.

237

ALAMEDA

SANTA   **CLARA**

Calaveras Res.

Rd.

130

Rd.

N

E

Liou's House

South Legend

Jacklin   Rd.   Evans Rd.

Milpitas

Abel   Calaveras

St.

Park

Victoria

Piedmont

Cropley Ave.

Rd.

Montague Expwy.

N.

880

Great America Pkwy.

Tasman   Lafayette   Zanker

1st   Dr.   Ex.pwy.

Sunnyvale

Bowers   Ave

Montague   Expwy.

San Tomas

Trimble   Rd.

G2

G4

Oakland   Rd.

Brokaw   Rd.

Lundy

Berryessa

King

Hostetter   Rd.

McKee   Rd.

Sierra   Rd.

Capitol   Ave.

White   Rd.

Rd.

Rd.

Rd.

Alum Rock

130

F

ALAMEDA

1

2

Tanto

Jang   Su Jang

Monroe

Sawa Sushi

Orenchi

Lawrence   Expwy.

Real

Ave.

NORMAN Y. MINETA SAN JOSE INTL.

Kabab & Curry's

Saratoga   Ave.

Santa   Clara

Park   Ave.

Hedding

Zona Rosa

Back A Yard

San   Carlos   St.

Smoking Pig BBQ

1st   St.

10th   St.

87

Julian   St.

Vung Tau

Santa   Clara   St.

SAN JOSE

82

Monterey

Alum   Rock   Ave.

Story   Rd.

King   Rd.

McKee   Rd.

White   Rd.

13D

101

Bun Bo Hue An Nam

Quimby   Rd.

Tully   Rd.

Aborn   Rd.

San Felipe   Rd.

Evergreen

Silver Creek   Rd.

Yerba Buena   Dr.

Rd.

3

Lawrence   Expwy.

Williams   Ave.

Zeni

Hamilton   Ave.

San Tomas   Expwy.

Winchester   Blvd.

Liquid Bread

Campbell

Naschmarkt

17

Bascom   Ave.

Union   Ave.

280

Meridian   Ave.

SW   Expwy.

Willow

Willow Glen

The Table

Fratello

Curtner   Ave.

Almaden   Expwy.

Hillsdale   Ave.

10th   St.

Senter   Rd.

Tully   Rd.

82

Capitol   Expwy.

Thiên Long

McLaughlin   Ave.

Aborn   Rd.

Hellyer   Ave.

Rd.

Monterey   Rd.

101

G2

Quito   Rd.

Winchester   Blvd.

Los Gatos   Blvd.

Rangoli

Camden   Ave.

Cambrian Park

Camden   Ave.

85

Blossom   Hill   Rd.

Alamitos

Camden   Ave.

Santa   Theresa   Blvd.

Almaden   Expwy.

Edenvale

G10   Rd.

Monterey   Rd.

85

101

Theresa

4

9

Los Gatos

Blossom   Hill   Rd.

G10

Donostia

Oak & Rye

Cin-Cin

Manresa

Dio Deka

Nick's Next Door

17

Lexington Res.

Gatos

Shannon   Rd.

Coleman   Rd.

Almaden   Expwy.

Camden   Ave.

McKean   Rd.

Guadalupe Res.

ALMADEN QUICKSILVER COUNTY PARK

SANTA THERESA COUNTY PARK

Rd.

D   **E**   **F**

Alexander's Steakhouse

Steakhouse 𝕏𝕏𝕏

C3

10330 N. Wolfe Rd. (at I-280), Cupertino

Phone: 408-446-2222

Web: www.alexanderssteakhouse.com

Prices: $$$$

Lunch Tue – Fri

Dinner nightly

Silicon Valley's pet steakhouse is a sprawling den complete with private dining nooks, a fireside lounge, and glass-enclosed aging room. Two exhibition kitchens pump out enough updated favorites to sate rollicking groups of executives savoring expensive Napa cabs at roomy tables—all on the company dime, of course.

From dry-aged to bone-in to Japanese A5, Alexander's shines the spotlight on beautifully marbled beef. These luscious cuts are brilliantly adorned, as in the bone marrow-potato confit and black garlic-tinged demi-glace served with the Porterhouse. Knockout starters like soft-shell crab tempura with green papaya salad and green curry are proof of the kitchen's high yielding talents. The same is the case with their intricately composed desserts.

Back A Yard

Caribbean 𝕏

E3

80 N. Market St. (bet. Santa Clara & St. John Sts.), San Jose

Phone: 408-294-8626

Web: www.backayard.net

Prices: 🥜

Lunch & dinner Mon – Sat

Though this Caribbean spot is located in the heart of downtown San Jose, dining here feels like a vacation thanks to cheerful murals, a lively soundtrack, and hospitable servers. Unlike its Menlo Park predecessor, which mainly does to-go orders, this location boasts a capacious brick dining room.

Back A Yard is a Jamaican term meaning "the way things are done back home," and the food doesn't disappoint on that count. Specialties include smoky, spicy, and tender jerk chicken, flavorful curry goat, and vinegar-marinated *escovitch* fish fillets, all accompanied by coconut rice and red beans, a side salad, and caramelized fried plantains. Cool off your palate with a glass of coconut water, then order a slice of dense, flan-like sweet potato pudding.

South Bay

Baumé ❀ ❀

B4

Contemporary 🍴🍴🍴

201 S. California Ave. (at Park Blvd.), Palo Alto

Phone: 650-328-8899
Web: www.baumerestaurant.com
Prices: $$$$

Lunch Fri – Sat
Dinner Wed – Sat

This single story building can seem nondescript, but a bright orange door catches everyone's eye and marks Baume's entrance. That same vibrant color carries through the interior with striped floor-to-ceiling curtains to keep tables semi-private in the two main dining areas. Inlaid marble floors, soft lighting, and a climate-controlled wine case complete the attractively unadorned look. Service is fuss-free and very professional—attributes that are ideal for their large business clientele.

Chef Bruno Chemel may be progressive, but his nightly menu never loses sight of taste, balance, and pleasure. Savor the likes of velvety and intensely fresh pea purée topped with sweet blue lobster from Brittany, garnished with more fresh peas, tendrils, and tarragon. Thin, fork-tender slices of beef loin prove the kitchen's magnificent talent: the meat is gorgeously pink from edge to edge and set over a pool of red wine-mace reduction alongside a coffee-crusted spear of salsify.

Desserts may tease the palate with bubbles of refreshing strawberry soda; then follow with an airy, nitrogen-frozen banana sabayon topped with a warm and boozy chocolate-rum ganache that freezes into a shell on contact.

Bun Bo Hue An Nam

F3

2060 Tully Rd. (at Quimby Rd.), San Jose

Phone: 408-270-7100   Lunch & dinner Thu – Tue
Web: N/A
Prices: 💲💲

Take a hint from the local Vietnamese families and head into this second San Jose outpost, a slightly more contemporary version of the original. Inside, walls hang with flat screens showing Vietnamese TV, and wooden tables and chairs sit atop tiled floors.

As the name suggests, *bun bo hue* soup is the specialty here, though it may be a pleasure limited to intrepid diners. This spicy beef noodle soup blazes with chili oil, lemongrass, scallions, and cilantro, yet remains slightly gamey and rich with ample portions of tripe, tendon, and congealed pork blood. An array of *pho* is also a popular choice. Folks can be found slurping down *pho dac biet*, a fragrant star anise and lemongrass broth overflowing with meat, served with lime, basil, and chilies.

Cascal

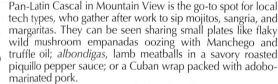

C2

400 Castro St. (at California St.), Mountain View

Phone: 650-940-9500   Lunch & dinner daily
Web: www.cascalrestaurant.com
Prices: $$

Pan-Latin Cascal in Mountain View is the go-to spot for local tech types, who gather after work to sip mojitos, sangria, and margaritas. They can be seen sharing small plates like flaky wild mushroom empanadas oozing with Manchego and truffle oil; *albondigas*, lamb meatballs in a savory roasted piquillo pepper sauce; or a Cuban wrap packed with adobo-marinated pork.

The food is always top-notch, but the vibe remains casual, with families enjoying dinner and couples with dogs in tow benefitting from the spacious patio. Efficient servers bustle between tables inside the colorful room, flooded with light thanks to walls of windows. Sharing is the ethos here, so there's no shame in saving room for a *tres leches* cake to split between friends.

Chez TJ ✤

Contemporary 🍴🍴🍴

C2

938 Villa St. (bet. Bryant & Franklin Sts.), Mountain View

Phone:	650-964-7466
Web:	www.cheztj.com
Prices:	**$$$$**

Dinner Tue – Sat

The modern Google office building next door may symbolize the current trajectory of Mountain View, but Chez TJ, housed in a quaint, historic bungalow, remains delightfully analog. Its warren of narrow rooms, each boasting its own style, is brought together by hand-blown colored glass lamps and professional servers in sharp black suits. A favorite for celebratory couples on date-night or suits gathering for business, it offers some of the area's finest food.

The nightly chef's tasting menu dances ably through numerous styles and cuisines, from a Spanish-inspired dish of *jamón ibérico* and beef tendon chips over romesco sauce, to a fluffy blini topped with duck confit and quenelle of Sauternes-infused duck liver mousse. Moist and flaky halibut cheeks are served over streaks of onion soubise, pickled mushrooms and shallots, and sweet English peas, then topped with a rich oxtail ragout.

A palate-cleansing glass of house-made hibiscus-rose soda is a gateway to the excellent desserts. Try a slice of the moist banana sponge cake with banana-chrysanthemum mousse and intense strawberry sorbet; or the Valrhona chocolate mousse with grapes, pistachio paste, and gold-dusted chocolate pearls.

Cin-Cin

International

368 Village Ln. (at Saratoga Los Gatos Rd.), Los Gatos

Phone: 408-354-8006
Web: www.cincinwinebar.com
Prices: $$

Dinner Mon – Sat

Sure, enjoy that well-priced Happy Hour (Monday-Saturday from 4:00-6:00 P.M.), but just make sure to stick around for the wonderfully diverse range of international small plates. Almost any craving can be quelled here, where Asian, American, Mexican, French, and Italian goodies are available for a sharing showdown.

The lively wine bar is styled in blonde woods, pale greens, and low lights, with two adjoining dining spaces and a primo lounge. To start, fill up on lettuce cups piled with cold soba noodles, shaved apple, fried shiitakes, and sauced with chipotle aïoli. Hamburger sliders on silver dollar rolls with grilled onion and aged cheddar fondue; or Korean tacos heaped with kimchi and shaved ribeye are a delightful balance of flavor and texture.

Dio Deka

Greek

210 E. Main St. (near Fiesta Way), Los Gatos

Phone: 408-354-7700
Web: www.diodeka.com
Prices: $$$

Dinner nightly

Dio Deka may specialize in Greek food, but this is no typical taverna, as the stylish dining room (complete with a roaring fireplace) ably demonstrates. A wealthy, well-dressed Los Gatos crowd flocks to the front patio on warm evenings, dining and people-watching beneath the vine-covered walls of the Hotel Los Gatos. The bar also draws a brace of cheery regulars.

Skip the dull mesquite-grilled steaks and keep your order Greek: think stuffed grape leaves with tender braised beef cheek, or a bright pan-seared local salmon with roasted yellow peppers, potatoes, and artichokes. The adventurous shouldn't miss out on the fun offering of Greek wines and sweet buffs should allow space for the *crema me meli*, a fantastic burnt-honey mousse with almond and lemon.

DishDash

Middle Eastern ✗✗

C2

190 S. Murphy Ave. (bet. Evelyn & Washington Aves.), Sunnyvale

Lunch & dinner Mon – Sat

Phone: 408-774-1889
Web: www.dishdash.com
Prices: $$

Dining on the run is certainly possible at this Middle Eastern favorite on historic Murphy Avenue—just ask the tech types flooding the to-go counter to bring food back to their desks. Families and small groups congregate in the colorful dining room. But you might want to linger on the front sidewalk patio, all the better to people-watch while savoring a bright, tangy, and healthy tabbouleh salad, or indulging in the tender-crisp falafel, redolent of spices, topped with whipped tahini. Served on griddled bread and topped with garlicky yogurt-parsley sauce, wraps like the incredibly tender, smoky, and juicy lamb shawarma are full-flavored and downright memorable. For dessert, try the *m'halabieh*, a floral rosewater and creamy pistachio pudding.

Donostia

Basque 📋

D4

424 N. Santa Cruz Ave. (bet. Andrews St. & Saratoga Los Gatos Rd.), Los Gatos

Dinner Tue – Sat

Phone: 408-797-8688
Web: www.donostiapintxos.com
Prices: $$

Donostia is the Basque name for San Sebastián, and in the same vein, oodles of Basque flavor is on offer at this sister spot to popular Italian wine bar Enoteca la Storia. Even the walls, packed with glowing blue geode slices, suggest the color of the ocean. Whether they're sipping crisp Albariño or fruity sangria, a crew of chic locals pack the bar, sharing plates of *pintxos* like *patatas bravas* drizzled with spicy *crema* and eggy *tortilla de patata*.
Those seeking heartier fare have choices like slow-cooked beef cheeks over chickpea purée and romesco. Most opt to make a meal of tapas, sharing such tempting treats as spicy gazpacho and creamy, golden brown cod *croquetas*. The staff is always happy to suggest a wine from their carefully crafted list.

Evvia 😋

A4

Greek ✗✗

420 Emerson St. (bet. Lytton & University Aves.), Palo Alto

Phone: 650-326-0983
Web: www.evvia.net
Prices: $$

Lunch Mon – Fri
Dinner nightly

As popular as ever, this downtown Palo Alto fixture draws a mix of suits by day and local couples by night, all of them bathed in the glow of the hearth that reflects off the hanging copper pans in the exhibition kitchen. This is an authentic Greek *estiatorio* experience, from the herbed feta that tops wood oven-baked *gigante* beans in tomato-leek sauce to the creamy *tzatziki* that enhances slices of tender roast lamb on house-made pita.

When it's warm in Palo Alto (as it often is), Evvia throws open its glass front doors, allowing the convivial staff to get a whiff of fresh air as they tend to a stream of regulars. At night, the experience is more intimate, providing a cozy environment for splitting a rich but devourable olive oil-semolina cake.

Fratello

E3

Italian ✗✗

1712 Meridian Ave. (at Lenn Dr.), San Jose

Phone: 408-269-3801
Web: www.fratello-ristorante.com
Prices: $$

Dinner nightly

Generous portions and a comfortable neighborhood vibe bring happy regulars to this casual Italian restaurant in San Jose's Willow Glen neighborhood. Its location at the edge of a shopping plaza is less than prepossessing, but the friendly staff and tasty dishes make up for any shortfalls. A live band sets up shop every Saturday, making it a particularly popular night for a visit.

Pastas—many of them homemade—star on the menu and include fettuccine in a ragù of grass-fed beef, Berkshire pork, and San Marzano tomatoes. Pizzas and hearty entrées like the pan-seared salmon with wild mushroom risotto and garlic spinach are also solid choices. For dessert, the tender, buttery apple tart is a tasty delight with sweet chunks of apple accented by cinnamon syrup.

Hachi Ju Hachi

C4

14480 Big Basin Way (bet. Saratoga Los Gatos Rd. & 3rd St.), Saratoga

Phone: 408-647-2258
Web: www.hachijuhachi88.com
Prices: $$

Dinner Tue – Sun

With a refined small plates menu of traditional washoku cuisine, Chef Jin Suzuki shows true dedication to his craft. Dishes are subdued and delicate, celebrating just a few ingredients, like soft morsels of eggplant marinated in sweet miso-mirin. Crunchy salads may toss large pieces of cucumber and bamboo shoots in an earthy and tangy fermented barley-miso vinaigrette. Simple pleasures underscore the *gyu-niku* teriyaki, served as slices of tender marinated filet of beef with enticing salty-smoky flavors.

The restaurant itself is a serene space filled with blonde wood furnishings and a long counter facing the kitchen. After a kaiseki meal here, take the chef's invitation to sign the wall, or just peruse the names of those who went before you.

Jang Su Jang

D2

3561 El Camino Real, Ste.10 (bet. Flora Vista Ave. & Lawrence Expwy.), Santa Clara

Phone: 408-246-1212
Web: www.jangsujang.com
Prices: $$

Lunch & dinner daily

Smoky Korean barbeque, luscious soft tofu stews, and enormous seafood pancakes are among the standards at this Santa Clara classic and Koreatown star. Its strip-mall façade may not seem enticing, but the interior is classier than expected, thanks to granite tables equipped with grill tops and ventilation hoods, and a glass-enclosed exhibition kitchen in back.

This is fiery flavored cuisine for gourmands who can stand the heat. A heavy-handed dose of kimchi flavors soft beef and pork dumplings, while the fierce red chili paste that slicks garlicky slices of marinated pork may actually cook the meat in *daeji bulgogi*. Cool down with *mul naeng myun*, a cold beef broth with tender, nutty buckwheat noodles, and a pot of roasted grain tea.

Kabab & Curry's

D3   Indian ✗

1498 Isabella St. (at Clay St.), Santa Clara

Phone: 408-247-0745   Lunch & dinner Tue – Sun
Web: www.kababcurrys.com
Prices: 💰

The appeal is in the name at Kabab & Curry's, which has become a dining destination among Indian and Pakistani expats missing the comforts of home. On lunch breaks from the local tech giants, they pack the all-you-can-eat buffet, filling up their plates with fragrant chicken *boti kababs*, coupled with creamy *dal makhani* and slabs of charred naan for soaking up those savory sauces.
Set in a white house with simple tile floors and orange walls, Kabab & Curry's is more about food than service. But, that doesn't deter the crowd of local families from gushing in for dinner or to pick up take-out. With to-go bags laden with rich chicken *tikka masala* and pungent lamb *kadahi*, it's clear that everybody loves this *desi* diner's bold and authentic flavors.

Liou's House

E1   Chinese ✗

1245 Jacklin Rd. (at Park Victoria Dr.), Milpitas

Phone: 408-263-9888   Lunch & dinner Tue – Sun
Web: N/A
Prices: 💰

Set in quiet Milpitas, this established hot spot rewards a regular crowd of families and tech execs with unique Hunan cooking.
The modest dining room is favored for lunch service, known for its fantastic value, tasty food, and signature dishes (some of which, like honey baked ham or crispy duck stuffed with sweet rice, require advance ordering). But, the regular menu continues to enjoy a fan-base for such authentic preparations as a bamboo stalk filled with sweet-sticky rice flavored with pork jus and layered with rich pork belly. Outstandingly crisp tea-smoked duck is served with steamed *bao*, hoisin, and scallions for making perfect little sandwiches, and *chow fun*—stir-fried with roasted chicken and veggies—is big in size and best for wary palates.

Liquid Bread

Gastropub ✗

D3

379 E. Campbell Ave. (bet. Central Ave. & Civic Center Dr.), Campbell

Dinner Tue – Sun

Phone: 408-370-3400
Web: www.liquidbreadcampbell.com
Prices: $$

Beer is serious business at this Campbell Avenue hot spot, which boasts a sizable menu of drafts and bottles. But the food is a step up from the typical brewpub, with dishes like an asparagus salad topped with shaved sunchokes, black garlic, and balsamic dressing; or roasted chicken breast over maple syrup-soaked waffles and garlicky escarole. Brews even show up on the food menu from time to time, as in the stout cream that crowns a fudgy chocolate brownie.

While it's far from a dive bar, Liquid Bread can get loud, making it better for sharing pints with friends than an intimate date-night. If the communal high-top tables, large front patio, and copious brews add up to a little too much fun, do as the regulars do and have a taxi handle the drive home.

Naschmarkt

Austrian ✗✗

D3

384 E. Campbell Ave. (bet. Central & Railway Aves.), Campbell

Dinner Tue – Sun

Phone: 408-378-0335
Web: www.naschmarkt-restaurant.com
Prices: $$

Named for the large produce market in Vienna known as the "city's stomach," this spot in Campbell is becoming a gastro-favorite. On weekends, find romantic couples savoring the contemporary space, boasting a wrap-around dining counter, open kitchen, exposed brick walls, and high ceilings.

The cuisine captures the true spirit of Austria by preparing its classics with modern style. Familiar traditions are found in Hungarian beef goulash braised in paprika with herbed spätzle; or classic wiener schnitzel with lingonberry sauce and potato salad. Innovations are clear in riesling-steamed black mussels with carrots and celery root. Stay for the sweet, as in a piping-hot and fluffy *salzburger nockerl* with tangy yogurt and stewed blueberry compote.

Manresa ✿✿

Contemporary 🍴🍴🍴

320 Village Ln. (bet. Santa Cruz & University Aves.), Los Gatos

Phone: 408-354-4330
Web: www.manresarestaurant.com
Prices: $$$$

Dinner Wed – Sun

The news is true: a terrible fire destroyed part of Manresa, resulting in its temporary closure. However, it is scheduled to re-open by early 2015 with a new kitchen and fresh coat of everything. The refurbished interior will surely come to reflect that same distinctive northern Californian style. The service team will be as synchronized, sharp, and welcoming as ever. And the talented kitchen will not have skipped a single beat.

The chef's one nightly tasting menu is unknown until it arrives at each guest's table—though servers ascertain dietary restrictions and preferences in advance. Expect dishes that showcase superlative ingredients and technique, like a delicate yuzu-tinged local milk panna cotta topped with abalone jelly and cubes of soy-sake braised abalone, garnished with radish flowers. Lightly smoked cherry salmon gains an almost creamy quality alongside roe, fennel, citrus segments, a chip of crisped salmon skin, and tiny fried sage leaves.

Save yourself for elegant desserts, like the slender bar of chocolate ganache paired with a quenelle of *fromage blanc* sorbet nestled into finely ground cookie crumbs, with lacy salted sourdough tuiles and squiggles of chocolate and caramel.

Nick's Next Door

American ✗✗✗

D4

11 College Ave. (at Main St.), Los Gatos

Phone: 408-402-5053

Web: www.nicksnextdoor.com

Prices: $$

Lunch & dinner Tue – Sat

Though it originally opened as the sibling to Chef Difu's Nick's on Main, Nick's Next Door is now his sole restaurant—even more confusing given that it's actually across the street from his original spot. One fact is evident, though: the crowd here has ritzy tastes, often flocking in from the high-end cigar shop next door and Bentley dealership down the street.

Upscale American bistro cuisine is the focus with dishes like seared pepper-crusted ahi tuna, a veal rib chop with creamy Tuscan white beans, and meatloaf with potatoes and wild mushroom gravy. Whether you dine in the cozy yet elegant dining room with its black-and-gray motif or on the beautiful patio at the foot of a towering redwood, you'll receive a warm welcome, often from Nick himself.

Oak & Rye

Pizza ✗✗

D4

303 N. Santa Cruz Ave. (bet. Almendra & Bachman Aves.), Los Gatos

Phone: 408-395-4441

Web: www.oakandryepizza.com

Prices: $$

Lunch Tue – Sun
Dinner nightly

A longtime *pizzaiolo* from Brooklyn's acclaimed Roberta's is behind the pies at this South Bay jewel, where a coppery wood-fired oven produces chewy, blistered crusts. The pies' toppings are as quirky and delightful as their monikers, like the Scottie 2 Hottie (*soppressata*, *pepperoncini* oil, tomatoes, mozzarella, honey) and the Truffle Shuffle (Gruyère, green onion, truffle oil, cornichon).

The menu is rounded out by a handful of small plates like a shaved Brussels sprout, lemon, and pecorino salad, but the real focus is the pizza, for which Oak & Rye has quickly become Los Gatos' go-to. Friendly and casual, with gregarious servers, its only drawback is the need to arrive early—reservations for parties fewer than 10 aren't accepted, and waits can get long.

Orenchi

Japanese   ✗

D3

3540 Homestead Rd. (near Lawrence Expy.), Santa Clara

Phone: 408-246-2955

Lunch & dinner Tue – Sun

Web: www.orenchi-ramen.com

Prices: ㊊㊅

Whether at lunch or dinner, this ramen specialist is known for its lines of waiting diners that curl like noodles outside its door. Even those who arrive before they open may face a long wait, so don't come if you're in a rush. Once inside, you'll be seated at a simple wood table or at the bar, collaged with Polaroid portraits of guests savoring their ramen.

The reason for the wait becomes clear when you're presented with a rich and utterly delicious bowl of *tonkotsu* ramen full of chewy noodles, roasted pork, and scallions. *Shoyu* ramen is equally delish, but make a point to show up early for spicy miso *tsukemen* or miso ramen as they're limited to only 15 and 20 servings, respectively, at lunch and dinner.

Check out Iroriya next door for *robata* dining.

Oren's Hummus Shop

Israeli   ✗

A4

261 University Ave. (bet. Bryant & Ramona Sts.), Palo Alto

Phone: 650-752-6492

Lunch & dinner daily

Web: www.orenshummus.com

Prices: ㊊㊅

For a quick trip to Israel, head over to Oren's Hummus Shop in Palo Alto. It's a casual stop catering to tech-types, Stanford University professors, and local families looking for incomparably authentic Israeli food. Fresh and healthy is the name of the game here, where delicious bites are fired up with all natural ingredients and a lot of homemade love.

Try the salad trio of traditional Middle Eastern appetizers: smoky roasted eggplant baba ghanoush; *labane* topped with olive oil and spices; and crispy, moist falafel balls served with tahini. Do not miss the signature hummus, drizzled with olive oil, paprika, and served with fluffy, warm pita bread. Or try the tender grilled chicken skewer, alongside salad and sweet potato fries.

Pampas

Brazilian 🍴🍴

A4

529 Alma St. (bet. Hamilton & University Aves.), Palo Alto

Phone: 650-327-1323
Web: www.pampaspaloalto.com
Prices: $$$

Lunch Mon – Fri
Dinner nightly

Pampas has a prime Palo Alto location across from the Caltrain, just steps from the shops on University Ave. The large brick façade is hard to miss, and judging by the half-off happy hour crowds, most yupsters don't. The voluminous, bi-level restaurant has the look of a sexy barn with dark masculine furnishings.

Pampas is a Brazilian *churrascaria* (carnivore heaven) where servers bring tender, well-seasoned, spit-roasted *rodizio* meat until you say "uncle." Standouts include the tenderloin filet seasoned with garlic and herbs; chicken legs marinated in garlic, chiles, and vinegar; and house-made chorizo with *harissa* and more chiles. In case this isn't enough, the sidebar buffet is unlimited. The slow-roasted pineapple makes an excellent finale.

Pastis

French 🍴

B4

447 S. California Ave. (bet. Ash St. & El Camino Real), Palo Alto

Phone: 650-324-1355
Web: www.pastispaloalto.com
Prices: $$

Lunch Tue – Sun
Dinner Tue – Sat

Parisian charm flowers in the heart of Silicon Valley at Pastis, a delightful Palo Alto French bistro. Compact and cheery with yellow walls, a sprinkling of tables, and specials on the chalkboard, it's every inch the European experience (just don't bring along a big group). You'll hear a lot of French spoken by both the staff and guests as it's a favorite with the expats—always a good sign for American gastronomes.

The low-key, laid-back menu is heavy on Gallic classics like fluffy, buttery quiche Lorraine; a grilled merguez sausage sandwich with roasted bell peppers and *harissa* mayonnaise; as well as a simple but perfect crème brûlée. *Le Benedict* and *les omelettes* are big draws for brunch, particularly when enjoyed on the lovely front patio.

Plumed Horse ✿

Contemporary ✗✗✗

14555 Big Basin Way (bet. 4th & 5th Sts.), Saratoga

Phone: 408-867-4711　　　　　　　　　　　　Dinner Mon – Sat
Web: www.plumedhorse.com
Prices: $$$$

Set in what appears to be a cozy bungalow that opens into a surprisingly large space, Plumed Horse's small-town surroundings are belied by the McLarens and Lamborghinis regularly parked out front. Tech money infuses the well-to-do suburb, and this show pony is a fine-dining favorite among wealthy local retirees.

But even if you have to save your pennies, you will enjoy the creative and delectable dishes on offer here. These include a crunchy phyllo cannoli shell stuffed with smoked trout-mascarpone mousse and dusted with chives; or velvety sweet corn soup with a tangy chow-chow of pickled vegetables, smoked duck, and popped sorghum. Flaky butter-basted salmon rests in a bed of earthy porcini and fava beans, while tender chicken roulades are accented by chanterelles and sweet corn. A quenelle of blackberry sorbet served over honey-flavored tapioca pearls makes for a rich yet very refreshing finale.

Some technical touches, like an iPad wine list and fiber-optic chandeliers, are a nod to the clientele. But, the vibe generally tilts towards classic luxury—from the attentive and professional staff, to the contemporary space with its enormous glass wine cellar and arched barrel ceiling.

Rangoli

Indian

D4

3695 Union Ave. (at Woodard Rd.), San Jose

Phone: 408-377-2222
Web: www.rangolica.com
Prices: $$

Lunch Sun – Fri
Dinner nightly

Located on the edge of San Jose, between Campbell and Los Gatos, Rangoli is a lovely and upscale Indian restaurant. Leagues ahead of its neighboring (read: pedestrian) *desi* diners, it is no wonder that elegant Rangoli is so popular among the local South Asians. The dining areas consist of half-partitions and little alcoves, and tabletops are adorned with pretty votive candles.

The restaurant offers a massive buffet, but the best option is to order à la carte. Try spice-sparked items like a tandoor-smoked eggplant appetizer blended with chilies; followed by lamb Madras—cubes of lamb stewed in a hearty red coconut curry; or juicy chicken in a nutty, creamy, and saffron-infused *korma*. As always, a chewy naan is the best way to sop up any leftover sauce.

Sakoon

Indian

C2

357 Castro St. (bet. California & Dana Sts.), Mountain View

Phone: 650-965-2000
Web: www.sakoonrestaurant.com
Prices: $$

Lunch & dinner daily

An Indian mainstay in Mountain View, Sakoon draws big techie crowds for its lunch buffet—and transforms into an upscale, contemporary dinnertime experience come sundown. Vibrant and cheerful, its oversized mirrors, modern furnishings, and brightly patterned banquettes delight the eye, as do the fiber-optic lights that pattern the ceiling with constantly shifting swirls of color.

The food and service are strikingly attentive and polished, with well-constructed dishes like *chaat ki parat* (fried shredded wheat topped with potatoes, chickpeas, red onion, and cilantro) and a flavor-packed Chettinad chicken curry. For an unusual and satisfying dessert-like bread, try the Kashmiri naan filled with rosewater-soaked shredded coconut and toasted chopped nuts.

Sawa Sushi

D3

Japanese ✗

1042 E. El Camino Real (at Henderson Ave.), Sunnyvale

Phone: 408-241-7292   Dinner Mon – Sat
Web: www.sawasushi.net
Prices: $$$$

Strict rules and big rewards unite at this zany, unusual and randomly located (in a mall) dive, where Chef Steve Sawa rules the roost. After going through the rigmarole of landing a reservation for his omakase-only affair, throw all caution to the wind and just go with the flow. Yes, the décor is nothing special and downright weird; however, the food is anything but so-so and the ad hoc prices are usually quite high.

So what draws such a host of regulars? Their pristine and very sublime fish, of course—from creamy Hokkaido sea scallops to delicious toro ribbons. Sawa is also an expert on sauces: imagine the likes of *yuzu kosho* topping kanpachi, or a sweet-spicy tamarind glaze on ocean trout. Finish with a top sake or cold beer and feel the joy seep in.

The Sea

B2

Seafood

4269 El Camino Real (at Dinah's Ct.), Palo Alto

Phone: 650-213-1111   Dinner nightly
Web: www.theseausa.com
Prices: $$$

Palo Alto's buzzy new arrival is brought to you by the folks behind Alexander's Steakhouse. Offering a sophisticated and capacious setting that boasts the finer touches and ample proportions, The Sea has already become a preferred destination for expense account meals and group dining.

Meanwhile, the kitchen's skilled chef and crew combine Asian accents, French technique, and Californian sensibility to produce a first-class roster of carefully sourced ingredients. Elegant appetizers include Dungeness crab salad with purple rice, blood orange, and ginger crème fraîche. Entrées reveal fish like seared mero, caught off the coast of Hawaii, neatly trimmed, nicely seared, and plated with sweet potato purée, caramelized *cipollini* onions, and a drizzle of Port.

Smoking Pig BBQ

Barbecue ✗

E2

1144 N. 4th St. (bet. Commercial St. & E. Younger Ave.), San Jose

Phone: 408-380-4784
Web: www.smokingpigbbq.net
Prices: 🪙🪙

Lunch & dinner daily

Identifiable by the aroma of wood smoke that surrounds it for a block in every direction, this barbecue-slinging dive is wildly popular. Read: plan on a wait in the smoker-ringed parking lot if you want to dine at prime meal times. Accommodations are beyond basic, with tattered booths and disposable servingware, but service is friendly, and something about the lack of ambience amplifies the gustatory pleasure.

Indeed, there is plenty of pleasure to be found on the combination plates, especially via the signature pork ribs—smoky and well-seasoned, they fall off the bone. Order them up in a combination plate of peppery brisket or juicy pulled pork, along with a cornbread muffin and tasty, smoky beans with burnt ends. This is pigging out at its finest.

South Legend

Chinese ✗

E1

1720 N. Milpitas Blvd. (bet. Dixon Landing Rd. & Sunnyhills Ct.), Milpitas

Phone: 408-934-3970
Web: www.southlegend.com
Prices: 🪙🪙

Lunch & dinner daily

In the Sunnyhills strip mall, packed with Chinese restaurants and Asian markets, South Legend stands out for its fiery and lip-numbing interpretations of classic Sichuan cooking. Though Chengdu-style dim sum provides a brief respite on weekend mornings, it's all about the heat the rest of the week in dishes like fried Chongqing chicken topped with piles of dried chilies.

Large and no-frills, South Legend is usually crammed with locals looking for an authentic taste of their Chinese childhoods, grungy dining room and dated décor be damned. They're too busy sweating out spicy pickled vegetables and enormous braised whole fish covered in still more chilies, then cooling off with some blander *dan dan* noodles and a pot of hot black tea.

Sumika

Japanese ✗

236 Plaza Central (bet. 2nd & 3rd Sts.), Los Altos

Phone: 650-917-1822
Web: www.sumikagrill.com
Prices: $$

Lunch Tue – Sat
Dinner Tue – Sun

Sumika is first and foremost an *izakaya*. There are just a handful of wood tables and the rest of the guests sit at a counter facing the kitchen, where they gaze longingly at the specialty—*kushiyaki*, skewers on a smoking grill set atop a charcoal fire. Lunch is a mellow meal frequented by local families. A noon spread likely includes fragrant miso soup, followed by a bowlful of white rice topped with crumbled chicken *tsukune* and a soft-cooked egg; or golden-fried chicken *katsu* matched with spicy Japanese mustard and smoky *tonkatsu* sauce.

At dinner, the place fills up with those seeking an easygoing vibe in which to enjoy beer and sake with their skewers of chicken heart or pork cheek. Small plates of deliciously crispy Japanese-style fried chicken anyone?

The Table

American ✗

1110 Willow St. (at Lincoln Ave.), San Jose

Phone: 408-638-7911
Web: www.thetablesj.com
Prices: $$

Lunch Fri – Sun
Dinner nightly

The casual, farm-to-table food that's standard fare in SF is harder to come by in San Jose, which explains why this ingredient-centric gathering place is always packed with diners. With long wood tables, large windows, a busy back bar, and lots of hard, modern surfaces—not to mention a bevy of craft cocktails fueling the crowds—it can get noisy. Read: don't plan an intimate evening here.

Instead, make The Table your spot to share bites and drinks with friends, like caramelized sourdough spaetzle with smoked butternut squash and pea tendrils, or sugar-dusted ricotta beignets with lemon curd. Brunch is so popular that it's offered on Fridays as well as weekends, but you should expect a wait to enjoy your omelette, hash browns, or more of those beignets.

Tamarine

Vietnamese ✕✕

A4

546 University Ave. (bet. Cowper & Webster Sts.), Palo Alto

Phone: 650-325-8500
Web: www.tamarinerestaurant.com
Prices: $$$

Lunch Mon – Fri
Dinner nightly

At Tamarine, contemporary Asian accents, low lighting, and walls showcasing works for sale by Vietnamese artists combine to fashion a swanky atmosphere that reflects the restaurant's modern take on Vietnamese cuisine.

All of this makes chic Tamarine a darling among Palo Alto's eclectic community. Corporate suits talk business in the large private dining room. Moneyed tech types fill up the front bar and share the likes of tender hoisin- garlic- and rosemary-glazed lamb chops, or *bánh mì roti* with spicy coconut Penang curry sauce for dipping those puffy crêpes. There is a quieter nook in the back where one might find ladies who lunch and couples sharing the outstanding sticky toffee pudding oozing hot caramel, or sipping refreshing Kaffir lime cocktails.

Tanto

Japanese ✕

D2

1063 E. El Camino Real (bet. Helen & Henderson Aves.), Sunnyvale

Phone: 408-244-7311
Web: N/A
Prices: $$

Lunch Tue – Fri
Dinner Tue – Sun

Lone rangers on tech-office lunch breaks pack this strip-mall Japanese spot, whose crowded parking lot belies its unimpressive façade. Waits are inevitable, but it's worth it to sit down to a steaming bowl of simple and flavorful udon. Indeed, all the standards are rendered beautifully here, from crisp vegetable tempura to tender, flaky grilled *unagi* set atop freshly steamed rice.

Tanto's menu expands a bit at dinner, bringing more grilled items and *izakaya*-style small plates. Pristine sushi and sashimi like albacore with ponzu are also a strong pick. You'll likely be seated at one of the closely-spaced dining room tables, but the occasional stroke of luck might land you in one of the curtained, semi-private alcoves popular with business diners.

273

Thiên Long

Vietnamese 🍴

F3

3005 Silver Creek Rd., Ste.138 (bet. Aborn Rd. & Lexann Ave.), San Jose

Phone: 408-223-6188   Lunch & dinner daily
Web: www.thienlongrestaurant.com
Prices:

There are plenty of Vietnamese restaurants catering to the local expats in San Jose, but Thiên Long stands out for its pleasant dining room presenting delicious cooking—as the numerous families filling the large space will attest. Tile floors and rosewood-tinted chairs decorate the space, while walls hung with photos of Vietnamese dishes keep the focus on food.

Begin with sweet-salty barbecued prawns paired with smoky grilled pork and served atop rice noodles. But, it is really the *pho* with a broth of star anise, clove, and ginger, topped with perfectly rare beef that is a true gem—even the regular-sized portion is enormous. English is a challenge among the staff, but they are very friendly; plus the faithful flavors make up for any inadequacies.

Vung Tau

Vietnamese 🍴🍴

E3

535 E. Santa Clara St. (at 12th St.), San Jose

Phone: 408-288-9055   Lunch & dinner daily
Web: www.vungtaurestaurant.com
Prices:

It's easy to see why Vung Tau is a longtime love and go-to favorite among South Bay locals: think elegant décor, hospitable service, massive menu, and tasty food. Inside, the large space combines several dining areas styled with soft beiges, wood accents, and pendant lights. Lunchtime draws in business crowds while dinner brings families, many of whom are of Vietnamese heritage.

Authenticity is paramount in such offerings as hearty *bun bo hue*—ask for Vietnamese not American style—which comes with sliced flank steak, beef tendons, and pork blood in a spicy, earthy broth, served with a side of fresh herbs, lime, onions, and bean sprouts. Delicately sweet and creamy pleasures abound in *bánh khot*, delightful coconut-prawn cups served with chili-fish sauce.

Zeni

Ethiopian ✗

D3

1320 Saratoga Ave. (at Payne Ave.), San Jose

Phone: 408-615-8282   Lunch & dinner Tue – Sun
Web: N/A
Prices: $$

Diners get to choose their own adventure at this Ethiopian standby located beside a shopping plaza. Zeni caters to expats as well as foodies of all stripes with traditional basket-like pedestals bounded by low stools. Regardless of your seat, you'll be served spongy, sour *injera* to scoop up delicious *yemisir wot* (red lentils with spicy *berbere*); *kik alicha* (yellow peas tinged with garlic and ginger); or beef *kitfo* (available raw or cooked), tossed with *mitmita* (an aromatic spice blend) and crowned with crumbled *ayib* cheese. Here, *injera* is your utensil so no need to ask for one; there's a sink in the back to clean up after.

Sip cool, sweet honey wine to balance the spicy food, or opt for an after-dinner Ethiopian coffee.

Zona Rosa

Mexican ✗

E3

1411 The Alameda (bet. Hester & Shasta Aves.), San Jose

Phone: 408-275-1411   Lunch Tue – Sun
Web: www.zonarosasj.com   Dinner nightly
Prices: $$

For food just like *abuela's* (but somehow even better), make a beeline to this soul-warming cantina, which makes its salsas, blue and white corn tortillas, and other timeless dishes by hand. Start with an *antojito* like *albondigas fundido,* then proceed to tacos filled with *guajillo*-braised pork ribs and tomatillo-avocado salsa or pan-seared skirt steak with vibrant and garlicky *chimichurri*. Another star: a roasted *chile relleno*, which is smoky, spicy, sweet, and earthy in equal measure.

What the space lacks in square footage, it makes up for in down-home appeal, with steaming clay *cazuelas* cradling the dishes and vintage glass and iron pendants hanging above. It isn't a great choice for those in a rush as the homespun service can get easily overwhelmed.

275

Wine Country

Wine Country

NAPA VALLEY & SONOMA COUNTY

Picnicking on artisan-made cheeses and fresh crusty bread amid acres of gnarled grapevines; sipping wine on a terrace above a hillside of silvery olive trees; touring caves heady with the sweet smell of fermenting grapes—this is northern California's wine country. Lying within an hour's drive north and northeast of San Francisco, the hills and vales of gorgeous Sonoma County and Napa Valley thrive on the abundant sunshine and fertile soil that produce grapes for some of North America's finest wines.

FRUIT OF THE VINE

Cuttings of Criollas grapevines traveled north with Franciscan *padres* from the Baja Peninsula during the late 17th century. Wines made from these "mission" grapes were used primarily for trade and sacramental purposes. In the early 1830s, a French immigrant propitiously named Jean-Louis Vignes (*vigne* is French for "vine") established a large vineyard near Los Angeles using cuttings of European grapevines *(Vitis vinifera)*, and by the mid-19th century, winemaking had become one of southern California's principal industries. In 1857, Hungarian immigrant Agoston Haraszthy purchased a 400-acre estate in Sonoma County, named it Buena Vista, and cultivated Tokaji vine

cuttings imported from his homeland. In 1861, bolstered by promises of state funding, Haraszthy went to Europe to gather assorted *vinifera* cuttings to plant them in California soil. Upon his return, however, the state legislature reneged on their commitment. Undeterred, Haraszthy forged ahead and continued to distribute (at his own expense) some 100,000 cuttings and testing varieties in different soil types. Successful application of his discoveries created a boom in the local wine industry in the late 19th century.

THE TIDE TURNS

As the 1800s drew to a close, northern California grapevines fell prey to phylloxera, a root louse that attacks susceptible *vinifera* plants, and entire vineyards were decimated. Eventually researchers discovered they could combat phylloxera by replanting vineyards with disease-resistant wild grape rootstocks, onto which *vinifera* cuttings could be grafted. The wine industry had achieved a modicum of recovery by the early 20th century, only to be slapped with the 18th Amendment to the Constitution, prohibiting the manufacture, sale, importation, and transportation of intoxicating liquors in the United States. California's winemaking industry remained at a near-standstill until 1933, when Prohibition was repealed. The Great Depression slowed the reclamation of vineyards and it wasn't until the early 1970s that California's wine industry was fully re-established. In 1976, California wines took top honors in a blind taste testing by French judges in Paris. The results helped open up a whole new world of respectability for Californian vineyards.

COMING OF AGE

As Napa Valley and Sonoma County wines have established their reputations, the importance of individual growing regions has increased. Many sub-regions have sought and acquired Federal regulation of place names as American Viticultural Areas, or AVAs, in order to set the boundaries of wine-growing areas that are distinctive for their soil, microclimate, and wine styles. Although this system is subject to debate, there is no doubt that an AVA like Russian River Valley, Carneros, or Spring Mountain can be very meaningful. The precise location of a vineyard relative to the Pacific Ocean or San Pablo Bay; the elevation and slope of a vineyard; the soil type and moisture content; and even the proximity to a mountain gap can make essential differences.

Together, Sonoma and Napa have almost 30 registered appellations, which vary in size and sometimes overlap. Specific place names are becoming increasingly important as growers learn what to plant where and how to care for vines in each unique circumstance. The fact that more and more wines go to market with a specific AVA flies in the face of the worldwide trend to ever larger and less specific "branded" wines. Individual wineries and associations are working to promote the individuality of North Coast appellations and to preserve their integrity and viability as sustainable agriculture. In recent decades, Napa Valley and Sonoma County have experienced tremendous levels of development. Besides significant increases in vineyard acreage, the late 20th century witnessed an explosion of small-scale operations, some housed in old wineries updated with state-of-the-art equipment.

Meanwhile, the Russian River Valley remains less developed, retaining its rural feel with country roads winding past picturesque wineries, rolling hills of grapevines, and stands of solid redwood trees. With such easy access to world-class wines, organic produce and cheeses from local farms, residents of northern California's wine country enjoy an enviable quality of life. Happily for the scores of visitors, those same products supply the area's burgeoning number of restaurants, creating a culture of gourmet dining that stretches from the city of Napa all the way north to Healdsburg and beyond.

Note that if you elect to bring your own wine, most restaurants charge a corkage fee (which can vary from $10 to as much as $50 per bottle). Many restaurants waive this fee on a particular day, or if you purchase an additional bottle from their list.

Napa Valley

GRAPES GALORE

Venerated as one of the most illustrious wine growing regions in the world, Napa Valley is a 35 mile-long and very luscious basin where wine is everything. Given its grape-friendly climate and impeccable location (extending north from San Pablo Bay to Mount St. Helena, between the Mayacama and Vaca mountain ranges), Napa unsurprisingly ranks with California's most prestigious wineries. With stretches of valley floor, knolls, canyons, dry creek beds, and glorious mountain vistas, the microclimates and soil types are the beginnings of their renowned wine. San Pablo Bay has a regulating effect on the valley's temperatures, and the mountains minimize the influence of the Pacific Ocean. In the valley, powerfully hot summer days and cool nights provide the perfect environment for cabernet sauvignon grapes, a varietal for which Napa is justifiably famous.

Among the region's many winemakers are names like **Robert Mondavi**, **Francis Ford Coppola**, and the **Miljenko "Mike" Grgich**. Originally from Croatia, Grgich rose to fame as the winemaker at **Chateau Montelena** when his 1973 chardonnay took the top prize at the Judgment of Paris in 1976, outshining France's best white Burgundies. This feat turned the wine world on its ear, and put California on the map as a bona fide producer of fine wines. Since then, Napa Valley's success with premium wine has fostered endless pride. Fourteen American Viticultural Areas (AVAs) currently regulate the boundaries for districts

such as Carneros, Stags Leap, Rutherford, and Los Carneros.

SPECIALTY FINDS

The Valley's wine-rich culture coupled with its noteworthy restaurants that are destinations in themselves, make Napa one of the world's most popular tourist attractions. Reclaimed 19th century stone wineries and Victorian homes punctuate the rolling landscape, and serve as a constant reminder that there were some 140 wineries here prior to 1890. Up from a Prohibition-era low of perhaps a dozen, the region today boasts over 400 growers and producers, all clustered along Route 29. This main thoroughfare runs through the western mountains, passing through the county's commercial hub and continuing north through the charming little burgs of Yountville, Oakville, Rutherford, St. Helena, and Calistoga. The lush wine terrain continues along Silverado Trail, which hugs the foothills of the eastern range and lends the farming community an idyllic look. Along both routes, picturesque spots for alfresco dining and specialty stores abound. Be sure to pick up some heirloom beans from **Ranch Gordo**, headquartered here in Napa. Serving as the main supplier to the area's top chefs, this spot is open to the public who always seem smitten and return time and again for their selection of beans. Looking for some inspiration? They can also instruct you on how best to cook them!

Picnic supplies are the main draw at **Oakville Grocery** (on Route 29); while **Model Bakery** in St. Helena and **Bouchon Bakery** in Yountville are wildly popular for freshly baked breads and extra-decadent pastries. The continued growth in wine production has spawned a special kind of food and wine tourism in Napa County, and tasting rooms, tours, and farm-fresh cuisine are de rigueur. **Olivier Napa Valley** is a quaint, very charming retail shop in St. Helena selling oils, vinegars, and local food products alongside beautiful handcrafted tableware and ceramics from Provence. Residents who aren't rejoicing over their wares may be found dining along Washington Street, where acclaimed chefs like Thomas Keller, Richard Reddington, Michael Chiarello, and Philippe Jeanty frequently rub elbows. Other well-known personalities like Cindy Pawlcyn and Hiro Sone also hail from around the way. Like the neighborhood itself, they have successfully raised their local-legend status to an international level.

SHOPPING TREATS

Visitors touring the Valley will spot fields of wild fennel, silvery olive trees, and rows of wild mustard that bloom between the grapevines in February and March. The mustard season kicks off each year with the **Napa Valley Mustard Festival** paying homage to the food, wine, art, and agricultural bounty of the region. Several towns host seasonal farmer's markets from around May through October, including one in Napa (held near Oxbow Public Market on Tuesdays and Saturdays); St. Helena (Fridays in Crane Park); and Calistoga (on Saturdays at Sharpsteen Museum plaza on Washington Street). On Thursday nights in the summer, the **Chef's Market** in Napa Town Center unites the community over cooking classes held by local chefs of world-famous status and draws folks from near and far for amazing food and wine pairings. Launched in early 2008, famed **Oxbow Public Market** is a block-long, 40,000-square-foot

Toffee Milk Chocolate

SugaRai

facility that is meant to rival the **Ferry Building Marketplace** across the bay. Flooded with food artisans and wine vendors from within a 100-mile radius of the market, and housed within a barn-like building, Oxbow keeps its fans returning for everything from farm-fresh produce, cheeses, charcuterie, and spices to olive oils, organic ice cream, and specialty teas. For those who may work up an appetite while combing its shelves, there is a spectrum of snacks available to take-away!

SIGHTS TO BEHOLD

Napa Valley's regional products, such as **St. Helena Olive Oil** and **Woodhouse Chocolates** on Main Street, also in St. Helena, have gained a large-scale national following. Three generations of one family run this charming chocolatier, also favored for tasty, handmade toffees. Just north of downtown St. Helena, the massive stone building that was erected in 1889 as Greystone Cellars, now houses the West Coast campus of the renowned **Culinary Institute of America (CIA)**. Their intensive training and syllabus ensures a striking lineup of top chefs in the making. With all this going for the wine-rich valley, one thing is for certain—from the city of Napa (the region's largest population center) north to the town of Calistoga known for its mineral mud baths and spa cuisine, this narrow yet noteworthy region is nothing short of nirvana for lovers of great food and fine wine.

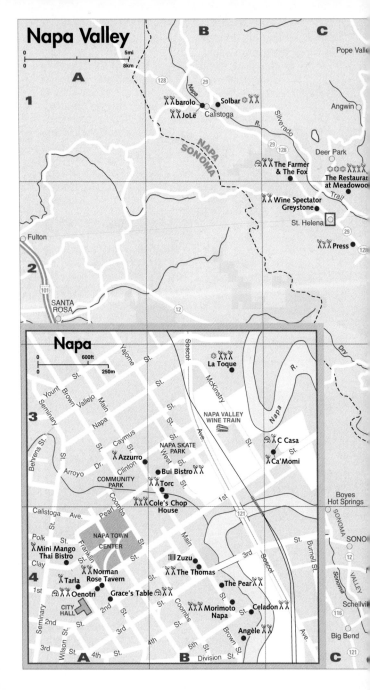

Napa Valley

0 — 5mi
0 — 8km

A **B** **C**

Pope Valley

1

Napa
128
29
✕✕ barolo
✕✕ JoLe
○ Calistoga
● Solbar ✳ ✕✕
Angwin ○

NAPA
SONOMA
Silverado
R.

29
128
Deer Park ○
✳ ✕✕ **The Farmer & The Fox**
✳✳✳ ✕✕✕✕
The Restaurant at Meadowood

✕✕ **Wine Spectator Greystone**
St. Helena □
Trail
29

2
Fulton ○
101
SANTA ROSA
12
✕✕✕ **Press**
128
Dry

Napa

0 — 600ft
0 — 250m

3
Yount St.
Brown St.
Vallejo St.
Seminary St.
Main St.
Napa St.
Behrens St.
Caymus St.
Clinton Dr.
✕ **Azzurro**
● **Bui Bistro** ✕✕
✕✕ **Torc**
✕✕✕ **Cole's Chop House**
Arroyo St.
COMMUNITY PARK
NAPA SKATE PARK
West St.
Soscol St.
McKinstry St.
NAPA VALLEY WINE TRAIN 🚂
✳ ✕✕✕ **La Toque**
Napa R.
✳ ✕ **C Casa**
✕ **Ca'Momi**
1st St.
Boyes Hot Springs

4
Calistoga Ave.
Polk St.
Clay St.
1st St.
2nd St.
3rd St.
Wilson St.
Seminary St.
✕ **Mini Mango Thai Bistro**
Franklin St.
Coombs St.
Pearl St.
NAPA TOWN CENTER
CITY HALL
✕ **Tarla**
✕ **Norman Rose Tavern**
✳ ✕✕ **Oenotri**
Grace's Table ✕✕
🍸 **Zuzu**
✕✕ **The Thomas**
Main St.
Coombs St.
3rd St.
4th St.
5th St.
Division St.
Brown St.
● **The Pear** ✕✕
✕✕✕ **Morimoto Napa**
Celadon ✕✕
Angèle ✕✕
Soscol Ave.
Burnell St.
SONOMA VALLEY
12
116
121
SONO
SONO
Schellvi
Big Bend
121

A **B** **C**

284

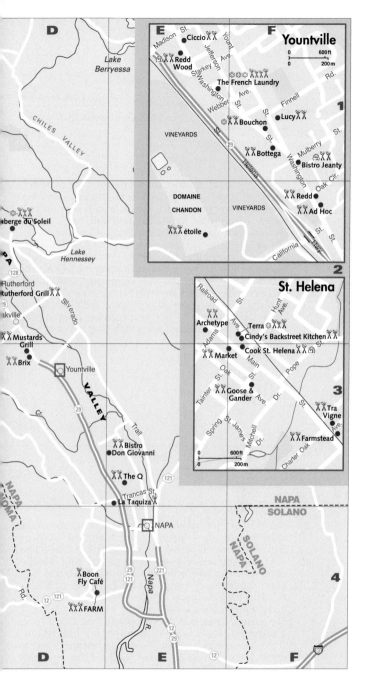

Yountville

Madison St.
Ciccio
Redd Wood
Jefferson St.
Starkey St.
Washington St.
Webber St.
Yount St.
Ave.

The French Laundry

Finnell Rd.

VINEYARDS

Bouchon

Lucy

St.

Bottega

Mulberry St.

Bistro Jeanty

Washington St.

Oak Cir.

DOMAINE
CHANDON

VINEYARDS

Redd

Ad Hoc

étoile

Helena Hwy.

California Dr.

0   600ft
0   200m

29

St. Helena

Railroad St.

Hunt Ave.

Archetype

Terra

Adams St.

Cindy's Backstreet Kitchen

Cook St. Helena

Market

Oak Ave.

Main St.

Pope St.

Goose & Gander

Tainter St.

Spring St.

James St.

Mitchell Dr.

Dr.

Tra Vigne

Ave.

Charter Oak Ave.

Farmstead

0   600ft
0   200m

Lake Berryessa

CHILES VALLEY

Auberge du Soleil

Lake Hennessey

128

Rutherford

Rutherford Grill

9

Oakville

Silverado

Mustards Grill

Brix

Yountville

NAPA VALLEY

29

Cr.

Trail

Bistro Don Giovanni

The Q

121

Trancas St.

La Taquiza

NAPA

NAPA
SOLANO

NAPA
SONOMA

Boon Fly Café

29
121

FARM

Rd.

12
121

Napa R.

221

12
29

12

SOLANO
NAPA

80

285

Ad Hoc

American ✗✗

F2

Wine Country ▶ Napa Valley

6476 Washington St. (bet. California Dr. & Oak Circle), Yountville

Phone: 707-944-2487   Lunch Sun
Web: www.adhocrestaurant.com   Dinner Thu – Mon
Prices: $$$

While the world clamors for a taste of Thomas Keller's renowned cooking, lucky Napa locals can make their way down the street from his flagships to easy breezy Ad Hoc. Hugely homey, this rustic-chic spot with wood residing everywhere is always crammed with locals and tourists.

The set menu is served family-style and may underscore such teasers as an elegant salad of little gem lettuces, romaine hearts, beets, and brioche croutons in a tangy herb vinaigrette. Buttered radishes and pea-and-potato salad finished with bacon crumbles and dill are perfect complements to the best fried chicken *ever*—crisp-skinned, briny, and moist. For the big win, dive into a cheese course revealing tangy cheddar and crisp puff pastry licked with vanilla-pear compote.

Angèle

French ✗✗

B4

540 Main St. (at 5th St.), Napa

Phone: 707-252-8115   Lunch & dinner daily
Web: www.angelerestaurant.com
Prices: $$

Nestled into a sun-splashed river bend adjacent to the Napa River Inn, Angèle is housed in a repurposed boathouse replete with wood panels and beams, French blue-framed windows, and linen-dressed tables topped with miniature olive trees. Not only is the setting of this downtown Napa bistro completely charming, but the impressive pedigree of its father-daughter team includes experience at key wine country destinations.

The menu is classic with a contemporary twist. Case in point: a seemingly simple apple salad that, at first bite, reveals a surprisingly complex composition of poached apples, roasted chestnuts, crumbled feta, and vanilla bean vinaigrette. Heartier items include a spot-on croque monsieur or roasted quail stuffed with bits of green chorizo.

Archetype

American ✗✗

E2

1429 Main St. (bet. Adams & Pine Sts.), St. Helena

Phone: 707-968-9200   Lunch & dinner daily
Web: www.archetypenapa.com
Prices: $$

While French Blue's farmhouse design turned heads, its fare didn't catch on with locals. No problem—the Solbar team was brought in to shake up its food and concept. Fittingly christened Archetype, the space is still a looker with an airy patio, wicker furniture, and light-flooded dining room. A stunning open kitchen, flanked by floor-to-ceiling cupboards, features an oak-fired grill and zinc bar.

The menu is a wide-reaching winner with dishes like buckwheat blinis topped with oozy burrata, followed by poached Delta asparagus with deviled eggs and trout roe. King salmon is roasted on barrel staves and topped with fried artichokes, while pillowy naan encases a lamb gyro with tomato jam. Chocolate-centric desserts and local wine amplify the pleasure factor.

Azzurro

Pizza ✗

A3

1260 Main St. (at Clinton St.), Napa

Phone: 707-255-5552   Lunch & dinner daily
Web: www.azzurropizzeria.com
Prices: $$

This casual, well-executed Napa Italian spot is the perfect place for a pizza and beer or glass of wine. The setting is semi-industrial with exposed ducts, polished concrete floors, and marble counters. Whether you dine with a group at the large wooden communal table or watch chefs toss arugula salads at the marble counter, you'll feel a brisk, friendly energy here.

Ten kinds of thin, crisp pizza are available, perhaps topped with slices of deliciously salty speck and creamy mozzarella, or the perennially popular *manciata*, a doughy crust topped with salad. (No health points for that one, sadly). Inventive and seasonal antipasti made with local produce and comforting desserts (think double-chocolate brownies) round out the top-notch offerings.

287

Auberge du Soleil ✿

Californian 🍴🍴🍴

D2

180 Rutherford Hill Rd. (off the Silverado Trail), Rutherford

Phone: 707-963-1211
Lunch & dinner daily

Web: www.aubergedusoleil.com

Prices: $$$$

Overlooking miles of vineyards and the stunning Mayacamas Mountains, the setting of this upscale auberge is quite literally picture-perfect. So it should come as no surprise that while the interior dining room is sumptuous in a laid-back California way with its timber accents and soft yellow color scheme, most diners prefer to sit *en plein air* on the expansive porch.

Executive Chef Robert Curry surpasses the challenge of ensuring the idyllic surroundings do not eclipse the cuisine; the cooking here is stunning in its own right. Expect to partake in ocean-raised Kona kampachi crudo, served over morsels of sushi rice and garnished with ripe avocado, strips of *kampyo*, drops of nori purée, and a succulent Hong Kong vinaigrette of soy, zesty ginger, and green onion. Local quail is presented pink, its crisped skin flecked with black pepper, and served alongside a cool salad of black quinoa, fresh hearts of palm, silken chanterelles, and Romano beans. A lick of well-seasoned jus is the ultimate finishing touch.

After dinner, sit back and savor the view over an impeccably crafted dessert such as the delicate roulade of pumpkin genoise and soft cinnamon marshmallow with espresso ice cream.

barolo

Italian ✗✗

B1

1457 Lincoln Ave. (bet. Fair Way & Washington St.), Calistoga

Phone: 707-942-9900   Dinner nightly
Web: www.barolocalistoga.com
Prices: $$

Set at the base of the Mount View Hotel & Spa in downtown Napa, this cheerful Italian restaurant is easily recognized—there's a Vespa scooter in the middle of the dining room. The pleasant space also combines red walls and white mosaic tiles with large, red-framed posters depicting pasta in all its glory. Local crowds flock to the small, close tables and expansive marble bar, which is perfect for solo dining.

The food spans all regions of Italy and unveils mozzarella- and pesto-stuffed fried risotto balls; rich spaghetti carbonara; and perfectly sautéed pork Milanese with mascarpone-Parmesan risotto and *salsa rossa*. In keeping with the name, the wine list is stocked with sublime (if pricey) Barolos, while the bar holds plenty of premium spirits.

Bistro Don Giovanni

Italian ✗✗

E3

4110 Howard Ln. (at Hwy. 29), Napa

Phone: 707-224-3300   Lunch & dinner daily
Web: www.bistrodongiovanni.com
Prices: $$

Located just off Highway 29, Bistro Don Giovanni can be easy to pass, but driving by would mean forgoing incredible Napa people-watching and superbly consistent Italian food. Park among the olive trees and grapevines, then take a seat in the airy, flower-decked dining room. If it's sunny, choose one of the rattan chairs on the peerless, postcard-perfect garden terrace.

A *pizzaiolo* mans the wood-burning oven in the front, firing up a selection of seasonal pies that are popular with families. Meanwhile, the more adult set opts for fried olives with warm Marcona almonds, *garganelli* with duck ragù, and seared salmon with tomato-chive butter, all washed down with local wines. Already conquered a number of wineries? Switch to a cocktail at the busy front bar.

Bistro Jeanty 🐾

F1

6510 Washington St. (at Mulberry St.), Yountville

Phone: 707-944-0103   Lunch & dinner daily
Web: www.bistrojeanty.com
Prices: $$

This cheery bistro in the heart of the culinary mecca that is Yountville is quintessentially French. Envision yellow walls, antiques, full flower boxes, and those woven café chairs and you will get the picture. And yet it also reeks of wine country charm by virtue of its welcoming staff and casual yet elegant demeanor.

The bistro's quality-ridden menu is exemplary, classic, and expertly prepared. For instance, a perfect and balanced rabbit pâté served with Dijon mustard and cornichons is beautifully chased by a supremely tender, slow-roasted pork shoulder paired with butternut squash gratin, caramelized Brussels sprouts, and bacon. One morsel of the crème caramel with a flaky Palmier on the gorgeous patio and you will be instantly transported.

Boon Fly Café

D4

4048 Sonoma Hwy. (at Los Carneros Ave.), Napa

Phone: 707-299-4870   Lunch & dinner daily
Web: www.thecarnerosinn.com
Prices: $$

Set amid the verdant pastures of the chic Carneros Inn, this rustic red barn is a friendly and unpretentious modern roadhouse, complete with a gracious staff. Fresh and well-made American standards include a classic Caesar with toasted onion, shaved Parmesan, and anchovy vinaigrette; or a generous Margherita flatbread pizza layered with mozzarella, tomatoes, and Italian sausage. Quesadillas and burritos are good, too. Be sure to check the blackboard for daily specials.

Though it's open from breakfast to dinner, Boon Fly Café's most popular meal is brunch, when parties wait on porch swings for eggs Benedict with jalapeño hollandaise. Whether they're locals in the know about its relaxed charm or travelers seeking a break, everybody leaves with a smile.

Bottega

Italian

F1

6525 Washington St. (near Yount St.), Yountville

Phone: 707-945-1050
Web: www.botteganapavalley.com
Prices: $$

Lunch Tue – Sun
Dinner nightly

Michael Chiarello is one of the original celebrity chefs, and his higher-end Napa outpost draws fans from around the globe seeking a glimpse of the *NapaStyle* star. Hopefuls are indeed likely to see him in the kitchen, drizzling olive oil on plates of creamy, almost liquid fresh burrata and marinated mushrooms; or pouring persimmon purée across thick slices of yellowfin tuna crudo. Even the wine list features his house blends, which pair nicely with pastas like whole-wheat *tagliarini* tossed in a pitch-perfect Bolognese.

Large and boisterous, Bottega's autumn-hued dining room welcomes crowds in comfy banquettes; find lovely outdoor seating by the firepit. A well-made tiramisu and espresso offer a fine *Italiano* end to the festivities.

Look for our symbol 🍇,
spotlighting restaurants
with a notable wine list.

Bouchon ✿

F1

French ✕✕

6534 Washington St. (at Yount St.), Yountville

Phone: 707-944-8037
Web: www.bouchonbistro.com
Prices: $$$

Lunch & dinner daily

Classic French fare feels fresher than ever at Thomas Keller's exuberant, theatrical brasserie, located just down the street from his iconic French Laundry. The chic dining room is the spitting image of a Parisian bistro, complete with lush potted palms, perfectly polished brass, and massive mirrors. An animated crowd energizes the space with laughter and conversation, and every plush banquette and stool at the bustling bar is full.

You'll want to grab a hunk or two of a perfectly fresh and crusty *epi* baguette as you peruse the appealing menu of pristinely executed favorites like steak frites and French onion soup. A warm chickpea salad tossed with chewy and sweet Medjool dates, tart pickled garlic, and grilled merguez is a light start. Then, move on to the decadently tender roast leg of lamb with quince and fall squash, or the meaty coquille St. Jacques nestled with mushroom duxelles in a perfectly browned crust.

While desserts like profiteroles and lemon tart may seem simple, you're not likely to find better execution anywhere else. Nor are you likely to encounter a friendlier staff: attentive, cheerful, and unobtrusive, they're polar opposites of the snobby Parisian waiters of legend.

Brix

Californian 🍴🍴

D3

7377 St. Helena Hwy. (at Washington St.), Napa

Phone: 707-944-2749   Lunch & dinner daily
Web: www.brix.com
Prices: $$$

This roadside gem overlooking the Mayacamas Mountains is almost as well-known for its extensive, 16-acre produce garden, vineyard, and sheltered terrace, as it is for its ultra-seasonal French and Italian cuisine. Dishes are eclectic and often refined as in beautifully crafted ricotta gnocchi cooked to a gentle gold in rosemary-browned butter, with creamy squash, plump Medjool dates, and almonds. The saffron and orange salmon arrives firm and pink with quail eggs, dill aïoli, and potato salad. An extensive Sunday brunch buffet highlights offerings from the wood-fired oven and charcoal grill.

The interior feels like a mountain ranch with stone walls, fireplaces, exposed beams, and clever chandeliers made of cutlery. Service is exceptional.

Bui Bistro

Vietnamese 🍴🍴

B3

976 Pearl St. (bet. Main St. & Soscol Ave.), Napa

Phone: 707-255-5417   Lunch & dinner Mon – Sat
Web: www.buibistro.com
Prices: 💰💰

Large and airy, Bui looks and feels like an upscale French bistro, rife with an Asian pantry serving Vietnamese cuisine… and so the fun begins! Clean-lined but not stark, the space contrasts olive-green walls with bright red booths and tall paper lanterns. Solo diners hit the bar for a chardonnay and plate of fried rice with well-seasoned tofu. Dishes like earthy banana flower with strips of tender chicken and cubes of juicy Bosc pear aren't Hanoi-authentic, but are tasty all the same. Purists might prefer the mild yet fragrant chicken curry, studded with lemongrass and ginger.

Delicious sautéed pea sprouts with olive oil and garlic are a favorite among vegetarians. For dessert, a Kaffir lime crème brulée underscores the fusion of the menu.

Ca'Momi

Italian ✗

C3

610 1st St. (at McKinstry St.), Napa

Phone: 707-257-4992
Web: www.camomienoteca.com
Prices: $$

Lunch & dinner daily

As if the Oxbow Public Market wasn't already teeming with temptation, this *enoteca*-cum-*pasticceria* is sure to grab your attention even before you've wandered twenty paces. The seating inside is housed within a private corner of the sprawling emporium, donning wrought-iron furniture and yellow-stained cabinetry. However, the spacious terrace is the best seat in the house.

Authenticity is the Italian menu's strong suit. From the listing, enjoy specialties highlighted by their region of provenance, such as a bowl of tagliatelle twirled with crushed fava beans, fresh mint, and lots of finely grated Pecorino Romano as prepared in Marche. The house pizza is certified Verace Pizza Napoletana, while slow-cooked items include poached beef tongue with salsa verde.

C Casa 😊

Mexican ✗

C3

610 1st St. (at McKinstry St.), Napa

Phone: 707-226-7700
Web: www.myccasa.com
Prices: 💲💲

Lunch & dinner daily

With a long line that marks it as one of the top destinations in the busy Oxbow Public Market, C Casa may look like a fast-food joint, but it's got serious sustainability credentials—all the more impressive given the reasonable prices.

Unique tacos are made to order and filled with the likes of mahi mahi or ground buffalo, then topped with plenty of fresh vegetables and garlic aïoli. If pork tacos with smashed white beans, cilantro, guacamole, and romaine don't appeal, then check out the daily specials on the small boards above the griddle and stoves. They might include rotisserie chicken with a pile of crisp Caesar salad or a rich duck *tostada*. Throw in a Mexican coffee, fresh juice, or glass of local wine, and you'll still have cash left over.

Celadon

International XX

B4

500 Main St., Ste. G (at 5th St.), Napa

Phone: 707-254-9690 Lunch Mon – Fri
Web: www.celadonnapa.com Dinner nightly
Prices: $$

Housed in the historic Napa Mill complex on the banks of the Napa River, Celadon is named for the comforting shade of gray-green that permeates its dining room. Inside, small tables, a quaint bar, and framed family photos lend charm, while a heated outdoor atrium with a corrugated aluminum roof lets in natural light by day and serene flickers from the brick fireplace at night. Oversized bottles of wine can be found throughout the dining room.

Chef Greg Cole is a Napa fixture and his signature global cuisine ranges from a nice rendition of classic Caesar salad, to plump and gently seared *togarashi*-crusted diver scallops set over creamy mashed potatoes. Friendly service adds to the appeal, as does the wide selection of local wines.

Ciccio

Italian XX

E1

6770 Washington St. (bet. Madison & Pedroni Sts.), Yountville

Phone: 707-945-1000 Dinner Wed – Sun
Web: www.ciccionapavalley.com
Prices: $$

A pleasant contrast to the sleek new spots around town, Ciccio's country-style curtains and slatted front porch are a ticket to another era. Its location (a wood-framed 1916-era grocery) could pass as some John Wayne film set, but Ciccio is more of a spaghetti Western, thanks to the focused Italian-influenced menu featuring a mega-rich pasta accented with fresh uni, crisp breadcrumbs, and generous dose of cream. Segue from carbs into the bone-in pork chop with fennel gratin, but don't miss the remarkable signature Ciccio sponge cake, soaked in citrus liqueur and topped with grapefruit and orange.

With turn-of-the-century square footage, tables are a hot ticket here. Expect a wait for even a lowly bar stool, happily passed with a glass of local pinot.

Cindy's Backstreet Kitchen

International 🍴🍴

F2

1327 Railroad Ave. (bet. Adams St. & Hunt Ave.), St. Helena

Phone: 707-963-1200　　　　　　　　　　Lunch & dinner daily
Web: www.cindysbackstreetkitchen.com
Prices: $$

Cindy's can be found in a historic 1800's house tucked along Railroad Avenue in quaint St. Helena. Locals and families enjoy its welcoming setting—loads of country charm infuses everything from the fruit-motif wallpaper, down to the cushioned banquettes and gracious service.

Under the spin of ceiling fans, a globally influenced menu of small plates, salads, sandwiches, and large plates is divulged. Expect the likes of achiote-roasted pulled pork tacos featuring white corn tortillas, avocado, and kicky red chile salsa; or a delightful duck burger flavored with ginger, topped with a shiitake mushroom reduction, smear of Chinese mustard, and served with crispy fries. But leave room for dessert or just save the homemade honey-glazed cornbread for last!

Cole's Chop House

Steakhouse 🍴🍴🍴

B3

1122 Main St. (bet. 1st & Pearl Sts.), Napa

Phone: 707-224-6328　　　　　　　　　　Dinner nightly
Web: www.coleschophouse.com
Prices: $$$$

Prime meat at prime prices is the modus operandi at Cole's, which gives diners their pick of deeply flavorful cuts like dry-aged California rib-eye or 21-day Chicago dry-aged New York strip. Faithful accompaniments like baked potatoes, creamed spinach, and crisp asparagus with Hollandaise round out the menu. Traditional desserts like a comforting bourbon bread pudding or perfect sugar-crusted crème brulée are a satisfying end to the meal. A selection of gutsy red wines, bourbons, and single-malt Scotches stand up to the steak.

In place of the clubby atmosphere of traditional steakhouses, Cole's (which shares ownership with nearby Celadon) is more refined, with a barn-like stone interior and cozy selection of booths and mezzanine tables inside.

Cook St. Helena 😊

F3

Italian ✗✗

1310 Main St. (bet. Adams St. & Hunt Ave.), St. Helena

Phone:	707-963-7088
Web:	www.cooksthelena.com
Prices:	$$

Lunch & dinner daily

A papier-mâché unicorn head hangs in this tiny Italian haven on St. Helena's main drag. Random? Not really, when one considers how rare solid cooking and sane prices can be in this tony burg. The cozy space has two seating options: a marble counter up front and tables stretching from front to back (the front tables, lighter and airier, are preferable).

The food is thoughtful and refined with a daily rotating risotto, house-stretched mozzarella and burrata, and glorious pastas like ricotta *fazoletti* married with a deeply flavored Bolognese. Grilled octopus salad with potatoes, olives, and tomato dressing is boosted by prime ingredients and careful seasoning. A strong red wine list tempts at dinner while bloody Mary's are all the rage for Sunday brunch.

étoile

E2

Contemporary ✗✗✗

1 California Dr. (off Hwy. 29), Yountville

Phone:	707-204-7529
Web:	www.chandon.com
Prices:	$$$$

Lunch & dinner Thu – Mon

The barrel-like curved wood ceilings at this lovely sanctum serve as a reminder of its owner—the famed sparkling wine producer Domaine Chandon. Tourists with cheeks flushed from wine tasting flock here for a glass of their rosé, perhaps selecting a treat from the oyster and caviar menu, before sampling artistic plates like Colorado lamb loin over Israeli couscous and eggplant.

Each dish at étoile contains a wealth of ingredients like sunchoke, spinach, beets, chard, orange, and brown butter that interplay beautifully with fleshy, pan-seared Arctic char. The informed staff can help navigate both the menu and 5,000+ bottles on the iPad-based wine list, but don't let them steer you away from a classic caramelized pear mille-feuille for dessert.

FARM

D4

4048 Sonoma Hwy. (at Old Sonoma Rd.), Napa

Phone: 707-299-4882   Dinner Wed – Sun
Web: www.thecarnerosinn.com
Prices: $$$

Just off a main road at the Carneros Inn, FARM exudes wine country style with cathedral ceilings, romantic banquettes, trendy fixtures, and the requisite fireplaces. Expect a mixed clientele of fancy locals, tourists, and hotel guests filling the main dining room and watching the chefs through the glassed-in kitchen.

Whether settling into a cushioned wicker seat in the outdoor lounge to sip local wines by the half-glass, noshing at the indoor bar, or going for the tasting menu in the dining room, the gorgeous surrounds will not disappoint. On the menu, expect interesting compositions like lobster risotto with Parmesan and Meyer lemon. Seasonal desserts can be a highlight, as in pumpkin pudding cake with sugar-sweet pumpkin and butternut frosting.

Farmstead

F3

738 Main St. (at Charter Oak Ave.), St. Helena

Phone: 707-963-9181   Lunch & dinner daily
Web: www.longmeadowranch.com
Prices: $$

Local winemakers love to dine at this former nursery barn, owned by the 650-acre Long Meadow Ranch, which also supplies all of its olive oil, beef, and other produce. Spacious and airy, with a cathedral ceiling and an open kitchen, this is a lively spot to savor a great glass of wine from Long Meadow or another local producer. As a result, the spacious dining room is nearly always full.

The sustainable, Southern-accented fare changes with the seasons, but might include a light and smooth tomato soup with tart goat cheese *crema*, generously portioned bone-in pork chops flanked by jalapeño grits, and a hearty wedge of Scharffen Berger chocolate cream pie. Recreate the experience by taking home some fresh produce and flowers from the outdoor farm stand.

The French Laundry ✿ ✿ ✿

Contemporary 🍴🍴🍴🍴

E1

6640 Washington St. (at Creek St.), Yountville

Phone: 707-944-2380
Web: www.frenchlaundry.com
Prices: $$$$

Lunch Fri – Sun
Dinner nightly

The name is synonymous with impeccable food and service, which is evident from the moment you step through the courtyard garden and into this venerable stone building. Inside, the décor is more neutral and homey than highfalutin, with windows peeking into a wine cave and well-spaced tables covered in fine damask. The ratio of servers to diners seems unprecedented; know that every need or whim will be met without question or delay. There is a certain buzzy hush to the dining room; guests are here for the food but also to enjoy themselves, and not just pay homage to the kitchen.

Luxury is present on every plate, especially the beautifully pink veal wrapped in a thin spinach pancake with a single spear of perfect asparagus and baby turnips, served with rich whole grain mustard and a Hollandaise-like Jidori egg mousse sauce. Each marvelous flavor tempers and enhances the next in fava bean agnolotti with vibrant green-white ricotta filling streaming into the plate, blending with sweet onion cream sauce, young fava beans, and crisp shallots.

The French Laundry will be closed for a number of months while team Keller builds what is sure to be a spectacular state-of-the-art kitchen.

Goose & Gander

American ✗✗

F3

1245 Spring St. (at Oak Ave.), St. Helena

Phone: 707-967-8779   Lunch & dinner daily
Web: www.goosegander.com
Prices: $$

In keeping with the proliferation of more casual restaurants in this upscale area, the former Martini House has been transformed into this British-inspired gastropub. Wooden floors, red walls, and leather banquettes upstairs give it the vibe of a mountain lodge crossed with a private club. The downstairs bar is cozier and centered around a large fireplace. The simple, rustic fare includes shared plates like cheese and charcuterie boards or sticky-moist Medjool dates stuffed with Gorgonzola; as well as entrées like moist, tender roast chicken or rich Scottish salmon. Though the upstairs closes at 10:00 P.M., a limited bar menu is available until midnight—perfect for soaking up the array of local wines and handcrafted cocktails on offer.

Grace's Table 🍜

International ✗✗

A4

1400 2nd St. (at Franklin St.), Napa

Phone: 707-226-6200   Lunch & dinner daily
Web: N/A
Prices: $$

Around the world in four courses without leaving wine country? It's possible at this bright, contemporary downtown Napa space that balances fun with excellence. Only here can a top-notch tamale filled with chipotle pulled pork, green chile, and black beans be followed by cassoulet that would do any Frenchman proud—thanks to its decadent mélange of butter beans, duck confit, and two kinds of sausage.

With Italian and American staples in the mix as well, it might sound too eclectic for one meal, but Grace's Table earns its name with charming service and a thoughtful, well-priced wine list to bridge any gaps between cuisines. Don't miss the satiny ganache-layered devil's food chocolate cake—a slice is big enough to split, and a winner in any tongue.

JoLē

Mediterranean ✗✗

B1

1457 Lincoln Ave. (bet. Fair Way & Washington St.), Calistoga

Phone: 707-942-5938   Dinner nightly
Web: www.jolerestaurant.com
Prices: $$

Located in the center of Calistoga, JoLē is owned and operated by a husband (chef) and wife (pastry chef) team. The dining room may be simple, but it is never silent. Dressed with wood furnishings, a small bar lined with solo diners, and an exhibition prep area, this Mediterranean marvel is always jamming with locals and visitors.

The farm-to-table food is prepared with seasonal and flavorful ingredients. A tasting menu unveils shredded kale stew, salty from ham and creamy from potatoes and Parmesan *fonduta*; while bruschetta is topped with fine fixings like wilted spinach, buttery chanterelles, and a quail egg. Glazed duck breast with eggplant and tofu is as tender as the cubes of lamb in a flavorful stew of carrots finished with pillows of gnocchi.

La Taquiza

Mexican ✗

E3

2007 Redwood Rd., Ste. 104 (at Solano Ave.), Napa

Phone: 707-224-2320   Lunch & dinner Mon – Sat
Web: www.lataquizanapa.com
Prices: 💲💲

For sustainable *sabor* that doubles as a budget-saver in pricey Napa, La Taquiza's upscale take on Mexican fast food is well worth a visit. Whether you prefer your fish California-style (flame-grilled) or Baja-style (battered and fried), you'll find no end to spicy, tangy, and savory options, available in heat levels from mild to spicy and in configurations from tacos to burritos to rice bowls.

However, the adventurous shouldn't stop at crisp corn tortillas—there's also a fine selection of snappy ceviches, grilled octopus, beer-battered oysters, and other delights from the sea. Counter service is friendly and prompt, and massive, colorful paintings from a local artist give the room a vibe almost as bright as their delicious strawberry *agua fresca*.

La Toque ✿

Contemporary 🍴🍴🍴

1314 McKinstry St. (at Soscol Ave.), Napa

Phone: 707-257-5157   Dinner nightly
Web: www.latoque.com
Prices: $$$

Upbeat yet relaxed, this Westin hotel restaurant is a swanky and sophisticated blend of leather-covered tables, soft rugs, tall banquettes, and vibrant artwork. Nothing seems opulent, but everything is precise, right down to the tailoring of the staff's suits. It's all very tranquil except for the ruckus in the vibrant, open kitchen, where Chef/owner Ken Frank is confidently blending tradition and innovation. Multiple, well-crafted dining options make it all the better for La Toque's upscale clientele to contemplate the elevated cuisine.

Here, kampachi tartare hints at what a talented kitchen can do with a rather ubiquitous dish: amazingly fresh fish mixes with cubed Asian pear, avocado, and ponzu-yuzu emulsion for a citrusy spark that heightens the full, clean flavors of the ocean. Pacific King salmon "tournedos" *a la plancha* arrive with a technically perfect and buttery Bordeaux reduction, oyster mushrooms, and sweet cipollinis. Finish with a warm, crumbly Gravenstein apple cake atop cool apple sauce, surrounded by "pearls" of chardonnay-poached apple, dots of caramel, and brown sugar-honey ice cream.

For a casual daytime meal, BANK Café and Bar (also from Ken Frank) is ideal.

Lucy

F1   Californian XX

6526 Yount St. (bet. Finnell Rd. & Mulberry St.), Yountville

Phone: 707-204-6030   Lunch & dinner daily
Web: www.bardessono.com
Prices: $$$

This modern restaurant in the eco-chic Bardessono hotel offers more adventure than many of its neighbors, while retaining the area's strict adherence to farm-to-table bonafides (including many ingredients grown in its own garden). Expect attractive compositions like a salad of orange and yellow carrots, some cooked until tender, some shaved into ribbons, all dressed in a curried carrot-shallot emulsion. Other dishes might include matcha-infused diver scallops, and a yuzu-accented strawberry shortcake with vanilla sorbet.

The sleek terrace features a Japanese aesthetic, overlooking verdant bamboo and a pond. The wine list highlights the area's best producers, while the courteous staff gladly helps hotel guests and tourists navigate the options.

Market

F3   American XX

1347 Main St. (bet. Adams St. & Hunt Ave.), St. Helena

Phone: 707-963-3799   Lunch & dinner daily
Web: www.marketsthelena.com
Prices: $$

St. Helena's scenic main drag is a trip back to the '50s, complete with quaint shops and an old-school movie theater. But, the food at this legendary downtown fixture is happily modern. Lobster rolls forgo buttered buns for Vietnamese-inspired rice paper with avocado and mango (all dipped in a delicious cilantro-basil-lime sauce); while a seared steak sandwich, loaded with onion and jack cheese, gets a spark from pickled jalapeño. Childhood-inspired s'mores for dessert end the meal on a nostalgic and graceful note.

The massive mahogany bar (a magnificent eBay find) is the heart of the pleasant space, which boasts stone-covered walls and big open windows for prime people-watching. Service is friendly and fuss-free, not unlike its picturesque surrounds.

Mini Mango Thai Bistro

A4

Thai ✗

1408 W. Clay St. (bet. Franklin and Seminary Sts.), Napa

Phone: 707-226-8884
Web: www.minimangonapa.com
Prices:

Lunch Tue – Sat
Dinner Tue – Sun

In an area where moneyed travelers seek Californian flavors and fine wines, good international restaurants can be hard to come by. So while this sweet, no-frills Thai spot may lack the proper heat level of a Bangkok street feast, it still earns its stripes for Napa.

Affordable favorites include tender sea bass topped with creamy Panang curry; steamed and seared radish cakes; or brightly flavored prawn, spinach, and lettuce wraps.

Though the dining room is small and comfortable with fresh plants and bamboo-covered walls, most diners head for the covered outdoor patio, all the better to enjoy the pristine wine country weather. Don't miss the chocolate-stuffed wontons with coconut ice cream for dessert—far from authentic, they're still close to divine.

Morimoto Napa

B4

Japanese ✗✗✗

610 Main St. (at 5th St.), Napa

Phone: 707-252-1600
Web: www.morimotonapa.com
Prices: $$$

Lunch & dinner daily

Beautiful Morimoto draws tourists and locals for its sleek industrial style and contemporary cuisine. The front room is best for groups and sports a sushi bar, stylish lounge, and large communal tables. The back area with its smooth wood tables and cushioned banquettes is ideal for a private party.

The innovative kitchen encourages sharing in dishes like sashimi towers (crafted from toro, salmon, eel, and tuna) painted with yuzu juice or barbecued eel sauce. Homemade tofu is prepared tableside and expertly coupled with mushroom sauce and bonito flakes; while a hearty pot pie with stewed abalone is comfort food at its best. Come with friends so you don't miss out on a fantastic sticky toffee pudding made with kabocha and topped with poached Asian pear.

Mustards Grill

American ✗✗

D3

7399 St. Helena Hwy. (at Hwy. 29), Yountville

Phone: 707-944-2424   Lunch & dinner daily
Web: www.mustardsgrill.com
Prices: $$

At Cindy Pawlcyn's iconic roadhouse, it's a joy to eat your greens. Lettuces are freshly plucked from the restaurant's bountiful garden boxes and tossed with tasty dressings including a shallot- and Dijon mustard-spiked Banyuls vinaigrette. Fish of the day may unveil grilled halibut sauced with oxtail reduction and plated with silken leeks, fingerling potatoes, and baby carrots. But, save room as this is not the place to skip dessert, and the lemon-lime tart capped with brown sugar meringue that is fittingly described on the menu as "ridiculously tall," doesn't disappoint.

It should come as no surprise that there's usually a wait for a table here. But no matter; use the time to take a stroll on the grounds for a preview of what the kitchen has in store.

Norman Rose Tavern

American ✗✗

A4

1401 1st St. (at Franklin St.), Napa

Phone: 707-258-1516   Lunch & dinner daily
Web: www.normanrosenapa.com
Prices: $$

Right in the heart of downtown Napa, this appealing gastropub offers something for everyone, from hearty bacon-wrapped meatloaf with a smoky coffee-barbecue glaze, to satisfying and soul-warming vegetable soup. Burgers, salads, and even a menu of dressed-up fries (from chili-cheese, truffle-Parmesan and sausage gravy to cheddar "disco" fries) are both appealing and affordable.

The open, wood-beamed space, with its rich leather banquettes and soft lighting, is ideal for both a beer-soaked game at the bar or group dinners in the bustling dining room. Solo diners will enjoy well-lit perches that peer into the kitchen, and charming servers are more than adept at keeping the party going until the last wedge of decadent, triple-layered carrot cake is devoured.

Oenotri 🎈

Italian ✗✗

A4

1425 1st St. (bet. Franklin & School Sts.), Napa

Phone: 707-252-1022
Web: www.oenotri.com
Prices: $$

Lunch Sat – Sun
Dinner nightly

There's no sweeter greeting than the aroma of wood smoke that beckons diners into this downtown standout. And with its Neapolitan pizza oven, sunny textiles, and exposed brick, Oenotri—from an ancient Italian word for "wine cultivator"—looks as good as it smells.

Chef/owner Tyler Rodde imbues the cooking of Southern Italy with a dash of Californian spirit and the resulting cuisine is nothing short of enticing. Options change with the season, but true fans know that pizza is a must. Mixed chicory salad with *mozzarella di bufala*, pickled red chilies, and house-cured *salametto* is also a crowd-pleaser. Not far behind the *torchio* or corkscrew pasta is presented with diced roasted winter squash, toasted pine nuts, fried sage, and a drizzle of brown butter.

Press

Steakhouse ✗✗✗

C2

587 St. Helena Hwy. (near Inglewood Ave.), St. Helena

Phone: 707-967-0550
Web: www.presssthelena.com
Prices: $$$$

Dinner Wed – Mon

This steakhouse-with-a-side-of-wine country is a hot ticket for sipping and supping. Hungry crowds gather in the peak-roofed setting, where a working fireplace, wood-fired grill, and rotisserie heat up the unbeatable ambience.

Though there are numerous distractions like the fantastic bread basket and a bacon listing that includes boar, duck, and candied strips, the focus here is on carefully sourced, impressively prepared meat. USDA Prime cuts of beef are offered along with thick chops, and sustainably raised lamb sirloin grilled over almond and cherry woods. Farm-to-table sides reveal leafy, wilted kale with diced persimmon; and even the dessert (New York-style cheesecake by way of California) is served with a generous dollop of huckleberry compote.

The Q

Barbecue ✗✗

E3

3900 D, Bel Aire Plaza (at Trancas St.), Napa

Phone: 707-224-6600   Lunch & dinner daily
Web: www.barbersq.com
Prices: $$

With its tight space in the congested Bel Aire shopping plaza, the busy Q makes the most of its location by offering as much seating outside as in. Potted hedges help separate the umbrella-topped patio tables from the parking lot, while the interior is more luxe with Italian marble, beveled mirrors, and black-and-white photos of local suppliers (namely, farmers and vintners).

"American heritage" cooking is on the menu, as in the Memphis-style brisket barbecue sandwich with slaw; Southern skillet of cornbread with honey butter; or Cajun hush puppies with cheddar and pickled peppers. Each table has a caddy of various hot sauces, and a bottle from the all-California wine list is ready to cool the burn.

Takeout is also a fine option if waits are long.

Redd

Contemporary ✗✗

F2

6480 Washington St. (at Oak Circle), Yountville

Phone: 707-944-2222   Lunch Wed – Mon
Web: www.reddnapavalley.com   Dinner nightly
Prices: $$$$

This low, minimalist, industrial-concrete building appears beautiful and peaceful in its setting of olive trees and ponds—an eye-pleasing study in contrasts. The food, on the other hand, is maximal comfort fare, from a wonderfully silky warm cauliflower purée with delicate chopped cranberries to a hearty New York steak sandwich filled with caramelized onions and a sharp horseradish aïoli.

More urban in feel than its neighbors, Redd is a tough reservation at dinner, when crowds imbue it with a perceptible buzz. Lunch is a more mellow affair, especially on the lovely patio with its gurgling fountain. It's a nice escape for a glass of local cabernet or to share a decadent chocolate mousse cake with peanut butter-praline—each bite is pure joy.

Redd Wood ☺

Italian ✗✗

E1

6755 Washington St. (bet. Madison & Pedroni Sts.), Yountville

Phone: 707-299-5030   Lunch & dinner daily
Web: www.redd-wood.com
Prices: $$

This offspring from Richard Reddington (of Redd down the street) is not just any old neighborhood pizzeria. Bespeaking a sophisticated-slash-industrial décor are high ceilings, dark-stained walls, tufted black leather banquettes, and a spectacularly lit bar area.

The Italian roster fulfills your wine country noshing needs. For a super start, indulge in golden-brown salt cod fritters served with batons of *panisse* and streaked with *harissa* aïoli; then move on to a thin-crust pizza topped with taleggio, prosciutto, and a farm-fresh egg. Bookend soft potato gnocchi joined by tender pieces of duck meat and caramelized pancetta, with a super sweet butterscotch semifreddo capped in a heady bourbon sauce. Sleep it off at the adjoining North Block hotel.

Rutherford Grill

American ✗✗

D2

1180 Rutherford Rd. (at Hwy. 29), Rutherford

Phone: 707-963-1792   Lunch & dinner daily
Web: www.hillstone.com
Prices: $$

As the crowds filter out of neighboring Beaulieu Vineyards and other Highway 29 wineries, they head straight to this upscale chain, which boasts long lines at even the earliest hours. Kudos to the amiable host staff for handling them smoothly. The dark wood interior is clubby yet accommodating, and a large patio offers drinks for waiting diners.

Every portion here can easily serve two, beginning with a seasonal vegetable platter boasting buttery Brussels sprouts, a wild rice salad, and braised red cabbage. For those looking to stave off tasting-induced hangovers, the steak and enchilada platter is *the* ticket with plenty of juicy tri-tip, yellow and red *escabeche* sauce, and a poached egg. A wedge of classic banana cream pie delivers the knockout punch.

The Restaurant at Meadowood ✿ ✿ ✿

Contemporary XXXX

C2

900 Meadowood Ln. (off Silverado Trail), St. Helena

Phone: 707-967-1205   Dinner Mon – Sat
Web: www.therestaurantatmeadowood.com
Prices: $$$$

Located in a sprawling verdant resort amid mountains and vineyards, this restaurant is the height of wine-country chic. The bar and lounge resemble a plush mountain lodge, thanks to fireplaces, vintage books, and soft leather seating. The remarkable dining room boasts a cleverly backlit vaulted ceiling over tables made with granite and columns of Canadian redwood. Every detail conveys American beauty and class. Service is usually faultless, anticipatory, and adept.

Chef Christopher Kostow's cuisine is not only stunning to behold but thoroughly delicious. Sample an autumnal "smashed pumpkin" presented on a thick, tree-like slab of pottery holding in a frozen shell of spicy-earthy *mole*, cracked tableside to reveal diced, roasted pumpkin, cheese curd, nasturtium leaves, and marigold petals.

The texture of tiny, meaty wedges of matsutake mushrooms perfectly mirror cuttlefish beneath a nest of young pine and silky, wilted enoki mushrooms surrounded by a hauntingly complex broth that may leave you speechless and amazed. A cup of squab tea (imagine sipping a bay leaf) may prepare your palate for dry-aged squab leg rubbed with spice bush, served with chunks of sweet beets topped with bonito flakes.

Solbar ✿

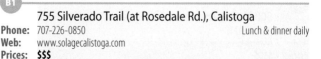

B1

Californian 🍴🍴

755 Silverado Trail (at Rosedale Rd.), Calistoga

Phone: 707-226-0850   Lunch & dinner daily
Web: www.solagecalistoga.com
Prices: $$$

Ensuring that you enjoy the journey as much as the meal, Solbar is accessed by walkways that wind past the fragrant rose bushes and gurgling fountains dotting the grounds of the Solage Calistoga resort. Once inside this airy dining room, you'll be treated to a panorama of distant mountains through large windows that complement the space's airy barn-meets-loft vibe.

Take a cue from locals who drink in the view from the chic lounge before heading to their luxuriously appointed terrace for alfresco dining. Offering plenty of reason to shift focus from the splendid vistas is Chef Brandon Sharp's Californian cooking—a hybrid of global accents and locally farmed produce. Proof is in the menu, where starters include a salad of red and golden roots laid over *garam masala*-spiked yogurt and topped with preserved lemon rind and pistachio meringue.

Solbar offers healthy eating at its finest, and the carte features hearty options displayed alongside simply prepared dishes like lemon-steamed halibut. Dressed *ribollita*-style with Castroville artichoke hearts, sweet black garlic, and San Marzano tomato broth, this zesty number proves there's no sacrificing satisfaction when choosing to dine light.

Tarla

M e d i t e r r a n e a n ✗

A4

1480 1st St. (at School St.), Napa

Phone:	707-255-5599
Web:	www.tarlagrill.com
Prices:	**$$**

Lunch & dinner daily

A stacked stone façade and orange sign indicate that you've found Tarla. This casual Mediterranean restaurant in Napa's hub boasts a modern décor with hints of rusticity—bright orange barn door panels line the walls. Guests can eat at the bar or at tables along a banquette. But, when the sun is out, alfresco seats on the sidewalk are most coveted.

Expect to see a mix of local business sorts at lunch and families for dinner devouring items that range in influence from Greek to Turkish. These have included a juicy lamb *kofte* burger layered with fava bean spread and white cheddar cheese, coupled with herb-strewn fries; or tasty beef *doner*, shavings of Turkish spit-roasted beef served on a pita coated with spicy mayonnaise and topped with a sumac salad.

The Farmer & The Fox 🕲

G a s t r o p u b ✗✗

C1

3111 St. Helena Hwy. N. (near Bea Ln.), St. Helena

Phone:	707-302-5101
Web:	www.farmerandfox.com
Prices:	**$$**

Dinner nightly

Burrowed within the 7-acre spread of Edwin and Stacia Williams' Cairdean Estate winery is this sophisticated taproom. Inside, soaring vaulted ceilings and wine country sunshine reflecting off the checkerboard marble floors are distinctly Californian features, set against the requisite backdrop of dark-stained wood and brown leather furnishings.

Chef Joseph Humphrey does gastropub cooking proud with his clever renditions of such old favorites including bar bites like popovers fresh from the oven and smoked duck wings with blue cheese and crunchy celery. Lamb tartare with fresh mint, fried shallots, and curry brioche; or rabbit Wellington featuring Swiss chard, spot-on puff pastry, and a classic red wine sauce are among the impressive items to be enjoyed.

Terra ❀

Contemporary 🍴🍴🍴

1345 Railroad Ave. (bet. Adams St. & Hunt Ave.), St. Helena

Phone: 707-963-8931   Dinner Thu – Mon
Web: www.terrarestaurant.com
Prices: **$$$**

This extraordinary but understated spot along a quaint stretch of St. Helena is housed in a 19th century building known as The Hatchery (it was once a hatchery). Today, the décor deftly embraces its earthy, rustic past to fashion a cozy but elegant room with floor-to-ceiling wine racks, exposed stone, terra-cotta floors, and chunky beams. The result is an experience that feels more old-world European than modern-day wine country.

Of course the cuisine is another story entirely. The seasons may be an initial inspiration, but whether this delicious and far-reaching cooking takes guests to Japan or off to explore the Mediterranean is entirely up to the talented Chef Hiro Sone. The fixed menus may begin with a nightly crudo presented as cool and terrifically fresh slices of sweet scallop, Kona kampachi, and uni artistically arranged with drops of ponzu, emerald-green olive oil, fine beads of black caviar, and watermelon radish shavings. Fresh pastas are expertly crafted and nicely chewy when tossed with a rich duck ragù, maitake mushrooms, and cipollinis. Heartier courses may feature a fantastic stew of slivered tripe.

Don't have a date? Head to Bar Terra next door for a more casual bite.

The Pear

Southern ✗✗

B4

720 Main St. (at 3rd St.), Napa

Phone: 707-256-3900   Lunch & dinner daily
Web: www.thepearsb.com
Prices: $$

The Pear is the brainchild of celebrated chef, Rodney Worth. He continues his love affair with Southern food at this Napa outpost, rife with stunning views of the promenade and river, a pristine exposed kitchen, and large dark wood tables. Speaking of *amour*, the Blues play in the background, further enhancing this sense of romance—look for the trumpet, violin, and saxophone, all hanging on pistachio-hued walls. Generous portions of great food including a creamy crab dip crusted with Parmesan and studded with baby artichokes plays into the Southern bent. Gumbo *ya ya* is an intensely flavorful stock bobbing with chicken and seasoned with andouille, tomato, and garlic. Bourbon-glazed baby back ribs with crushed peanuts evoke Louisiana in all its glory.

The Thomas

Californian ✗✗

B4

813 Main St. (bet. 2nd & 3rd Sts.), Napa

Phone: 707-226-7821   Lunch & dinner daily
Web: www.thethomas-napa.com
Prices: $$$

The first West Coast venture from the owners of NYC's Public, this historic building was most notoriously known as a bar called Fagiani's, which shuttered after an infamous 1974 crime (solved in 2010). The Thomas may have kept the previous owner's bright neon sign, but the interior is completely fresh with a downstairs bar, upstairs bistro with chunky tables, and an open kitchen, as well as a third-floor roof terrace.

The seafood-centric menu is varied, perhaps including fleshy grilled squid, an extensive (read: inviting) raw bar, and wood-grilled salmon. The brined and crusted pork chop is succulent and notable. And the bar, hugely popular for cocktails, also serves the full menu.

Sunday is a good day to visit, with a well-regarded brunch.

Torc

American ✗✗

B3

1140 Main St. (bet. 1st & Pearl Sts.), Napa

Phone: 707-252-3293
Web: www.torcnapa.com
Prices: $$

Lunch Sat – Sun
Dinner nightly

Torc may be Gaelic for "boar," but the food from Chef Sean O'Toole (who boasts the aforementioned boar on his family crest) is definitely not Irish. The large menu offers dishes with globe-trotting influences: Italian-leaning gnocchi with peas and favas; swordfish with artichokes and calamari; as well as a free-range roast chicken for two are some of his signatures. Classic desserts include a highly-refined milk-chocolate caramel bar, and the wines are great too—look to the warm and genuine staff to recommend a well-priced bottle from the moderately-sized list.

As for the ambience, the former Ubuntu space remains quite the looker with its exposed brick walls, highly-coveted banquettes (complete with views of the open kitchen), and industrial-barn vibe.

Tra Vigne

Italian ✗✗

F3

1050 Charter Oak Ave. (off Hwy. 29), St. Helena

Phone: 707-963-4444
Web: www.travignerestaurant.com
Prices: $$$

Lunch & dinner daily

Cal-Italian cuisine got its start with Chef/owner Michael Chiarello and this Napa grand-dame remains a tourist favorite. The vine-covered stone exterior could have been plucked out of Umbria, were it not for the surprisingly timeless, airy, light-filled dining room it contains. Service is less appealing, heavy on suggestions and smiles that wow the tour-bus crowds but may disappoint others.

The cadre of servers will push the mozzarella *al minuto*, memorable and famous in its own right, but find more modern offerings like enticingly chewy, palate-awakening kale and farro salad. Pasta courses may feature black tagliatelle with Meyer lemon, *bottarga*, and poached tuna. Worthy entrées include pan-seared wild cod over tender artichoke hearts.

Wine Spectator Greystone

Californian ✗✗

C2

2555 Main St. (at Deer Park Rd.), St. Helena

Phone: 707-967-1010   Lunch & dinner Tue – Sat
Web: www.ciarestaurants.com
Prices: $$$

The kitchen is the classroom at the Culinary Institute of America's West Coast training restaurant, housed (along with the school) in the former Christian Brothers château. The big, visually impressive room—with stone walls, copper lighting, and display of oversized spoons and whisks—is a comfortable perch in which to watch students at work in the open kitchen.

Each day's three-course prix-fixe is conceived and prepared solely by them, while an à la carte menu is more focused. Though dishes will change daily, expect the likes of roast quail, moist with lightly crisped skin, served with carrot-parsnip purée and squash ribbons. Swordfish arrives fresh and meaty, accompanied by lemon risotto and a bisque-like sea urchin broth packed with flavor.

Zuzu

Spanish

B4

829 Main St. (bet. 2nd & 3rd Sts.), Napa

Phone: 707-224-8555   Lunch Mon – Fri
Web: www.zuzunapa.com   Dinner nightly
Prices: $$

There's a sultry authenticity to this delightful tapas spot, which blends Mediterranean and South American influences with skill and care. Dishes include the signature *boquerones*, stuffed with the flavors of white anchovy, egg, and remoulade; or tender lamb chops in a minty-sweet Moroccan barbecue glaze. Daily specials might reveal a rich and spicy seafood stew. At a recommended three plates per diner, there are opportunities to sample numerous dishes.

The space is better than ever after a brief closure for earthquake retro-fitting, with a colorful, brightly tiled floor and artfully rusted Mexican tin tiles on the ceiling. Other attractions include their extensive list of sherry or wines by the glass, and dinner served until 11:00 P.M. on weekends.

VALLEYS AND VINTNERS

Bordering the North Bay, Sonoma County boasts around 76 miles of Pacific coastline and over 250 wineries. Eclipsed as a wine region by neighboring Napa Valley, this area's wineries understand and know how to take full advantage of some of California's best grape-growing conditions. Agoston Haraszthy established northern California's first premium winery, **Buena Vista**, just outside the town of Sonoma in 1857. Today, thirteen distinct wine appellations (AVAs) have been assigned in this area, which is slightly larger than the state of Rhode Island itself. These vintners continue to produce a groundbreaking range of varietal wines.

Along Highway 12 heading north, byroads lead to isolated wineries, each of which puts its own unique stamp on the business of winemaking. Named after the river that enabled Russian trading outposts along the coast, **The Russian River Valley** is one of the coolest growing regions in Sonoma, largely due to the river basin that acts as a conduit for coastal climates. While refined and popular grapes like pinot noir and chardonnay headline here, syrah is quickly catching up. At the upper end of the Russian River, **Dry Creek Valley** yields excellent sauvignon blanc as well as more chardonnay and pinot noir. This region is also justifiably famous for zinfandel,

a grape that does especially well in the valley's rock-strewn soil. Winery visits in Dry Creek are a study in contrasts as palatial modern vineyards rise up along the same rural roads that were once home to independents for generations. Young grapevines trained into laser-straight rows are juxtaposed against the dark, gnarled fingers of old vines. Sonoma County's most inland AVAs are **Knights Valley** and **Alexander Valley**. These two regions are marked by warm climates and highlight cabernet sauvignon. Nestled between the Mayacamas and Sonoma mountain ranges, the 17-mile-long Sonoma Valley occupies the southern portion of the county. At its center is the town of Sonoma, founded in 1823 and the site of California's northernmost and final mission—the San Francisco Solano Mission. At one time, the mission included a flourishing vineyard before secularization and incorporation into the Sonoma State Historic Park system occurred around 102 years ago, when the vines were uprooted and transplanted elsewhere in the county.

The town's eight-acre plaza continues to be surrounded by 19th century adobe buildings, most of them now occupied by shops, restaurants, and inns. Of epicurean note is the fact that building contractor Chuck Williams bought a hardware store in Sonoma in 1956. He gradually converted its stock from hardware to unique French cookware, kitchen tools, and other novelty items. Today, **Williams-Sonoma** has over 200 stores nationwide, and visits are considered obligatory among cooking enthusiasts around the world. Located just south of Sonoma is a portion of the Carneros district, named for the herds of sheep (*los carneros* in Spanish) that once roamed its hillsides. Carneros is best known for its cool-climate grapes, notably pinot noir and chardonnay.

PASTORAL PLEASURES

Throughout scenic and bucolic Sonoma County (referred to as SoCo to savvy locals), vineyards rub shoulders with orchards and farms. These in turn take advantage of the area's fertile soil to produce everything from apples and olives to artisanal cheeses. The words "sustainable" and "organic" headline these local farmer's markets, which herald the spring (April or May) in Santa Rosa, Sebastopol, Sonoma, Healdsburg, and Petaluma. Within these open-air bazaars, find every item imaginable from just-picked heirloom vegetables to sea urchin so fresh that it may still appear to be moving. Also from the sea, some of the best oysters are found off of the Sonoma Coast and enthusiasts may drive along Highway 1 to sample as many as varieties as possible—from **Tomales Bay Oyster Company**, **The Marshall Store**, and **Hog Island Oyster Company**, to **Drakes Bay Oyster Farm** in Inverness. Of course, Sonoma County boasts much more than mollusks. Start off

your day by following the locals and visitors from miles around as they head to **The Fremont Diner** for *the* most delicious and hearty breakfasts in town. The fact that every dish here is crafted with ingredients sourced from regional producers makes the experience all the more special. While here, try their very popular Bellweather Farms ricotta pancakes and find out what all the fuss is about.

Quench these hearty delights by heading straight to **Bear Republic Brewing Company Pub & Restaurant**—a family-owned operation in Healdsburg. Celebrated for such local, award-winning brews as Ricardo's Red Rocket Ale, brewery tours (by appointment only) are now an essential part of the experience here. And what goes best with beer? Barbecue, of course. While Sonoma may be little known for these smoky, deliciously charred eats, fans of **BubbaQue's** over in Petaluma might beg to differ. Large smokers on the side of Bodega Avenue and lined in front of a deli-liquor market mark the entrance to this serious take-out barbecue spot, famous for turning out the likes of pulled pork or pork ribs with a side of "Linda's" beans. Serious home gardeners should be sure to stop by the **Petaluma Seed Bank**, located in the historic Sonoma County Bank Building, as it happily counts motivated gardeners and farmers among their patrons. Find these artisans rejoicing in their selection of over 1500 rare and heirloom seeds. Prolong this love affair with local, hand-crafted treats at the original Powell's **Sweet Shoppe** in Windsor. This old-fashioned

candy store carries both the old classics as well as a massive variety of modern creations that can all be purchased in one spot. Pick up a pail at the door and fill it up! If that doesn't have you crawling up the walls,

look for their creamy, delicious scoops of gelato. In addition, numerous ethnic food stands bring world cuisines to this wine-centric community, with offerings that have their roots as close as Mexico and far away as India and Afghanistan. Thanks to Sonoma County's natural bounty, farm-to-table cuisine takes on new heights in many of its surrounding restaurants and some chefs need go no farther than their own on-site gardens for fresh fruits, vegetables, and herbs. With such easy access to local products like Dungeness crab from Bodega Bay, poultry from Petaluma, and cheeses from the **Sonoma Cheese Factory**, it's no wonder that the Californian cuisine here has attracted such high-levels of national attention.

SHED
HealdsburgShed.com

OPEN WED·MON: 8AM-7PM &

= COFFEE BAR =
Breakfast Pastries
Cookies and Ice Cream

= CAFE =
- Breakfas
8-11AM

- Lunch
1130AM-3
changing M

- Brunc
Saturdays·S
8AM-3

= FERMENTATION BAR =
Local Wines, Beers,
Kombuchas and other
Fermented Beverages
Afternoon Savories
Flatbreads Charcuterie
and Cheese Plates

= LARDER & PANTRY =
Farmhouse Cheeses, Charcuterie
Vinegars, Freshly Milled Flours, Ar
Breads, Local Produce, Prepared Fo

HOUSEWARES
Traditional Wares Focusing on
Cooking and Food Preservatio

= FARM & GARDE
Quality Tools, Supplies and

= COMMUNITY & PRIVATE
Workshops, Classes, Sundae
Private Events & Tasting

= 25 NORTH ST. 707·4

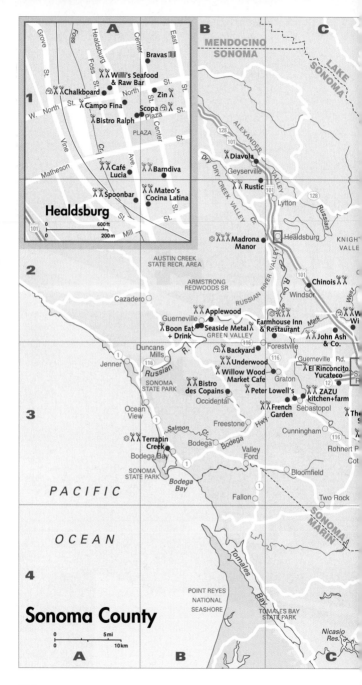

Healdsburg

A
- Bravas
- Willi's Seafood & Raw Bar
- Chalkboard
- Zin
- Campo Fina
- Scopa
- Bistro Ralph
- Café Lucia
- Barndiva
- Spoonbar
- Mateo's Cocina Latina

0   600ft
0   200m

B   MENDOCINO
     SONOMA

C   LAKE
     SONOMA

128
101   ALEXANDER   VALLEY

Diavola

DRY   Geyserville

DRY   CREEK   Rustic   101   Lytton   128   Russian

VALLEY   Healdsburg   KNIGHT'
                        VALLE

Madrona Manor

AUSTIN CREEK
STATE RECR. AREA

ARMSTRONG
REDWOODS SR

RUSSIAN   RIVER   VALLEY   Chinois   W
                            Windsor   Wi

Cazadero

Applewood   John Ash
Guerneville   Farmhouse Inn   & Co.
Boon Eat   Seaside Metal   & Restaurant   Mark
+ Drink   GREEN VALLEY   116   Forestville   Guerneville Rd.
Duncans   116   El Rinconcito   S.
Mills   Backyard   Yucateco   R.
Jenner   Russian   Underwood   Graton   12
            Willow Wood   ZAZU
            Market Cafe   kitchen+farm
SONOMA   Bistro   Peter Lowell's   The
STATE PARK   des Copains   S.
Ocean   Occidental   French   Sebastopol
View   Garden
        Freestone   Cunningham   116
Terrapin   Salmon   Hwy
Creek   Bodega   Bodega   Valley   Rohnert P
Bodega Bay   Ford   Cot
SONOMA
STATE PARK   Bloomfield
Bodega
Bay   Fallon   Two Rock

PACIFIC   SONOMA
              MARIN

OCEAN

POINT REYES
NATIONAL
SEASHORE

Sonoma County

TOMALES BAY
STATE PARK

0   5mi
0   10km   Nicasio
                Res.

A   B   C

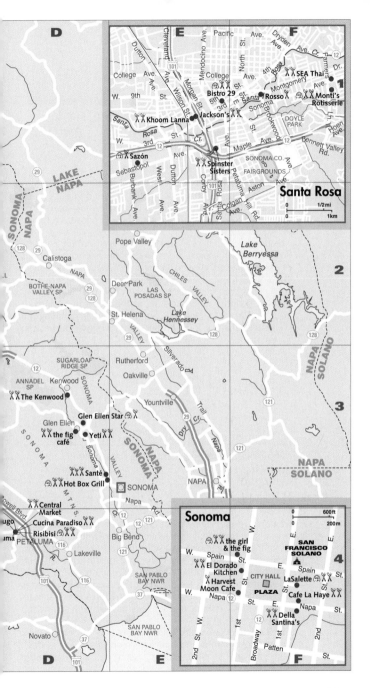

Santa Rosa

D

E   Pacific   F

Cleveland   Dryden   Ave.   Farmers Dr.

Dutton   Mendocino Ave.   North   St.   Ave.

College   Ave.   101   College   Ave.   4th   Ave.   12

W.   9th   St.   Morgan St.   Wilson St.   6th   St.   Santa   Montgomery   **SEA Thai**

Bistro 29   3rd   St.   Sonoma   **Rosso**   **Monti's Rotisserie**

Santa   **Khoom Lanna**   **Jackson's**   Brookwood   **1**

Rosa   St.   Cr.   Ave.   Maple   DOYLE PARK

W.   3rd   Ave.   12   101   Ave.   Bennett Valley Rd.

Sazón   Dutton   West   Corby   **Spinster Sisters**   SONOMA CO.   Hoen Ave.

Sebastopol   Ave.   Petaluma   FAIRGROUNDS

Burbank   Ave.   Santa Rosa   Aston   Ave.

Ave.   Colgan   Ave.   Hill Rd.

Santa Rosa

0   1/2mi

0   1km

2

Pope Valley   Lake Berryessa

Calistoga   NAPA   CHILES   VALLEY

BOTHE-NAPA VALLEY SP   29   Deer Park   LAS POSADAS SP   128   128

128   St. Helena   Lake Hennessey   128   SOLANO

VALLEY   29   128

SUGARLOAF RIDGE SP   Rutherford   Silverado   NAPA   SOLANO   **3**

ANNADEL SP   Kenwood   SONOMA   Oakville   Trail   121

The Kenwood   Yountville   29   Cr.   121

Glen Ellen Star   Dry   Napa   R.

Glen Ellen   SONOMA   NAPA   121

the fig café   **Yeti**   VALLEY   NAPA SOLANO

SONOMA   Sonoma

Santé   SONOMA

Hot Box Grill   SONOMA

Napa   Rd.

Powell Blvd   **Central Market**   MTNS   12   **Sonoma**

Cucina Paradiso   12   121

ugo   **Risibisi**   Big Bend   0   600ft

uma   PETALUMA   116   121   0   200m

Lakeville   **the girl & the fig**   SAN FRANCISCO SOLANO

101   116   SAN PABLO BAY NWR   Spain   St.   Spain   St.   **4**

37   **El Dorado Kitchen**   CITY HALL   **LaSalette**

Harvest Moon Cafe   PLAZA   **Cafe La Haye**

SAN PABLO BAY NWR   Napa   St.   Napa   St.

Della Santina's

Novato   37   101   1st   Broadway   Patten   St.   2nd   St.

D   E   F

Applewood

Californian ✗✗

B2

13555 Hwy. 116, Guerneville

Phone: 707-869-9093   Dinner Wed – Sun
Web: www.applewoodinn.com
Prices: **$$$**

With a sweeping view over well-manicured orchards, a top-notch spa, and 19 romantic rooms, Applewood is as much an appealing getaway as it is a destination restaurant. The talented kitchen prepares each dish with care, resulting in delightful starters like seared scallops set over fresh Mendocino uni in sumptuous, tangy saffron-butter sauce. Follow this with cocoa nib-coated lamb chops over lardons of sherry-braised chorizo and mint *chimichurri*. Dine à la carte or explore the tasting menu with wine pairings.

The dining room is quiet and barnlike with soft music, fireplaces, and couples soaking in the views of an interior courtyard from the enclosed sun porch. After sampling the well-curated list of local bottles, many choose to check in for the night.

Backyard

Californian ✗

B3

6566 Front St. (bet. 1st & 2nd Sts.), Forestville

Phone: 707-820-8445   Lunch & dinner Wed – Mon
Web: www.backyardforestville.com
Prices: **$$**

Centered in the sleepy main drag of serene Forestville, this hyper-local restaurant from a husband-and-wife team aims to make the most of Sonoma's seasonal and sustainable foods. Even some of the serving dishes are made from salvaged hazelnut and redwood. With credits for purveyors taking up more than half its length, the menu prominently features house-made pasta, sausage, and *salumi*. Begin with starters like deliciously creamy chicken liver mousse with sourdough points.

The butter-yellow walls of the open dining room display old window frames and hanging succulents. The red-brick courtyard offers seating under a giant oak and live music on weekends. Family-style fried chicken Wednesdays are popular, as is the succinct list of local wines.

Barndiva

Californian ✗✗

B1

231 Center St. (bet. Matheson & Mills Sts.), Healdsburg

Phone: 707-431-0100   Lunch & dinner Wed – Sun
Web: www.barndiva.com
Prices: $$

It's all kinds of wine country-chic here at Barndiva. From the rising vaulted ceilings and rustic wood tables in the dining room, to the gorgeous tree-shaded patio, this beguiling little number is the epitome of California-style sophistication. It's no surprise that many a wedding and private party take place here, so call ahead for reservations.

The exquisite menu has featured delights like creamy lobster risotto and luscious pork belly with bean cassoulet. Dig into crispy young chicken, perfectly prepared, seasoned, and served over roasted artichoke hearts, root vegetables, and smoky pancetta, with a soft ricotta-egg yolk *raviolo* perched on top. The warm peach- and almond-frangipane tart with vanilla bean-thyme ice cream is a dream come true.

The BBQ Spot

Barbecue ✗

C3

3448 Santa Rosa Ave. (bet. Robles Ave. & Todd Rd.), Santa Rosa

Phone: 707-585-2616   Lunch & dinner Tue – Sun
Web: www.thebbqspot.net
Prices: ⊜⊜

This Santa Rosa respite has a no-frills locale and is situated next to a tattoo parlor, but don't let the lack of ambience dissuade you—the little restaurant is turning out some seriously good barbecue. Its bill of fare has all the heavy hitters like succulent, falling-off-the-bone pork ribs that are smoky and caramelized with a sweet glaze; and tender pulled pork that is delicious on its own or drizzled with house-made spicy sauce. With sides like homemade baked beans and coleslaw to choose from, your barbecue sampler is complete. The restaurant is simple and causal with colorful linoleum floors, flat-screen TVs on the walls, and disposable utensils. Despite a planned move this fall, expect a low-key, local crowd to continue to frequent this spot.

Bistro des Copains

French   ✗✗

B3

3782 Bohemian Hwy. (at Occidental Rd.), Occidental

Phone: 707-874-2436   Dinner nightly
Web: www.bistrodescopains.com
Prices: **$$**

In the quaint town of Occidental, in a small cottage off of the main street, is Bistro des Copains. Take in the cheery yellow walls, wood burning oven, and red floral tablecloths. Vintage photos of the French countryside will have you instantly transported to Roquefort, where one of the owners spent part of his childhood at his grandparent's sheep farm.

Perfecting the setting is very traditional French bistro fare that might include onion soup to start; followed by *poisson du jour*, perhaps a simple and deliciously browned pan-roasted halibut, served over a pool of beurre blanc, and paired with a potato galette. One bite into raspberry shortcake filled with sweet whipped cream and plump berries, and you might even believe those memories are your own.

Bistro Ralph

Californian   ✗

A1

109 Plaza St. (bet. Center St. & Healdsburg Ave.), Healdsburg

Phone: 707-433-1380   Lunch daily
Web: www.bistroralph.com   Dinner Mon – Sat
Prices: **$$**

Set on the square in Healdsburg's central plaza, Chef/owner Ralph Tingle's California-French charmer draws plenty of locals for a light lunch or laid-back dinner. Though the menu is seasonal, afternoon standbys include crisp and spicy Sichuan calamari, a classic salad *Lyonnaise*, and a succulent lamb burger. In the evening, braised rabbit with egg noodles and a chocolate-caramel-espresso "animal-style" sundae are among the more substantial options.

Though there are two patio tables, the prime seating is inside, with whitewashed brick walls and an open kitchen with a concrete bar. Martinis are a special focus, with a big selection of vodkas and gins for mixing. Local wines, including some nice late-harvest dessert options, are also represented.

Bistro 29 😊

French 🍴🍴

E1

620 5th St. (bet. D St. & Mendocino Ave.), Santa Rosa

Phone: 707-546-2929   Dinner Tue – Sat
Web: www.bistro29.com
Prices: $$

This charming French bistro-meets-crêperie in downtown Santa Rosa specializes in the authentic dishes of Bretagne in the northwest of France. Bistro 29 has a traditional look to match the menu with deep red-painted walls, dark-framed mirrors, and crisp white linen. It is popular with locals and families and the diminutive spot is hopping at sundown.

Expect such faithful bistro items as a half head of butter lettuce massaged with a creamy *fromage blanc* dressing and then liberally sprinkled with chopped herbs. This is best trailed by a savory crêpe *Lyonnaise* filled with smoked lardons, caramelized onions, and melting cave-aged Gruyère. A runny egg tops this classic rendition and may leave you wondering how you got here without a passport.

Boon Eat + Drink

Californian 🍴

B2

16248 Main St. (bet. Armstrong Woods Rd. & Church St.), Guerneville

Phone: 707-869-0780   Lunch Thu – Tue
Web: www.eatatboon.com   Dinner nightly
Prices: $$

Its setting on cheerful Main Street may suggest small-town Americana, but Boon's fare is globally inflected. This is clear from the cool and refreshing toasted cumin yogurt that enlivens a tender Moroccan lamb stew, to the tang of buttermilk in an enticingly sour panna cotta with blueberry-thyme compote and plenty of vanilla. A large chalkboard offers numerous specials, tempting the crowds that flock here each evening.

The petite space is lovingly pitched between old-fashioned and modern, with extraordinary tables cut straight from large trees and aluminum bistro chairs. With lots of demand, even the outdoor seats are a hot ticket. French-press pots of locally roasted coffee and glasses of cabernet adorn each tabletop throughout the day.

Bravas

B1

420 Center St. (bet. North & Piper Sts.), Healdsburg

Phone: 707-433-7700
Lunch & dinner daily
Web: www.starkrestaurants.com
Prices: $$

This latest project from Willi's Wine Bar legends Mark and Terri Stark is named for the classic Spanish potato dish. Given their longstanding expertise with small plates, a truly Spanish tapas spot is right in their wheelhouse. Located in a small, quaint cottage two blocks north of Healdsburg's central plaza, the orange-walled dining room draws lines for first-come first-serve seats at the metal bar. Psychedelic posters and a beaded curtain evoke the '70s.

Bites are traditional yet flaunt California flair, perhaps beginning with a refreshing yet bold tuna belly salad with squid-ink vinaigrette, or a rich *jamón Serrano* and Manchego *bocadillo*. Spanish wines and sherries figure prominently, and soft-serve ice cream provides a fun end to the lively meal.

Cafe La Haye

F4

140 E. Napa St. (bet. 1st & 2nd Sts.), Sonoma

Phone: 707-935-5994
Dinner Tue – Sat
Web: www.cafelahaye.com
Prices: $$

For 17 years, Café La Haye has been a standby off the square in downtown Sonoma. One bite of its luscious burrata, surrounded with Early Girl tomatoes and crispy squash blossoms in summer, or vinaigrette-dressed pea shoots in spring, proves it hasn't aged a day. The small, modern space is still charming, with large windows and lots of mirrors. Stunning local artwork for sale decorates the walls.

The food spans cultural influences, including a delicate risotto with pine nuts in a cauliflower broth, or soy-sesame glazed halibut atop whipped potatoes and braised kale. A postage stamp-sized bar pours glasses of Sonoma chardonnay and cabernet, perfect with rich *strozzapreti* tossed in braised pork ragù, Grana Padano, and toasted breadcrumbs.

Café Lucia

Portuguese ❌❌

A1

235 Healdsburg Ave., Ste. 105 (bet. Matheson & Mill Sts.), Healdsburg

Phone: 707-431-1113

Web: www.cafelucia.net

Prices: $$

Lunch & dinner daily

Tucked just outside of Healdsburg's main plaza, this sibling to LaSalette shares its emphasis on authentic Portuguese ingredients, like seafood, stewed meats, tomatoes, garlic, and olive oil. Day boat scallops seared with a thin crust of *chouriço* sausage set over mashed Japanese sweet potatoes, and tender wood-oven roasted sea bass are among the delicious options.

A serene, plant-lined, interior courtyard leads to an airy dining room with a dark red horseshoe bar and prints of the owners' hometown, São Jorge, in the Azores. Settle into one of the espresso leather banquettes and be rewarded with cumin- and cinnamon-tinged dinner rolls, just like the chef's mother used to make—perfect for savoring over generous flights of Portuguese or Sonoma wine.

Campo Fina

Italian ❌

A1

330 Healdsburg Ave. (bet. North & Plaza Sts.), Healdsburg

Phone: 707-395-4640

Web: www.campo-fina.com

Prices: 🍴

Lunch & dinner daily

Just as card games inspire Scopa, this sister restaurant features a highly coveted patio for backyard bocce during the sunny months (expect a wait). The long, narrow dining room combines brick walls, Edison bulbs, and a wood-burning pizza oven, then gives way to the patio's arched twig roof for a lovely balance of sun and shade.

An antipasto like roasted and chilled spicy-sweet cherry peppers stuffed with tuna salad or burrata with grilled bread are great for savoring with a Negroni or black-walnut Manhattan. Sandwiches like *il Nonno* with house-made *soppressata*, rapini, fried egg, salsa verde, and Calabrian chilies make for a hearty lunch. At dinner, the Neapolitan pies take center stage, while a rich *shakerato* iced coffee is perfect anytime.

Central Market

Wine Country ▶ Sonoma County

D4   Mediterranean ✗✗

42 Petaluma Blvd. N. (at Western Ave.), Petaluma

Phone: 707-778-9900   Dinner nightly
Web: www.centralmarketpetaluma.com
Prices: **$$**

This is a relaxed but packed spot in downtown Petaluma where huge painted canvases of cows adorn the walls. Chef Tony Najiola is the welcoming proprietor walking through the dining room chatting with guests, many of whom are regulars. He is clearly passionate about his menu, which includes first-rate ingredients sourced from his own farm.

Foodies aim for seats facing the open kitchen where the chef can be seen creating Mediterranean-inspired dishes with care and precision. Starring local ingredients is a kale salad dressed in a light vinaigrette, tossed with shaved Parmesan, walnuts, and topped with a superbly fresh farm egg; or rainbow trout stuffed with wilted spinach, olives, and garlic, served with crispy paprika-seasoned potatoes.

Chalkboard 😊

A1   Contemporary ✗✗

29 North St. (bet. Foss St. & Healdsburg Ave.), Healdsburg

Phone: 707-473-8030   Lunch Sat – Sun
Web: www.chalkboardhealdsburg.com   Dinner nightly
Prices: **$$**

The space that long housed Cyrus now presents Chalkboard—enter Hotel Les Mars, pass by a gracious hostess, and head straight to this contemporary bistro adorned with vaulted ceilings, hardwood floors, casual banquettes, and very snug tables. The open kitchen may be ubiquitous but fits in beautifully with California's sensibility.

This small plates venue underlines an organic, seasonal menu capped off by local ingredients. The result is an excellent marriage of technique and flair as seen in hamachi crudo accented with fruity olive oil, sea salt, and ruby red grapefruit; or well-executed *strozzapretti* twirled with spicy sausage and leafy *broccolini*. A warm vanilla bean cake crested with Cointreau-and-crème fraîche sherbet makes for a perky finish.

Chinois

Asian 𝕏 𝕏

C2

186 Windsor River Rd. (at Bell Rd.), Windsor

Phone: 707-838-4667
Web: www.chinoisbistro.com
Prices: $$

Lunch Mon – Fri
Dinner Mon – Sat

Pan-Asian fare is given the fresh, seasonal California treatment at this Windsor bistro. The menu offers everything: plump, flavorful Filipino *lumpia*; Chinese dim sum; calamari and prawns in a peppy Cambodian garlic sauce. Thai curries, Taiwanese honey prawns, and even Indian *roti prata* are also represented, but the dance between cuisines is elegant and streamlined, not muddled.

The entry features a small wine bar that's great for solo dining, while the modern dining room is marked by red and white barrel light fixtures. The wine list is respectable (thanks to the surroundings); beer and sake or *sochu* cocktails are also strong. Happy hour, with $5 dishes and drinks, packs in crowds until 6:30 P.M. on the dot—get there early to savor it all.

Cucina Paradiso

Italian 𝕏 𝕏

D4

114 Petaluma Blvd. N. (bet. Washington St. & Western Ave.), Petaluma

Phone: 707-782-1130
Web: www.cucinaparadisopetaluma.com
Prices: $$

Lunch & dinner Mon – Sat

Set adjacent to the art galleries, boutiques, and theaters of Petaluma's delightful downtown, a meal at this farmhouse-style restaurant is like a jaunt to the Italian countryside. Deep yellow walls lined with wine bottles, embedded arches, and dark wood trestles set the rustic scene, while a large windowed façade gives diners a showcase view of the pedestrians strolling by.

Dinner always commences with fluffy house-made focaccia, a favorite among regulars. From there, choose from other delectable offerings like deliciously briny spaghetti with clams and mussels or tender, lightly crisped veal cutlets Saltimbocca, oozy with *Prosciutto di Parma* and provolone. Pair your meal with a bottle of great Italian wine, which the warm servers will happily recommend.

Della Santina's

Italian XX

F4

133 E. Napa St. (bet. 1st & 2nd Sts.), Sonoma

Phone: 707-935-0576   Lunch & dinner daily
Web: www.dellasantinas.com
Prices: $$

Just a few steps off the main square, through an iron gate, and down a brick pathway lies Della Santina's—a family-owned and operated Italian restaurant where guests are treated like part of the family. Coziness abounds from their garden patio with wisteria and olive trees, to the simple furnishings and family photographs.

The home-style dishes are prepared with skill and may be exactly what your Italian grandmother would make. And you'd happily heed her urge to *mangia* with dishes such as the restaurant's signature *gnocchi della nonna* (super soft gnocchi in an herbaceous tomato sauce), and a hearty *panino* of garlicky pork sausage and roasted peppers, served with a side of rosemary potatoes. Have a glass of wine and enjoy the warmest of welcomes.

Diavola

Pizza X

B1

21021 Geyserville Ave. (at Hwy. 128), Geyserville

Phone: 707-814-0111   Lunch & dinner daily
Web: www.diavolapizzeria.com
Prices: $$

Folks far and wide know to come to Geyserville for Dino Bugica's artisan-cured meats and pizzas. Once a brothel, the room's original wood floors, tin ceilings, and exposed brick exude history. And as for its decidedly tamer wares, find artisan hams, with whole legs hanging up front, as well as fresh sauces, sausages, and imported cheese available to take home.

A rosy pizza oven from Italy is hard at work at the end of the lengthy marble bar, where thin-crust pies are one-size-fits-all and decked with toppings ranging from the simple Margherita to smoked pork belly, meatballs, pine nuts, and raisins. Salads may include pomegranate, persimmon, and *ricotta salata*. Roasted bone marrow or crispy beef tongue are at the ready if pizza isn't your thing.

El Dorado Kitchen

Californian ✗✗

F4

405 1st St. W. (at Spain St.), Sonoma

Phone: 707-996-3030   Lunch & dinner daily
Web: www.eldoradosonoma.com
Prices: $$

A stone's throw from the grassy Sonoma town square and tucked away in the El Dorado Hotel, this stylish yet always casual canteen is a wine country hot spot, and deservedly so. Dressed in earthy shades, the spacious and attractively rustic dining room contrasts dark wood furnishings with bright white walls and isn't the slightest bit cliché. Meanwhile, a central communal table loved by large groups offers a view into the busy exhibition kitchen.

Utilizing the region's bounty, the kitchen turns out the likes of fried green tomatoes with pineapple salsa, or flaky Alaskan halibut with corn pudding, pea shoots, and shaved asparagus. The cheese plate sticks to West Coast producers, and desserts like warm rhubarb crisp make a strong case for seasonality.

El Rinconcito Yucateco

Mexican ✗

C3

3935 Sebastopol Rd. (bet. Campoy St. & Wright Rd.), Santa Rosa

Phone: 707-526-2720   Lunch & dinner Tue – Sun
Web: N/A
Prices: ⊜⊜

This small dining room specializes in dishes from the Yucatán region of Mexico. The spot may be fuss-free, casual, and basic, but the family who runs the place is super welcoming and convivial.

All meals start with homemade chips and spicy roasted chili salsa for dipping. *Auténtico* is to be found in the Yucatán specialty, *cochinita pibil panuchos*—black been purée sandwiched between two corn tortillas and topped with deliciously tender achiote-marinated roasted pork. Fresh tomato and pickled onions complete the flavorful creation. Fine fixings abound in the pineapple- and chili-marinated *al pastor panucho*; while the grilled chicken topped with cool, creamy avocado is simply *delicioso*! For those in a hurry, there is a weekend taco stand out front.

Farmhouse Inn & Restaurant ✿

Californian 🍴🍴🍴

C2

7871 River Rd. (at Wohler Rd.), Forestville

Phone: 707-887-3300
Web: www.farmhouseinn.com
Prices: $$$

Dinner Thu – Mon

The steep roads winding through the rugged landscape to this quaint yellow colonial heightens the anticipation of what is sure to be a great meal. The staff does everything in their power to assure every guest's enjoyment. Each of several dining rooms is polished and very attractive, with French doors, coffered ceilings, a crackling fireplace, and mirrors with whitewashed log frames. The setting, carefully orchestrated service, and most of all Chef Steve Litke's superb cooking have made this farmhouse a renowned destination.

Inventiveness and sublime quality appear on the plate again and again, beginning with mushroom soup capped with foam (an outstanding version of mushroom cappuccino); or *burrata alla panna*, an orb of mozzarella stuffed with whipped cream served with olive oil-braised leeks, chanterelles, mustardy breadcrumbs, and trumpet royale chips. Heartier options include the spoon-tender thigh confit and pan-roasted breast of Grimaud Farms guinea hen accompanied by mushroom-studded bread pudding and truffled root vegetable gravy.

The best way to handle dessert is just get one of each—don't miss the autumnal apple pie à la mode with sticky cider caramel and *mimolette* ice cream.

French Garden

International ✗✗

C3

8050 Bodega Ave. (at Pleasant Hill Ave.), Sebastopol

Phone: 707-824-2030
Web: www.frenchgardenrestaurant.com
Prices: $$

Lunch & dinner Wed – Sun

With "garden" in the name, it's no surprise that this local fixture is surrounded by manicured plants and a trickling fountain. Pull yourself away to enter an equally attractive dining room filled with white linen-topped tables. Its Southern France vibe is heightened by large windows that provide views back to their lovely garden.

Eclectic touches define the food here, like the creamy tomato sauce that enlivens a wild-mushroom mac and cheese; or the hint of saffron that perks up a dish of fresh Prince Edward Island mussels in fennel-leek broth. The restaurant boasts its own 30-acre farm, from which it gets nearly all of its produce. You'll be able to taste the difference this makes in the pecorino-accented shortcake with fresh berries and lavender cream.

Glen Ellen Star

Californian ✗

D3

13648 Arnold Dr. (at Warm Springs Rd.), Glen Ellen

Phone: 707-343-1384
Web: www.glenellenstar.com
Prices: $$

Dinner nightly

The country charm of this quaint cottage belies the level of culinary chops that will impress even a hardened city slicker. With knotty pine tables, well-worn plank floors, and a wood-burning oven, the space is delightful. A perch at the chef's counter affords a great view of the selections.

Seasonal dishes can include large and plump wood-roasted asparagus with thin shards of *lavash* crackers and shaved radish over a tangy hen egg emulsion; or chicken cooked under a brick with creamy coconut curry and sticky rice. The daily pizzas like the tomato-cream pie with Turkish chilies are also a must. Save room for the excellent, freshly churned house-made ice cream in flavors like vanilla maple bourbon, salted peanut butter, and peach verbena.

Hana

Japanese ✕

C3

101 Golf Course Dr. (at Roberts Lake Rd.), Rohnert Park

Phone: 707-586-0270
Web: www.hanajapanese.com
Prices: $$

Lunch Mon – Sat
Dinner nightly

For the full experience, park it at the sushi bar where the obliging chefs can steer you through the best offerings of the day. Rohnert Park denizens are wising up to this little gem of a spot, tucked in a hotel plaza next to the 101, and run by affable owner, Chef Ken Tominaga, who sees to his guests' every satisfaction.

Traditional, fresh sushi and Japanese small plates are the secret to Hana's success, though simply exquisite items like pan-seared pork loin with ginger-soy jus, and pots of steaming udon also hit the spot. The chef's omakase is a fine way to go—six pieces of nigiri which could include toro, hamachi belly, kampachi, *tai* snapper, halibut with ponzu sauce, or sardine tangy from lemon juice and sprinkled with Hawaiian lava salt.

Harvest Moon Cafe

Californian ✕

F4

487 1st St. W. (bet. Napa & Spain Sts.), Sonoma

Phone: 707-933-8160
Web: www.harvestmooncafesonoma.com
Prices: $$

Dinner Wed – Mon

Harvest Moon Cafe is located on the main town square in Sonoma. Without an obvious façade, this place has become popular by word of mouth. Featuring a pleasant crowd of locals, connoisseurs, and tourists, the café serves Californian fare made from local, seasonal ingredients. Some may choose to start a meal with gypsy pepper and potato soup with crème fraîche and sage. Others may embark with a crisp chicory salad tossed in a tangy blue cheese dressing with caramelized grilled onions and smoky-salty bacon; before moving on to the likes of house-made *boudin blanc* with collard greens and whole grain mustard sauce.

Adorned with wildflowers, this charming café features an open kitchen and bar, as well as an outdoor patio for warm summer evenings.

Hot Box Grill 😊

American 🍴🍴

D3

18350 Sonoma Hwy. (bet. Calle Del Monte & Hawthorne Ave.), Sonoma

Phone: 707-939-8383   Dinner Wed – Sun
Web: www.hotboxgrill.com
Prices: $$

To call Hot Box Grill "charming" would fail to express the warmth and care this Boyes Hot Springs darling expresses with every dish. The small room features a bustling front area, where patrons wait with glasses of Sonoma chardonnay for one of the handful of tables and settle into unencumbered window views of the Sonoma Highway,
The elegant seasonal fare begins with stunning mixed green salads adorned with the freshest local produce, followed by crisp focaccia topped with immaculate white anchovies, hard-boiled eggs, and aïoli. Swordfish steaks are seared over an open flame, brushed with *salmoriglio*, then set over rich and piquant romesco sauce made of smoky-spicy dried Spanish peppers pounded with tomatoes, garlic, almonds, vinegar, and olive oil.

Jackson's

American 🍴🍴

E1

135 4th St. (at Davis St.), Santa Rosa

Phone: 707-545-6900   Lunch & dinner daily
Web: www.jacksonsbarandoven.com
Prices: $$

Chef/owner Josh Silver's menu is created with families in mind. Still, the room is mighty sleek and curvy, adorned with soaring ceilings; while an espresso-brown and deep crimson shade the walls. Contemporary wood tables and chairs look upon bright paintings, many of which were actually done by one of the chefs.
The open kitchen with its shiny fire-engine red wood-burning oven is loved for more than just pizza. An oven-roasted Cornish game hen shares the menu with a daily changing hot dog, and sandwiches too. Lamb meatballs, mac and cheese, oysters, and mussels all get the roaring fire treatment.
While the kids enjoy a giant carrot cake cupcake for dessert, moms and dads can choose from their list of Scotch, Ports, and stickies.

John Ash & Co.

C2

Californian ✗✗

4330 Barnes Rd. (off River Rd.), Santa Rosa

Phone: 707-527-7687   Dinner nightly
Web: www.vintnersinn.com
Prices: $$$

The Vintner's Inn's restaurant—where the terra-cotta walls, wrought-iron chandeliers, and a flickering fireplace lead to acres of vineyards—exudes the romance of a Tuscan farmhouse. Yet even solo diners can enjoy a taste of John Ash thanks to the clubby Front Room, where the hunting-lodge vibe meets a chic bar menu of sweet-and-sour meatballs or avocado fries.

The food here emphasizes seasonal ingredients, and on-site gardens provide much of the produce. Expect the likes of zippy tuna tartare with *sriracha* aïoli and house-pickled ginger, or chorizo-crusted sea bass over beans and roasted cauliflower. Noted Sonoma winery Ferrari-Carano may own the inn and dominate the wine list, but other fine local and international selections are also available.

The Kenwood

D3

Californian ✗✗

9900 Sonoma Hwy. (near Libby Ave.), Kenwood

Phone: 707-833-6326   Lunch & dinner Wed – Sun
Web: www.kenwoodrestaurant.com
Prices: $$

This local favorite has been in operation for over 25 years, but recently changed ownership. The good news is that the hand-over was gentle enough that The Kenwood has preserved its fond place in the hearts of true-blue Sonoma residents.

Located just off the highway and surrounded by vineyards, this simply done beige space is a comfy setting in which to partake of Chef Anthony Paone's locally inflected cooking. Grilled wild King salmon collar marinated with sherry and sweet maple syrup and paired with an herb salad is finger-licking good. Meanwhile, house-made rabbit sausage arrives with green garlic spaetzle and tangy sauerkraut. Large plates are less daring, as in organic grass-fed ribeye with red wine-shallot butter and horseradish mashed potatoes.

Khoom Lanna

Thai ✗✗

E1

107 4th St. (bet. Davis & Wilson Sts.), Santa Rosa

Phone: 707-545-8424 Lunch & dinner daily
Web: www.khoomlannathai.com
Prices: $$

Although this Thai jewel might seem pricey to some, Khoom Lanna's generous use of fresh vegetables and unique ingredients in each of its dishes merits the expense. A brick façade (flanked by a wood awning adorned with windows and greenery) marks the entry into this charming yet rustic Asian burrow.

Countering its vibe (mauve walls, linen-lined tables, lush flower arrangements, and Thai artifacts), servers are candid and casual. If *pad si-ew* (noodles stir-fried with vegetables, tofu, eggs, and splashed with dark soy); or *plah gung* (succulent, smoky prawns tossed in tangy lime juice and dusted with toasted rice powder) aren't as fiery as you'd hoped, up the spice ante in a hearty dish of basil lamb glazed with garlic and red chilies.

LaSalette 😊

Portuguese ✗✗

F4

452-H 1st St. E. (bet. Napa & Spain Sts.), Sonoma

Phone: 707-938-1927 Lunch & dinner daily
Web: www.lasalette-restaurant.com
Prices: $$

LaSalette is a passage to Portugal just off Sonoma's town square. While wooden Port wine crates and pumpkin-hued walls may aim to transport, you'll feel right at home thanks to Chef/owner Manuel Azevedo and his wife, Kimberly, who bring the flavors of his native Azores Islands to wine country. Peek into the open kitchen where a wood-burning oven roasts a variety of small plates for sharing. Try the linguiça with *queijo fresco*—a piece of pork-and-garlic sausage crowned with farmer's cheese and a Portuguese olive. A lunch special of *caldeirada* (fisherman's stew) unveils a fragrant lobster-saffron broth teeming with fresh seafood and fingerling potatoes; while *piri piri* fries are dusted with chile powder and served with a creamy garlic-herb aïoli.

337

Luma

D4

500 1st St. (at G St.), Petaluma

Phone: 707-658-1940   Lunch & dinner Tue – Sun
Web: www.lumapetaluma.com
Prices: $$

A glowing presence in its industrial neighborhood, Luma's attractive red-and-yellow neon sign (the handiwork of owner Tim Tatum) is immediately recognizable. The artsy atmosphere meshes well with sunny orange walls and deep chocolate booths, though it can get a bit noisy. For a quieter meal, request a table in the front corner nook. This is a friendly, crowd-pleasing, neighborhood destination drawing local families to dine on crispy build-your-own pizzas and other comforting delights.

Consider your pizza options while indulging in guilt-ridden starters like "friends of the devil," a duo of prosciutto-wrapped figs and bacon-wrapped dates filled with goat cheese. Follow your pizza with chocolate-raspberry crêpes and excellent French-press coffee.

Mateo's Cocina Latina

B2

214 Healdsburg Ave. (bet. Matheson & Mill Sts.), Healdsburg

Phone: 707-433-1520   Lunch & dinner Wed – Mon
Web: www.mateoscocinalatina.com
Prices: $$

On a warm Sonoma day, it's hard to beat the patio at Mateo's, unquestionably one of the area's most captivating. Surrounded by planter beds and protected by Sunbrellas, guests have a full view into the kitchen. And if the weather takes a turn, the interior, full of rustic wood furnishings and soft lighting, is just as beautiful as the outdoors.

Flavors of the Yucatán abound here, from a heap of succulent *cochinita pibil*, to *panucho* pockets filled with a delicious black bean purée and topped with chicken and avocado. For extra heat, add a drop or two of the house-made habanero sauces. If you love them, you can buy bottles to take home—and if you can't handle the heat, a tall glass of hibiscus-raspberry *agua fresca* will cool things down.

Madrona Manor ✿

Contemporary ✕✕✕

1001 Westside Rd. (at W. Dry Creek Rd.), Healdsburg

Phone: 707-433-4231
Web: www.madronamanor.com
Prices: $$$

Dinner Wed – Sun

With its sweeping sense of romance and grandeur, this Victorian beauty is an unexpected home to a forward-looking kitchen. It's the kind of place that makes one want to dress up—just a little bit—to fully engage in the art of dining. Settle yourself in one of several rooms gilded in carved wood, marble, silks, and more.

The Asian-influenced contemporary cooking features a few bells, whistles, and "pop rocks" that can make it seem like a departure from the traditional setting but is nonetheless fantastic. Beautifully seared and evocative of the salty sea, a glistening mackerel fillet sits over a whoosh of dashi-simmered kabocha squash topped with daikon purée and micro greens. Lobes of dense uni star in a composition of chilled kombu-dashi sprinkled with lily bulb, flower petals, and puffed wild rice for perfect texture. Tender abalone atop grated radish and buckwheat emulsion underscores the kitchen's absolute competence, with the clear flavors of kelp adding to each bite.

Desserts like an apple spice cake are delicious fun—picture a bombshell of thin green apple gelée encasing apple mousse sitting over a crumbled spice cake surrounded by more "crumbs" of pecans and luscious caramel dots.

Monti's Rotisserie 😋

American 🍴🍴

F1

714 Village Court (at Sonoma Ave.), Santa Rosa

Phone: 707-568-4404   Lunch & dinner daily
Web: www.starkrestaurants.com
Prices: $$

With the scent of wood smoke hanging in the air, it seems impossible to resist ordering the day's offering hot off the rotisserie. Those smoked prime ribs or pomegranate-glazed pork ribs do not disappoint. But the oak-roasted chicken is a perennial favorite and deserves a visit all its own. Succulent auburn skin, lusciously seasoned flesh, heirloom carrots, smashed fingerling potatoes, and crisped pancetta render this dish a thing of beauty. End your meal with baby lettuces with Point Reyes blue cheese, candied walnuts, and shallot vinaigrette; and butterscotch pudding for lip-smacking comfort food, Monti's-style.

Set within Santa Rosa's Montgomery Village, this spot is dressed up with wrought-iron accents and a quirky collection of decorative roosters.

Peter Lowell's

Californian 🍴

C3

7385 Healdsburg Ave. (at Florence Ave.), Sebastopol

Phone: 707-829-1077   Lunch & dinner daily
Web: www.peterlowells.com
Prices: $$

With a devoted following in an artsy neighborhood, Peter Lowell's finely tuned design, staff, food, and philosophy are entirely in sync. The lofty, minimalistic space has a modern pantry-like vibe, with comfortable nooks for relishing the Italian-inspired Californian food.

Hyper-local, largely organic produce arrives in starters like caramelized acorn squash tossed with spiced chickpeas and chard from the restaurant's own farm. Then, move on to smoked-trout ravioli with apples, fennel, and whole-grain mustard. Or, feast on a carefully grilled swordfish steak basted with herb-infused olive oil over red quinoa, matsutake, and shiitake mushrooms.

Bring home some muffins with house Meyer lemon marmalade from the adjacent café for the morning after.

Risibisi 😊

Italian ✕✕

D4

154 Petaluma Blvd. N. (bet. Washington St. & Western Ave.), Petaluma

Phone: 707-766-7600
Web: www.risibisirestaurant.com
Prices: $$

Lunch & dinner daily

Though it's named for a comforting dish of rice and peas, Risibisi's seafood-heavy take on Italian cuisine is a bit more sophisticated. A meal here might begin with tissue-thin morsels of fresh salmon carpaccio with julienned celery, or blanched potato salad in orange-herb vinaigrette and zesty horseradish cream. Gnocchi with chunky wild boar ragù are so light and tender that it somehow seems easy to finish the generous portion. Finish with house-made tiramisu or cannoli, and you'll feel like you've been transported to Italy. The three-course lunch prix-fixe is a steal.

A makeshift picture gallery constructed out of salvaged Tuscan chestnut window frames, wine barrels, and wagon wheels bring character to the brick-walled dining room.

Rosso

Pizza ✕

F1

53 Montgomery Dr. (at 3rd St.), Santa Rosa

Phone: 707-544-3221
Web: www.rossopizzeria.com
Prices: $$

Lunch & dinner daily

Red wine, red sauce, and red meat are only the beginning at this pizzeria and wine bar. In fact, you're just as likely to go on to enjoy a fresh crab Louie, tender fried calamari and green beans with a green chili aïoli, or a Caesar salad with Gorgonzola dolce. Crunchy, uniquely-topped pizzas fly out of the wood oven and may feature a braised short rib number topped with gooey cheddar and tomato marmalade.

Set in a small shopping mall, Rosso is identifiable by the locals dining on its terrace, many of whom sign on for the restaurant's regular schedule of cooking classes. Rely on the upbeat staff for friendly advice on the Californian/Italian wine selection, all of which is also available to-go—an ideal alternative given their strong takeout business.

Rustic

B2

Italian 🍴🍴

300 Via Archimedes (off Independence Ln.), Geyserville

Phone: 707-857-1485
Web: www.franciscoppolawinery.com
Prices: $$

Lunch & dinner daily

Those Godfather Oscars certainly could have funded a posh restaurant for Francis Ford Coppola, but the director has kept it relatively simple at his enormous Geyserville eatery, offering Italian classics from his childhood. Savory *pettole* doughnuts in a paper bag kick off the meal, followed by crispy chicken *al mattone* sautéed in olive oil with strips of red pepper.

Coppola's personality is a big part of Rustic's appeal, with walls covered in film memorabilia as well as his own wines, recitations to accompany the food. The real reason for the crowds, though, is the Italian-American music, games, and nostalgia that define the past of Coppola and his many customers. Tuesdays are known not only for the special prix-fixe, but when waiters don vintage garb.

Santé

D3

Californian 🍴🍴🍴

100 Boyes Blvd. (at Hwy. 12), Sonoma

Phone: 707-939-2415
Web: www.santediningroom.com
Prices: $$$

Dinner nightly

Fresh off a major renovation, this classic spot in the Fairmont Sonoma Mission Inn looks better than ever. With exposed log rafters, thick stone walls, and a dramatic view of a lit pool outside, it's a dark and sultry space perfect for the diverse wine country clientele. Service is attentive, right down to the complimentary valet parking for diners.

Start your meal with a palate-pleasing cauliflower custard topped with briny caviar and served in a warm eggshell, then indulge in a plate of Carnaroli risotto with forest mushrooms that boasts both chopped black truffles and white truffle foam. Dessert delivers a thick and vanilla-rich Bavarian cream, accented by Riesling-poached pears, crumbled chocolate crêpe, and a touch of Roquefort ice cream.

Sazón 😊

Peruvian ✕

E1

1129 Sebastopol Rd. (at Roseland Ave.), Santa Rosa

Phone: 707-523-4346   Lunch & dinner daily
Web: www.sazonsr.com
Prices: 😊😊

A menu full of appealing choices makes for difficult decision-making at this cute Peruvian spot. Whether you select the tilapia ceviche with an acidic and spicy *leche de tigre* leavened by sharp red onion and cubes of sweet potato, or a meatier dish like marinated free-range chicken followed by wok-fried tenderloin, you're sure to enjoy the signature sweet and spicy flavors. At lunch, the selection of sandwiches and highly popular sweet potato fries are big hits.

Sazón's teeny space has just a handful of tables, but framed photos of Machu Picchu and Peruvian landscapes set the scene, and the friendly staff (it's family-run) make it homey. A pisco sour or passion fruit-infused sangria nicely complement the meal. Finish with a fresh-brewed Peruvian coffee.

Scopa 😊

Italian ✕

B1

109A Plaza St. (bet. Center St. & Healdsburg Ave.), Healdsburg

Phone: 707-433-5282   Dinner nightly
Web: www.scopahealdsburg.com
Prices: $$

The house always wins at Scopa, which is named for a bluff-centric Italian card game. Patrons will happily concede victory after their first bite of the heady spaghettini with a deeply flavored, spicy Calabrese beef and pork rib sugo. Fans of rarely seen Italian treats like thick-skinned, munchable *lupini* beans or *ciambella*, a cornmeal cake studded with citrus and cranberries, have definitely met their match.

Loud and dimly lit, Scopa's cool, railroad-narrow space quickly fills with bar-goers looking to achieve the other sense of its name ("scoring"—and, ahem, we don't mean points in a card game). Glasses of local cabernet sauvignon fuel the meeting and eating, though perfectly pulled espressos are always available for a little sobering up.

Seaside Metal

B2

16222 Main St. (bet. Armstrong Woods Rd. & Church St.), Guerneville

Phone: 707-604-7250   Dinner Wed – Sun
Web: www.seasidemetal.com
Prices: $$

Quaint Guerneville has gotten an infusion of cityside-chic thanks to this younger sibling of SF favorite, Bar Crudo. Located in the heart of town, its relaxed vibe and kind service draw both tourists and locals. They perch at the white marble counter, where an extensive raw bar is displayed alongside jars of house-pickled vegetables and a sizable cookbook collection.

You'll definitely want at least one raw item to start, whether it's fresh, briny Walker Creek oysters from nearby Point Reyes, or a vibrant yellowtail crudo with lemon curd, crispy shallots, and basil. Move on to the outstanding smoked shellfish platter of Dungeness crab, shrimp, and scallops that arrives on a wood board with crostini, coarse mustard, and those tangy pickled veggies.

SEA Thai

F1

2323 Sonoma Ave. (at Farmers Ln.), Santa Rosa

Phone: 707-528-8333   Lunch & dinner daily
Web: www.seathaibistro.com
Prices: $$

Sophisticated and sleek, SEA has spawned two spinoffs from Chef/owner Tony Ounpamornchai, but the mothership remains a Sonoma favorite thanks to its rich, fragrant, and spicy Thai fare. The cooking is much more unapologetically creative than authentic, yet perfectly balanced and delicious. The red-and-gold dining room is tasteful and inviting, especially the bar that faces the dramatic flames in their tidy open kitchen.

Quality is evident in custardy cubes of fried tofu over a complex soy-glazed cucumber salad and the fresh and earthy tangle of eggplant, basil, and mushroom in the angel chicken. Black noodles may not be black, but they're still a dark-horse favorite, thanks to a complex array of sauces, spices, and fresh vegetables.

Spinster Sisters

A m e r i c a n   ✕✕

E1

401 S. A St. (at Sebastopol Ave.), Santa Rosa

Phone: 707-528-7100
Web: www.thespinstersisters.com
Prices: $$

Lunch daily
Dinner Tue – Sun

This terra cotta-tinged bungalow is housed on a residential block off the city center, and flaunts a very hip and modern vibe as evidenced in concrete walls and a large circular wood counter. The urban respite also reeks of good taste—not only in design but also in their delicious range of food crafted from local Californian produce.

Open from breakfast to dinner, Sonoma County crowds come swarming in for Spinster Sisters' enticing cocktails impeccably paired with updated but serious American cuisine. A substantial wilted kale salad tosses creamy goat cheese, smoky bacon, pickled onion, and moist slices of chicken. The well-priced wine selection is as luring as a flaky quiche with gooey fontina, spicy sausage, and lemon vinaigrette.

Spoonbar

C o n t e m p o r a r y   ✕✕

A2

219 Healdsburg Ave. (bet. Matheson & Mill Sts.), Healdsburg

Phone: 707-433-7222
Web: www.spoonbar.com
Prices: $$

Dinner nightly

The dining room of the h2hotel brings an infusion of cool, lofty glamor to the rolling vineyards of quaint Healdsburg. Polished concrete and floor-to-ceiling windows frame the indoor-outdoor open space that is always bright with turquoise seating and stained glass accents.

Chef Louis Maldonado's menu is fittingly contemporary to suit the setting. Expect spirited cooking that applies seasonality and often complex global notes to meals that have started with roasted until gently charred but still crisp romaine hearts brushed with seaweed butter. Move on to entrées such as pan-roasted sea scallops atop shellfish bordelaise with baby turnips and crisped potatoes. Edgy desserts might include a Japanese-style cheesecake with yuzu curd and cocoa nib streusel.

Sugo

D4

Italian ✗

5 Petaluma Blvd. S. (at B St.), Petaluma

Phone: 707-782-9298
Web: www.sugopetaluma.com
Prices: $$

Lunch & dinner daily

A family-friendly, farm-to-table ethos is embodied in this cute Italian-American trattoria, brought to you by a husband-and-wife team. Housed in a petite, blink-and-you'll-miss-it strip mall, Sugo is decorated with vibrant photos including those of roosters (a tribute to Petaluma's agricultural past). The walls may be plain brick, but they are adorned with chalkboards that offer insight into the colorful display of wine bottles.

Straightforward dishes here include panzanella with chunks of grilled ciabatta, tomato, and fresh mozzarella; as well as a creamy fettuccine Alfredo intertwined with poached salmon, cherry tomatoes, and wilted spinach. A lovely *affogato*, vanilla ice cream drowned with espresso, can be enjoyed on the front patio on warmer nights.

the fig café

D3

Californian ✗✗

13690 Arnold Dr. (at O Donnell Ln.), Glen Ellen

Phone: 707-938-2130
Web: www.thefigcafe.com
Prices: $$

Lunch Sat – Sun
Dinner nightly

Look no further than this homey, relaxed spot after a long day of wine tasting—which generously waives corkage for its patrons. The quaint décor, with its green walls bearing antique crocks and blackboards trumpeting the well-priced prix-fixe menu, adds to the warm vibe, as do the chatty regulars and the flames dancing in the open kitchen.

Food is tasty and unfussy, from a spicy seafood pasta with chunks of tomato and smoky chorizo, to a fluffy, tender, deep-fried chickpea panisse cake served over curried squash purée and braised collard greens. The bright and boozy-sweet persimmon cake is a must. Check out the unique artwork on the walls, which blends colors and contours to create a calming sense of place, also beautifully echoed in the food.

Terrapin Creek ✧

Californian 🍴🍴

B3

1580 Eastshore Rd. (off Hwy. 1), Bodega Bay

Phone: 707-875-2700   Dinner Thu – Mon
Web: www.terrapincreekcafe.com
Prices: $$

Terrapin Creek isn't easy to find, but those who persevere will be rewarded with a delightful little hideaway bearing delicious cuisine. Dramatically situated high above Bodega Bay, this lovely restaurant provides glorious views of the water. (During the January-March whale-watching season, you might even catch a glimpse of these gentle giants bobbing in the Pacific.)

The upbeat, sun-filled dining room, done in bright orange and yellow and filled with big, bold paintings, is clean and unfussy. The small-town staff are every bit as warm as the space, and treats everyone like a regular. A meal might begin with a mixed-green salad topped with creamy goat cheese, sweet persimmon, bits of prosciutto, and a tart cherry vinaigrette; then segue into a nest of al dente linguine twirled with crumbled merguez and minty feta in a spicy tomato broth. A tender local ribeye is accented by creamy bordelaise and buttery potatoes, then strewn with sautéed *broccolini* and mushrooms; paired with a Napa red blend, it's equal parts modern and classic.

Be sure not to miss the fluffy, velvety German chocolate cake, full of crunchy-chewy pecans and coconut that give it a powerful, but never heavy, flavor.

the girl & the fig 🐷

Californian 🍴🍴

110 W. Spain St. (at 1st St.), Sonoma

Phone: 707-938-3634   Lunch & dinner daily
Web: www.thegirlandthefig.com
Prices: $$

It is easy to see why this restaurant is a favorite with both locals and tourists. Her fresh and seasonal Californian fare is prepared with top ingredients and not a ton of fuss. Frilled with a beautiful garden patio, the quaint country house décor features pastel-hued walls and mini lamp sconces. A beautiful carved wood bar completes the experience with inventive cocktails.

A California-and-French influenced menu may divulge a delicate smoked trout salad—moist, flaky, and mingled with pea tendrils and baby red and golden beets; or pastis-scented steamed mussels with crispy frites. If you're looking for the fluffiest quiche Lorraine ever (studded with bacon and Gruyère and served with ultra-thin herbed matchstick fries), you've come to the right spot.

Underwood

International 🍴🍴

9113 Graton Rd. (at Edison St.), Graton

Phone: 707-823-7023   Lunch Tue – Sat
Web: www.underwoodgraton.com   Dinner Tue – Sun
Prices: $$

Graton may be little more than a cluster of restaurants and shops, but Underwood is where local winemakers gather to celebrate the harvest or make deals over good food and wine. The nickel bar has a saloon feel, especially when laden with classic cocktails and oysters; and red, riveted banquettes alongside zinc-topped tables in the dining room conjure a French bistro. Yet, the cuisine is decidedly international.

The menu ranges from cheeses and salads to an eclectic selection of globe-trotting small plates like hoisin-glazed baby back ribs, or Thai lettuce cups full of lemongrass- and mint-seasoned pork, served with cucumbers, roasted peanuts, and rice noodles.

The Willow Wood Market Cafe across the street has the same owner and is a bit more rustic.

Willi's Seafood & Raw Bar

Seafood ✗✗

A1

403 Healdsburg Ave. (at North St.), Healdsburg

Phone: 707-433-9191   Lunch & dinner daily
Web: www.starkrestaurants.com
Prices: $$

"Eat oysters, love longer," reads a cheeky neon sign above the raw bar at Willi's, and seafood fans certainly feel affection for local restaurant mavens Mark & Terri Stark's love boat. The eclectic seafood offerings are designed for smiles, as in the crisp-fried oyster over jicama kimchi and Key lime aïoli, or bamboo skewers of plump bacon-wrapped scallops with tamarind-barbecue glaze.

The quirky space is a fun blend of tropical and New England accents. This is a favorite for groups, trading sips of cocktails and tasty bites of grilled fish tacos topped with plenty of salsa and avocado. The diet-conscious and landlubbers will find enticing options, as will the environmentalist: all the fish and shellfish served here is Safe Harbor certified.

Willi's Wine Bar

International ✗✗

C2

4404 Old Redwood Hwy. (at Ursuline Rd.), Santa Rosa

Phone: 707-526-3096   Lunch Tue – Sat
Web: www.starkrestaurants.com   Dinner nightly
Prices: $$

This roadhouse is easily missed when racing down the old tree-lined highway, if not for the packed parking lot. The name comes from a spot in Paris that pioneered serving American wines to the French 30 years ago. Nowadays, Willi's serves over 40 wines by the glass and an eclectic menu of smaller plates. Inside, find a series of small, wood-accented rooms with a romantic and a ruby-red glow.

The multi-cultural menu is divided into Surf, Earth, and Turf— and if the Ibérico pork loin is on offer, get it. In addition, try the skewered brick chicken with *harissa*, *tzatziki* sauce, and fried onion salad; Moroccan lamb chops; or goat-cheese fritters with smoked paprika and lavender honey.

Aspiring oenophiles should belly up to the bar for a real wine education.

Willow Wood Market Cafe

Californian ※

C3

9020 Graton Rd. (at Edison St.), Graton

Phone: 707-823-0233
Web: www.willowwoodgraton.com
Prices: $$

Lunch daily
Dinner Mon – Sat

Hospitality always pairs well with food—especially in California where that casual and cozy comfort is a distinct local pleasure. And stepping into the Willow Wood Market Cafe feels like returning to a welcoming home, or maybe a quirky sundries store stocked with good wine. Obscure specialty items for foodie friends and revolving local artworks hanging on the buttery yellow walls all combine to enhance this quaint eatery's charms.

Salads and sandwiches are tasty, but the menu focuses on many different homey renditions of piping-hot polenta. This creamy cornmeal goodness has many guises including garlicky rock shrimp with roasted peppers; or simple with goat cheese, sweet-roasted red onions, and pesto. Just about everything comes with garlic bread.

Yeti

Nepali ※※

D3

14301 Arnold Dr., Ste. 19 (in Jack London Village), Glen Ellen

Phone: 707-996-9930
Web: www.yetirestaurant.com
Prices: $$

Lunch & dinner daily

Historic Jack London Village, with its gristmill from the mid-1800s, may seem like an unlikely spot for a Nepali restaurant, but somehow, this odd combination works. Pass a 25-foot water wheel to find the quaint Yeti. Inside, large barn windows open for fresh air and garden-views, while Himalayan and some Indian influences are patent in the artifacts and fabrics—and cooking, of course.

This is a peaceful spot to enjoy superlative native preparations like *momos*, heart-warming Himalayan-style dumplings filled with ground meat and spices; trailed by a Himalayan pepper pot soup. Their version of chicken *tikka masala* (yogurt- and *garam masala*-marinated chicken in creamy tomato sauce) is above par, especially when paired with that piping-hot garlic naan.

ZAZU kitchen+farm

American ✗✗

C3

6770 McKinley St., Ste. 150 (bet. Bronw & Morris Sts.), Sebastopol

Phone:	707-523-4814	Lunch Wed – Sun
Web:	www.zazukitchen.com	Dinner Wed – Mon
Prices:	$$	

A fun change from the rustic décor seen in much of wine country, this big and bright industrial space is practically translucent, thanks in large part to its garage-like doors and glossy cement floors. Natural wood tables and huge wild flower arrangements keep it from feeling chilly, as do surprisingly great acoustics—you won't struggle to be heard, even if the massive 20-seat family table is full.

Pork is the priority here, as evidenced by the sharp, spicy, and addictive Cuban sandwich with house-made mortadella. Vegetarians will delight in the tart tomato soup with an oozing Carmody grilled cheese, or the black beans with baked eggs. But the real key for carnivores is to bring home the bacon; it's $13 for a package, and worth every penny.

Zin

American ✗

B2

344 Center St. (at North St.), Healdsburg

Phone:	707-473-0946	Dinner nightly
Web:	www.zinrestaurant.com	
Prices:	$$	

A narrow window at the door lined with jars packed with preserved goodies is a portent to the homemade goodness inside. Casual with polished concrete floors and walls hung with bright agrarian scenes, high ceilings overlook cork-lined tables below. The co-owners are sons of farmers, and that upbringing has not been forgotten in the cuisine.

The seasonal menu is laced with fresh spins on American classics, and their tempura-fried green beans with mango salsa are legendary in these parts. Southwestern zeal is evident in the crispy duck leg with pepper jelly or shrimp and grits with andouille sausage. Different blue-plate specials every night celebrate Americana.

There are always zinfandel tasting flights, with a half-dozen available by the glass.

● Where to **Eat**

Alphabetical List of Restaurants

Y

Yank Sing	⊛ 米米	155
Yeti	米米	350
Yuzuki	⊛ 米	89

Z

ZAZU kitchen+farm	米米	351
Zeni	米	275
Zen Peninsula	米	244

Zero Zero	⊛ 米米	155
Zin	米	351
Zona Rosa	米	275
Zuni Café	米米	37
Zut!	米米	197
Zuzu	▤	315
Z & Y	⊛ 米	105

Restaurants by Cuisine

Afghan

Helmand Palace	✗✗	96
Kabul	✗✗	230
Kamdesh	✗	182

American

Ad Hoc	✗✗	286
aliment	✗	95
Archetype	✗✗	287
Blue Plate	✗✗	75
Bluestem Brasserie	✗✗	141
Boon Fly Café	✗	290
Brick & Bottle	☺ ✗✗	205
Brown Sugar Kitchen	✗	167
Buckeye Roadhouse	✗✗	205
Bungalow 44	✗✗	206
FIVE	☺ ✗✗	176
Goose & Gander	✗✗	300
Homestead	✗	179
Hopscotch	✗	180
Hot Box Grill	☺ ✗✗	335
Jackson's	✗✗	335
Market	✗✗	303
Mason Pacific	☺ ✗✗	99
Monti's Rotisserie	☺ ✗✗	340
Mustards Grill	✗✗	305
Nick's Cove	✗✗	212
Nick's Next Door	✗✗✗	265
Norman Rose Tavern	✗✗	305
Park Chow	✗	128
Park Tavern	✗✗	115
Prospect	✗✗✗	148
Rutherford Grill	✗✗	308

Salt House	✗	149
Sir and Star	☺ ✗✗	215
Spinster Sisters	✗✗	345
Table (The)	✗	272
Torc	✗✗	314
Town Hall	✗✗	152
Wexler's	✗	53
ZAZU kitchen+farm	✗✗	351
Zin	✗	351

Argentinian

Lolinda	✗✗	81

Asian

Chino	☺ ✗	76
Chinois	✗✗	329
Hawker Fare	✗	179
house (the)	✗	112
Osmanthus	✗✗	186

Austrian

Leopold's	✗✗	99
Naschmarkt	✗✗	263

Barbecue

BBQ Spot (The)	✗	323
Cathead's BBQ	✗	141
4505 Burgers & BBQ	✗	31
Q (The)	✗✗	307
Smoking Pig BBQ	✗	271

International

Celadon	✗✗	295
Cin-Cin	▤	258
Cindy's Backstreet Kitchen	✗✗	296
French Garden	✗✗	333
Grace's Table	☺ ✗✗	300
Radio Africa & Kitchen	✗	86
The Peasant & The Pear	✗✗	194
Underwood	✗✗	348
Willi's Wine Bar	☺ ✗✗	349

Israeli

Oren's Hummus Shop	✗	266

Italian

Acquerello	✿✿ ✗✗✗	94
Albona	✗✗	110
A16	☺ ✗✗	57
Barbacco	✗✗	43
barolo	✗✗	289
Bellanico	☺ ✗✗	165
Beretta	✗	74
Bistro Don Giovanni	✗✗	289
Bottega	✗✗	291
Ca'Momi	✗	294
Campo Fina	✗	327
Chiaroscuro	✗✗	44
Ciccio	✗✗	295
Cook St. Helena	☺ ✗✗	297
Corso	☺ ✗	171
Cotogna	☺ ✗✗	112
Cucina Paradiso	✗✗	329
Delarosa	✗	60
Delfina	☺ ✗✗	77
Della Santina's	✗✗	330
Desco	✗✗	173
Donato Enoteca	☺ ✗✗	227
54 Mint	✗✗	144

Florio	✗✗	61
flour + water	☺ ✗	77
Frantoio	✗✗	208
Fratello	✗✗	260
La Ciccia	✗✗	79
Locanda	✗✗	80
Locanda Positano	✗✗	233
Oenotri	☺ ✗✗	306
Oliveto	✗✗	186
Osteria Coppa	✗✗	236
Osteria Stellina	✗✗	212
Pasta Moon	✗✗	237
Perbacco	☺ ✗✗	52
Pesce	✗✗	22
Picco	✗✗	213
Poggio	✗✗	214
Prima	✗✗	189
Quattro	✗✗	237
Quince	✿✿ ✗✗✗✗	116
Redd Wood	☺ ✗✗	308
Risibisi	☺ ✗✗	341
Riva Cucina	✗	190
Rustic	✗✗	342
Scopa	☺ ✗	343
Seven Hills	✗✗	102
Sociale	☺ ✗✗	65
SPQR	✿ ✗✗	66
Sugo	✗	346
Tosca Café	✗✗	118
Trattoria Contadina	✗	119
Trattoria da Vittorio	✗✗	130
Tra Vigne	✗✗	314
Vespucci	✗✗	242

Japanese

Akiko's	✗	42
Domo	☺ ✗	30
Hachi Ju Hachi	✗	261
Hana	✗	334
Ichi Sushi + Ni Bar	✗✗	79

Southern

Boxing Room	✗✗	29
Brenda's	✗	30
Picán	✗✗✗	188
The Pear	✗✗	313

Spanish

Bravas		▤	326
Contigo	⊛	✗✗	18
Coqueta	⊛	✗✗	46
Duende		✗✗	174
Iberia		✗✗	229
Zuzu		▤	315

Sri Lankan

1601 Bar & Kitchen	⊛	✗✗	151

Steakhouse

Alexander's Steakhouse	✗✗✗	254
Bourbon Steak	✗✗✗	43
Cole's Chop House	✗✗✗	296
El Paseo	✗✗	207
Epic Roasthouse	✗✗	143
Press	✗✗✗	306

Thai

Arun	✗	203
Bangkok Jam	✗✗	163
Grand Avenue Thai		✗✗	177
Khan Toke Thai House		✗	127
Khoom Lanna		✗✗	337
Kin Khao	⊛	✗	48
Manora's Thai Cuisine		✗	147
Mini Mango Thai Bistro		✗	304
Modern Thai		✗	100
R'Noh Thai		✗✗	214
SEA Thai		✗✗	344
Sweet Basil		✗	240
Thai House	⊛	✗✗	194
Thep Phanom		✗	35

Vegan

Millennium	✗✗	51

Vegetarian

Encuentro	✗	175
Greens	✗	62

Vietnamese

Bui Bistro	✗✗	293
Bun Bo Hue An Nam	✗	256
Slanted Door (The)	✗✗	52
Tamarine	✗✗	273
Thiên Long	✗	274
Vung Tau	✗✗	274

Cuisines by Neighborhood

370

Indexes ▶ Cuisines by Neighborhood

SOUTH BAY

Napa Valley

Indexes ▲ Cuisines by Neighborhood

Starred Restaurants

Within the selection we offer you, some restaurants deserve to be highlighted for their particularly good cuisine. When giving one, two, or three Michelin stars, there are a number of elements that we consider including the quality of the ingredients, the technical skill and flair that goes into their preparation, the blend and clarity of flavours, and the balance of the menu. Just as important is the ability to produce excellent cooking time and again. We make as many visits as we need, so that our readers may be assured of quality and consistency.

A two or three-star restaurant has to offer something very special in its cuisine; a real element of creativity, originality, or "personality" that sets it apart from the rest. Three stars – our highest award – are given to the choicest restaurants, where the whole dining experience is superb.

Cuisine in any style, modern or traditional, may be eligible for a star. Due to the fact we apply the same independent standards everywhere, the awards have become benchmarks of reliability and excellence in over 20 countries in Europe and Asia, particularly in France, where we have awarded stars for 100 years, and where the phrase "Now that's real three-star quality!" has entered into the language.

The awarding of a star is based solely on the quality of the cuisine.

ॐ ॐ ॐ

Exceptional cuisine, worth a special journey

One always eats here extremely well, sometimes superbly. Distinctive dishes are precisely executed, using superlative ingredients.

Benu	XXX	140
French Laundry (The)	XXXX	299
Restaurant at Meadowood (The)	XXXX	309
Saison	XXX	150

ॐ ॐ

Excellent cuisine, worth a detour

Skillfully and carefully crafted dishes of outstanding quality.

Acquerello	XXX	94
Atelier Crenn	XX	58
Baumé	XXX	255
Coi	XXX	111
Manresa	XXX	264
Quince	XXXX	116

ॐ

A very good restaurant in its category

A place offering cuisine prepared to a consistently high standard.

All Spice	XX	222
Ame	XXX	138
Auberge du Soleil	XXX	288
Aziza	XX	124
Bouchon	XX	292
Boulevard	XX	142
Campton Place	XXX	45
Chez TJ	XXX	257
Commis	XX	172
Farmhouse Inn & Restaurant	XXX	332
Gary Danko	XXX	113

Bib Gourmand

😋 This symbol indicates our inspectors' favorites for good value.
For $40 or less, you can enjoy two courses and a glass of wine or a dessert
(not including tax or gratuity).

Brunch

Credits

Michelin is committed to improving the mobility of travellers

ON EVERY ROAD AND BY EVERY MEANS

Since the company came into being – over a century ago – Michelin has had a single objective: to offer people a better way forward. A technological challenge first, to create increasingly efficient tires, but also an ongoing commitment to travelers, to help them travel in the best way. This is why Michelin is developing a whole collection of products and services: from maps, atlases, travel guides and auto accessories, to mobile apps, route planners and online assistance: Michelin is doing everything it can to make traveling more pleasurable!

→ *Michelin Apps*

Because the notions of comfort and security are essential, both for you and for us, Michelin has created a package of six free mobile applications—a comprehensive collection to make driving a pleasure!

→ *Michelin MyCar* • *To get the best from your tires; services and information for carefree travel preparation.*

→ *Michelin Navigation* • *A new approach to navigation: traffic in real time with a new connected guidance feature.*

→ *ViaMichelin* • *Calculates routes and map data: a must for traveling in the most efficient way.*

→ *Michelin Restaurants* • *Because driving should be enjoyable: find a wide choice of restaurants, in France and Germany, including the MICHELIN Guide's complete listings.*

→ *Michelin Hotels* • *To book hotel rooms at the best rates, all over the world!*

→ *Michelin Voyage* • *85 countries and 30, 000 tourist sites selected by the Michelin Green Guide, plus a tool for creating your own travel book.*

A tire...
→ what is it?

Round, black, supple yet solid, the tire is to the wheel what the shoe is to the foot. But what is it made of? First and foremost, rubber, but also various textile and/or metallic materials... and then it's filled with air! It is the skilful assembly of all these components that ensures tires have the qualities they should: grip to the road, shock absorption, in two words: 'comfort' and 'safety.'

1 TREAD
The tread ensures the tire performs correctly, by dispersing water, providing grip and increasing longevity.

2 CROWN PLIES
This reinforced double or triple belt combines vertical suppleness with transversal rigidity, enabling the tire to remain flat to the road.

3 SIDEWALLS
These link all the component parts and provide symmetry. They enable the tire to absorb shock, thus giving a smooth ride.

4 BEADS
The bead wires ensure that the tire is fixed securely to the wheel to ensure safety.

5 INNER LINER
The inner liner creates an airtight seal between the wheel rim and the tire.

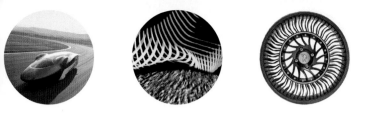

Michelin
→ *innovation in movement*

Created and patented by Michelin in 1946, the belted radial-ply tire revolutionized the world of tires. But Michelin did not stop there: over the years other new and original solutions came out, confirming Michelin's position as a leader in research and innovation.

→ *the right pressure!*

One of Michelin's priorities is safer mobility. In short, innovating for a better way forward. This is the challenge for researchers, who are working to perfect tires capable of shorter braking distances and offering the best possible traction to the road. To support motorists, Michelin organizes road safety awareness campaigns all over the world: "Fill up with air" initiatives remind everyone that the right tire pressure is a crucial factor in safety and fuel economy.

The Michelin strategy:
→ *multi-performance tires*

Michelin is synonymous with safety, fuel saving and the capacity to cover thousands of miles. A MICHELIN tire is the embodiment of all these things – thanks to our engineers, who work with the very latest technology.

Their challenge: to equip every tire – whatever the vehicle (car, truck, tractor, bulldozer, plane, motorbike, bicycle or train!) – with the best possible combination of qualities, for optimal overall performance.

Slowing down wear, reducing energy expenditure (and therefore CO_2 emissions), improving safety through enhanced road handling and braking: there are so many qualities in just one tire – that's Michelin Total Performance.

MICHELIN
Total Performance

Every day, **Michelin** is
working towards
sustainable
mobility

OVER TIME,
WHILE
RESPECTING
THE PLANET

Sustainable mobility
→ *is clean mobility... and mobility for everyone*

Sustainable mobility means enabling people to get around in a way that is cleaner, safer, more economical and more accessible to everyone, wherever they might live. Every day, Michelin's 113,000 employees worldwide are innovating:

• by creating tires and services that meet society's new needs.

• by raising young people's awareness of road safety.

• by inventing new transport solutions that consume less energy and emit less CO_2.

→ *Michelin Challenge Bibendum*

Sustainable mobility means allowing the transport of goods and people to continue, while promoting responsible economic, social and societal development. Faced with the increasing scarcity of raw materials and global warming, Michelin is standing up for the environment and public health. Michelin regularly organizes 'Michelin Challenge Bibendum', the only event in the world which focuses on sustainable road travel.

Notes

Notes

Notes

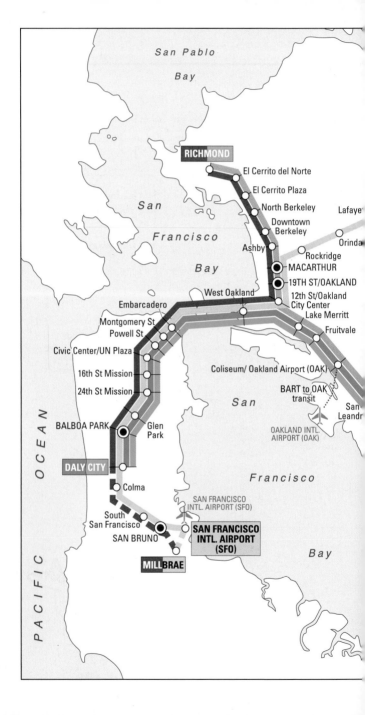

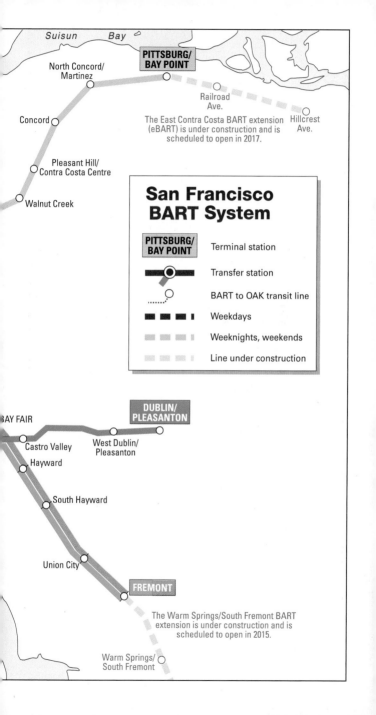

Suisun Bay

PITTSBURG/
BAY POINT

North Concord/
Martinez

Concord

Railroad
Ave.

The East Contra Costa BART extension
(eBART) is under construction and is
scheduled to open in 2017.

Hillcrest
Ave.

Pleasant Hill/
Contra Costa Centre

Walnut Creek

San Francisco
BART System

PITTSBURG/
BAY POINT   Terminal station

                   Transfer station

                   BART to OAK transit line

                   Weekdays

                   Weeknights, weekends

                   Line under construction

DUBLIN/
PLEASANTON

BAY FAIR

Castro Valley   West Dublin/
                 Pleasanton

Hayward

South Hayward

Union City

FREMONT

The Warm Springs/South Fremont BART
extension is under construction and is
scheduled to open in 2015.

Warm Springs/
South Fremont

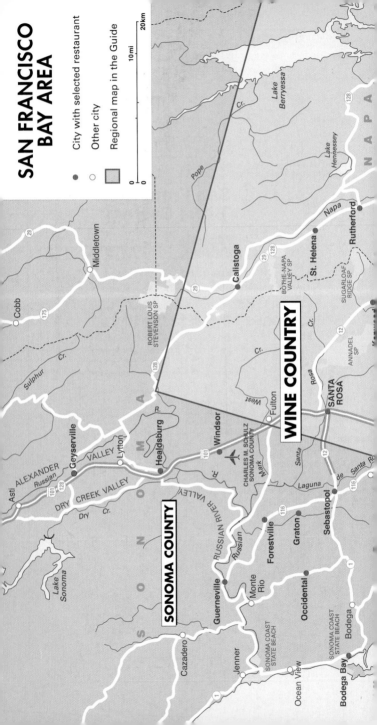